The Russian Intelligentsia

The Russian Intelligentsia

From Torment to Silence

Vladimir C. Nahirny

Routledge
Taylor & Francis Group

LONDON AND NEW YORK

First published in paperback 2018
by Routledge
711 Third Avenue, New York, NY 10017

and by Routledge
2 Park Square, Milton Park, Abingdon, Oxon OX14 4RN

*Routledge is an imprint of the Taylor & Francis Group, an informa
business*

© 2018 Taylor & Francis

The right of Vladimir C. Nahirny to be identified as author of this
work has been asserted by him in accordance with sections 77 and 78
of the Copyright, Designs and Patents Act 1988.

First published 1983 by Transaction Publishers

Library of Congress Cataloging-in-Publication Data
Nahirny, Vladimir C., 1928-
The Russian intelligentsia.
Includes bibliographical references.
1. Intellectuals—Soviet Union. 2. Soviet Union—Intellectual life.
1. Title.
HM213.N34   305.5'52'0947   82-4796

ISBN: 978-0-87855-463-8 (hbk)
ISBN: 978-1-4128-6532-6 (pbk)
ISBN: 978-1-351-31864-8 (ebk)

Typeset in Times New Roman
by Servis Filmsetting Ltd, Stockport, Cheshire

Table of Contents

Acknowledgments

No words of acknowledgment can fully convey the debt I owe to my teacher, Professor Edward Shils of the University of Chicago, to whom this book is gratefully dedicated. Without his sustained attention, encouragement, and counsel this book would not have been written. Professors Daniel Bell and Richard Pipes of Harvard University, and Professor Michael Confino of the University of Tel-Aviv, have been kind enough to read the manuscript and to offer invaluable suggestions and criticisms. Thanks are also due to Professor John Cuddihy of Hunter College for his incisive comments on the manuscript. The staff of Transaction, Inc. has been most helpful and cooperative. I am particularly grateful to Professor Irving L. Horowitz for his supportive reading of the manuscript, and Ms. Kerry Kern for her fine editorial assistance. It seems hardly necessary to add that I alone am responsible for the views expressed and conclusions reached in this study.

I am indebted to the editors of *American Journal of Sociology* and *Comparative Studies in Society and History* for permission to use in a revised form some material that has appeared in articles in their journals.

The intelligentsia cannot but be conscious of its imperfect, halfway situation; there must be at least a vague realization of this. If the intelligentsia closes itself off, withdraws into some idea or dogma, it begins to disappear, to be effaced. In the end, all ideological rivers flow into the swamp of philistinism: some in a direct, simple fashion, others after shelves and waterfalls, asceticism and quixotism. Having ceased to be a working hypothesis, the idea becomes an idol. It is to this idol that man is sacrificed.

The intelligentsia cannot pass by political events which touch its moral sense, but in submerging itself in politics, it loses itself and becomes a political counterelite, inside-out bureaucracy.

This happens very simply. A situation that gives birth to cowards also gives birth to heroes. The heroes, having entered the battle against despotism, come to the conclusion that everything is permitted for them in their holy battle. It is for this reason that fighters for freedom become accustomed to consider themselves above the law and middle class morality. Having achieved power, they easily take up the executioner's axe and continue the tradition against which they themselves rebelled.

G. Pomerantz
"Man Without an Adjective"

Having got over one bout of enthusiasm, Nerzin—whether definitively or not—understood the people in a new way, a way he had not read about anywhere; the people is not everyone who speaks our language, nor yet the elect marked by the fiery stamp of genius. Not by birth, not by the work of one's hands, not by the wings of education is one elected into the people.

But by one's inner self.

Everyone forges his inner self year after year. One must try to temper, to cut, to polish one's soul so as to become a human being.

Aleksandr I. Solzhenitsyn
The First Circle

And it was with tragic clarity that the sacred law of all life defined itself: freedom of the individual human being is higher than anything else, and there is no goal, no purpose in the world, for which it may be sacrificed.

Vasily Grossman
Forever Flowing

Introduction

The Russian intelligentsia has been examined from a variety of historical perspectives. It would not be putting the matter too strongly to say that most of the studies of the intelligentsia have been historical in orientation. The specific subjects of these studies range from the origin of the intelligentsia, to the nature of its significance, to the use of the term itself. But the major concern of the literature on the intelligentsia has been the ideas and ideals held by various groups of the intelligentsia, often combined with the life histories of their members. With scarcely an exception, therefore, this literature represents a mixture of intellectual history and biography.

The present work is not intended to be another history of the intelligentsia. Rather, it is an effort to develop a sociological perspective on the intelligentsia. Although it covers some of the same ground that one would find in a historical account of the intelligentsia, it is far from that. What this study seeks to accomplish is at once narrower and broader: narrower in that it deals in a persistent fashion with one major problem—the ideologization of the intelligentsia; broader in that it examines this problem with an eye to constructing a conceptual framework vital to the sociology of ideologically based relations and groups. In this sense, then, the present study may be said to offer a conceptually focused view of the intelligentsia as a distinct type of social group. No interpretive scheme presently available to sociology can account plausibly for the nature of the relations that characterize social groups whose members orient themselves to one another in terms of some central symbols—be they those of Zion, *patrie, Volk, narod,* or proletariat. The very fact that sociologists still tend to place these groups on the continuum of *Gemeinschaft* and *Gesellschaft* lends support to this contention. The same observation applies with equal force to such a historical particular as the Russian intelligentsia. It is not without good reason that at least one student of Russian history has voiced the following complaint:

> No recognized system of social analysis, either those known to the intelligentsia itself, or those elaborated since by modern sociology, makes provision for a "class" held together only by the bond of "consciousness," "critical thought," or "moral passion."[1]

The first chapter of this study is primarily an overview of the Russian literature on the intelligentsia. The chapter also seeks to unravel the dominant conception of the intelligentsia from the recurrent controversy over its place and role in Russian society. Chapter 2 traces the formation of the cultural elite in Russia by comparing data from various sources on the ethnic and social origins of the writers, artists, scholars, and professional people. Chapters 3, 4, and 5 highlight three different types of the intelligentsia: men of letters, men of ideas, and men of convictions. In chapter 5 an attempt is also made to construct the "ideal type" of the intelligentsia in terms of the mode of orientation to ideas and the nature of social bonds prevalent among its members. Chapter 6 focuses on the well-tried theme of the social context of ideas held by the intelligentsia; more specifically, it analyzes the relationship between the social position of the intelligentsia and its vision of ideal society. In chapter 7, in turn, there is an extended discussion of the intelligentsia's relationship to *narod* and proletariat—two key symbols in the ideology of the populist and Marxist intelligentsia. Finally, the concluding chapter examines critically the conventional explanations of the radicalization of the intelligentsia. The chapter also makes an effort to determine how far the social origins, life histories, and structural location of the members of the intelligentsia can account for their association within a distinct type of social groups. These are ideological groups that typically require their members to relate to one another in the light of ideas and beliefs rather than in the light of personal qualities or specific functions they perform. I have attempted to capture the essence of this type of relationship by constructing a set of dimensions that are contrasted with Parsons' well-known scheme of pattern variables. Whatever the implications of this procedure, the salient point is that the very decision to introduce this new conceptualization was based primarily on historical facts brought to light in the process of studying the intelligentsia. These facts could be neither meaningfully interpreted nor coherently related in terms of traditional typologies that pertain at best to personal groups and functional associations. Needless to say, the value of the interpretive scheme developed here is that of any constructive typology—the capacity to relate in a meaningful fashion hitherto unrelated facts.

Note

1. Martin Malia, "What Is the Intelligentsia," *Daedalus* (Summer 1960), p. 445.

1   The Russian Intelligentsia: The Problem and Its Background

The Russian intelligentsia poses one of the most exasperating problems in the social history of Russia. It has continued to engage the unabated attention of Western and Russian authors alike and has equally challenged the imagination of many creative men of letters. Not only has the intelligentsia been the object of varied analyses ranging from scholarly studies to "musical" edifications,[1] it has also been passionately attacked by many a detractor and no less passionately defended by many a partisan. So diverse and competing are these images of the Russian intelligentsia during the past century that their comprehensive review would require a separate study. It has been branded by some a "crazy class of semi-Europeans"[2] and exalted by others as that "beautiful class" which lends "life, warmth and beauty to the whole organism of Russia, to all her elements and classes of society."[3] It has been likened to "oil with which all wheels of the Russian state and public life are lubricated"[4] as well as compared to a "dung-hill" addicted to the parrot-like refrain on a syllogistic theme: "All Russian *intelligenty* are beautiful and great. I am the *intelligent*, consequently, I am beautiful and great."[5] Some authors, like those of *Vekhi,* likened the intelligentsia to a "leprous dog" and "afflicted crowd"[6] estranged from the Russian people, whereas others, like Merezhkovsky, bemoaned as unfortunate the very fact that these alleged foreigners in their own land were "too much Russian, indeed, exclusively Russian."[7] Finally, the same intelligentsia has been credited by some with the creation of Russian representative culture, only to be diagnosed by others as "crippled souls" suffering from the chronic malaise of "intellectual paralysis."

All these and other conflicting assessments of the intelligentsia seem to be so divergent as to be logically exclusive. For to contend with Gorky that the intelligentsia traditionally performed the role of "crabs" in Russian life "always moving backwards,"[8] and, at the same time, assert, as did Fedotov, that it made up the "general staff"[9] of the Russian Revolution, amounts to maintaining two inconsistent views of the intelligentsia. Some authors go so far as to attribute to the intelligentsia a decisive role in the revolution:

The moral lever of the movement was in the hands of the intelligentsia, with its own peculiar outlook, habits, tastes, and social stamp. The *intelligenty* themselves, naturally will not confess it, because they are *intelligenty*—each in accordance with his own particular catechism will name this or that class of society as the sole driving force of the revolution.[10]

To be sure, such rival evaluations of the intelligentsia are partly to be accounted for by the excessive sallies of the polemicists, which often made them too prone to use the same catchword—the intelligentsia—but refer to different groups of people. Yet, even if this is conceded, there lurks behind this formal and definitional lack of consensus the more basic problem of the normative disagreement over the very raison d'être of the intelligentsia, or its role and place in the Russian society. Disagreements of this kind reflected a search for collective identity, one of those truly "cursed questions" that the Russian intelligentsia never tired of raising. Over half a century ago, the author of the *History of the Russian Intelligentsia* referred to this untiring preoccupation of the intelligentsia as follows:

> In civilized countries the intelligentsia, that is, the educated and enlightened segment of society … constitutes, if one may use the phrase, an incontestable value. The intelligentsia simply carries on its work there, without posing the ingenuous query: What is the intelligentsia and what is the meaning of its existence?[11]

This unabated quest for collective self-definition lays the ground for suspecting that the Russian intelligentsia must have been devoid of a firmly established intellectual tradition capable of mitigating its sense of bafflement, so appropriately expressed by "What is to be done?" But even more suggestive of this sense of bafflement is the frozen certainty with which the intelligentsia answered these "cursed questions" and which made the whole debate dangerously resemble a determined attempt to end all debates. In one sense, at least, this particular dream of the intelligentsia, epitomized by a paltry rhyme, "Let us give simple answers to cursed questions,"[12] has definitely come true. At present, the problem of the intelligentsia in the Soviet Union has been decreed settled: both "cursed questions" and "simple answers" have become obsolete. And, if we are to believe the Soviet authors, the intelligentsia has no longer any legitimate reason to raise "cursed questions," let alone engage in dissent or complain of its estrangement from the people. For it has become "organically bound" to the people as well as "selflessly devoted to the cause of socialism."[13]

From the very beginning of its appearance in Russian literature, the term *intelligentsia* conveyed a wide range of meanings and was used to designate different but overlapping groups of people: (1) the educated and half-educated public in general, (2) creative scholars, scientists, and artists, and (3) ideologically oriented men of letters, publicists, and their votaries from the school-going youth.[14] The first usage of the term was loose enough to lump together all people who carried briefcases and distinguished themselves from the populace by their soft white hands and their starched shirts. In his *Strange Story,* Turgenev used the intelligentsia in this broad sense when he subsumed under the term marshals of nobility, officials, and other educated members of provincial society. "Day after tomorrow ... there is to be a ball in the Assembly of the Nobility. I advise you to go. We do not lack beauties here. And you will see all our intelligentsia, too."[15] It was this loose usage of the word that led Mikhailovsky to complain that the "Russian intelligentsia is often confounded with Russian society, educated people, privileged and ruling classes."[16] For this reason, he continued, "Fonvizin's Mitrofan, unable to distinguish the noun from the adjective; Mme. Prostakova, denying the value of the science of geography; and Griboedov's Skalozub, proposing the sergeant for another Voltaire ..."[17] found themselves in the company of the intelligentsia. Suggestive of the open texture of this term was the tendency of nineteenth-century authors to extend the use of intelligentsia with the help of such adjectives as "landowning," "bourgeois," "propertied," "provincial," "working," "serving," "toiling," "professional," or "technical."[18]

The second usage of the word—despite ostensive stipulations to the contrary—was never generally accepted in Russian literature, since the name of "intelligentsia" has been rarely accorded to creative scholars, scientists, and artists. Rather, it has been closely associated with those educated and half-educated persons who carried the torch of ideological enlightenment and served various causes: *narod* (people), proletariat, progress, or revolution. In this last sense, then, the intelligentsia was a quasi-normative term which was used on occasions with such adjectives as "true," "best," or "young."[19] The varied definitions of "true" intelligentsia tended, thus, to be persuasive in nature, carrying along with them definite attitudes and ideological preconceptions.

In this narrow sense of the word, the intelligentsia was concerned not so much with the creation of cultural values as with the ideological enlightenment of the people—peasants or workers. If we inquire into the nature of "goods" the members of the intelligentsia dispensed, most of their critics would have identified them as doctrines, myths, or ideologies. To be sure, these were goods that were not to be confused with special knowledge, or with expert information to be handed to the school-going youth, or to illiterate peasants and workers. They did not consist primarily of popularly presented ideas on hygiene, on the latest techniques of land cultivation and crop improvement, or on any other subject deemed valuable for the Russian peasant and the worker. Even if they started off the enlightenment of the people, as some populist authors proposed, with Laplace's astronomy and passed quickly through physics, chemistry, and physiology, these were only the first stepping stones, designed to warm up the audience and to be crowned ultimately with the grand vision of the world. If these goods contained interspersed bits of special knowledge, they were built into the specious comprehension of the social order.

Little would be gained and much lost, however, if we took for a starting point of this study an extensive analysis of the various usages of the term *intelligentsia.*[20] Rather we shall begin by trying to unravel the dominant conception of the intelligentsia from the recurrent controversies over its place and role in the society at large. A comprehensive review of the literature on the subject reveals at least two major waves of debate clustering around *narod,* class, and revolution. These three words, with multivalent symbolic power, are considered basic because they poignantly express the dominant theme in the controversy, as well as take into account the shifts in topical emphasis. By no means do they exhaust the foaming torrent of abstractions devised by the intelligentsia, since many other concepts—such as *pravda* (truth), *mirosozertsanie* (world view), consciousness and spontaneity, tsardom of truth and tsardom of justice, despotism of the people and dictatorship of the proletariat, the vanguard of idea and revolutionary vanguard—have been widely and recurrently used by its members. Nevertheless, hidden under this long cortege of high-sounding words is a narrow outlook, so narrow, in fact, as to suggest that the Russian intelligentsia had managed to resolve all subjects into one. The overriding issue continued to remain the intelligentsia's relationship to *narod* (the populist debate) or class (the Marxian debate) or to social processes such as progress or revolution.

The Populist Debate: Intelligentsia and Narod

The problem of intelligentsia has been inextricably wedded to the history of ideological movements in Russia. The word itself gained currency in the Russian literature during the heyday of populism; so too, the rise of the populist movement in Russia triggered a major controversy over the intelligentsia and *narod,* pointing to what may be termed the "relational nature" of the problem of intelligentsia. *Narod,* of course, far from being a partner in the controversy, was not even a passive participant; indeed, it could in no way distinguish the intelligentsia from the representatives of official Russia. Nevertheless, the debate was carried on under the aegis of two cabalistically vague catchwords: intelligentsia and *narod.* Almost all Russian men of letters and publicists of that period turned their attention to *narod:* some devoted their literary works—stories, plays, verses, and even prayers—to *narod,* others sought to unravel the "system of truth" that supposedly lay unshapen in *narod,* and still others devised schemes of how to relate to the object of their adulation.

It was during this preoccupation with *narod* that the populist conception of "true" intelligentsia became fully crystallized and differentiated from both the "civilized crowd" (the educated public) and the "uncivilized crowd" (the populace). As a rule, this "true" intelligentsia was called in the populist literature by such edifying appelations as "critically thinking individuals," "thinking individuals," "men of convictions," "conscious actors of historical progress," "conscious fighters for truth and justice," "fighters for social ideals," "social fighters," and "intellectually and morally developed minority."

At least two salient characteristics served to define the populist conception of "true" intelligentsia: (1) its unsettled position in the class structure, and (2) its ideological mode of orientation (commitment to the "system of truth"). As a distinct group of people, the intelligentsia admittedly stood above, and outside of, the established social order—its class and estate system. By virtue of this position, the members of the intelligentsia were neither bound together by class or occupational interests nor formed a status group of individuals enjoying definite rights and immunities derived from custom and/or law. To that extent the intelligentsia differed from conventional social formations—personal cliques, occupational status groups, associations of professional people, or corporate bodies. Although it is true that the matrix of the intelligentsia was the educated stratum of society, individual members of this stratum belonged to the ranks of the intelligentsia neither by virtue of their education and professional competence, nor their intellectual accomplishment alone. Just as "not every one that saith unto me, Lord, Lord, shall enter into the kingdom of heaven," wrote Lavrov, "not every educated person can become a member of the group of critically thinking individuals."[21] Since education and diploma were deemed inadequate for joining the intelligentsia, even a "half-learned peasant" could become a member if appropriately tutored and enlightened. Nor was intellectual creativity in the spheres of science and art a necessary attribute of the intelligentsia.

> Neither literature, nor art, nor science saves one from immoral indifference. By themselves they do not include nor determine progress. They only provide it with tools. They accumulate strength for it. But only that writer, artist, or scholar served progress who did all that he could to apply his energies to the dissemination and strengthening of the civilization of his time, who struggled with evil, embodied his artistic ideals, scientific truths, philosophical ideas, publicistic strivings in creations which were fully infused with the life of his times, and in activities which strictly corresponded to the amount of his energies.[22]

Steeped in "immoral indifference," which Lavrov, Mikhailovsky, and others consistently confounded with "ethical neutrality," most of the scholars and writers excluded themselves from the "ranks of conscious actors of historical progress."[23] Such creative intellectuals were often branded in the populist literature as "spiders," "servants of cultural fetishes," "civilized crowd," "savages with higher culture," "philistines of the learned world," or simply *meshchane* (bourgeois Philistines). The whole of "cultured society" was admittedly infested with them:

> … they control the capital; they form for the most part the public opinion; they preside over societal institutions and constituent assemblies; they control most of the press; they are professors in the universities and preempt positions of authority in scholarly societies and academies.[24]

Similarly, the professional world abounded with *meshchane*—all those physicians, lawyers, and teachers who looked at their respective professions as mere occupations and failed to see in them the "elements of social mission."[25] When a suggestion was once made that literature should descend from its pedestal and be treated like any other profession, and that in this there would be no humiliation, it was received as the most disgusting form of profligacy.[26]

Only those educated and half-educated individuals who consciously labored for the triumph of progressive social order and the "rational forms" of collective life, only those who uncompromisingly fought on behalf of ideals and principles consistent with the "system of truth" deserved the name of intelligentsia. Not intellectual creativity or erudite knowledge, but commitment to the "system of truth" was required of the "true" intelligentsia. This "system of truth" was also referred to in the populist literature as *obshchie mirosozertsanie* (common world view), "triumphant idea," "social ideal," *profession de foi,* or simply "creed." According to one populist author:

> It is not enough for him (the *intelligent*) to have a political program, a social theory; he must find in this program and this theory a place for himself, his personality, his sentiments, his conscience. He must understand how his personality is linked to things generally, to society, to the universe. These are the questions which in Russia are called social questions.[27]

To the populist intelligentsia, the "system of truth" represented a body of cognitive ideas, moral standards, and action-oriented ideals and beliefs. Accordingly, it provided: (1) a "guiding thread" in the analysis of the surrounding world, (2) a "guiding thread" in practical activity, and (3) a creed capable of eliciting "religious fervor."[28] As custodians of such an overarching doctrine, the members of the intelligentsia acted solely in the name of an ostensibly rational cry for life and were, to that extent, expected to assert themselves against the established order by criticizing all conventional institutions. This critical posture was considered a necessary hallmark not only of the intelligentsia but of all those deserving the name of "developed individuals." What animated the intelligentsia to play at iconoclasm was not so much its penchant for negation as the commitment of its members to the "system of truth" or "creed," without which they appeared loath to take a single step. As a "critically thinking individual," the *intelligent* criticized the social world around him for the sake of reaffirming the ideological commitment, since he was convinced that the "more severe, thorough, impassionate and comprehensive was the criticism, the more powerful and fervent would become his belief."[29] This critique of existing social arrangements served still another function: it laid the ground for truly enlightened action—action that would be informed by ideological beliefs rather than personal considerations, conventional values, or habits of "routine life." Far from being simply an ideologically inspired critic, the *intelligent* was a man of action who sought to translate the "system of truth" into practice in order to secure its triumph in collective life. In this sense, then, he not only preached the truth but also served the cause, fighting against its enemies and rejoicing over its victories. And it was this service to the cause that entailed a form of enlistment, since it required of the "critically thinking individuals" that they band together for the sake of organizing "something strong and solidary, but strong as a collective force and solidary by virtue of abstract unity."[30] Lavrov called this kind of social group the "party of fighters for truth and justice."[31] But whatever name was accorded to this group, the significant fact is that its members— the "critically thinking individuals"—were expected in their new roles of "fighters" to relinquish their individualities and "disappear in a common thought and common plan of action."[32] Except for the inconsequential, they were deprived of the freedom of action; at best, they were to engage in self-criticism by appraising critically their own actions in the light of ideas whose truth value was now determined by the party. All those of its members who dared to ignore the constraints imposed on their freedom, by naively assuming that they belonged to a "scholarly society," would be promptly branded as the enemies and dealt with accordingly. Against such enemies the "party of the fighters" was to direct all the power of its organization, "fighting like one man and employing all the means available to it."[33]

> A careful and uncompromising struggle against the enemies testifies to the viability of the party, as the unity of thought forms the basis of this viability, and the mutual defense of its members the main bond of the party.[34]

The crux of the populist conception of the intelligentsia may be summarized as follows: it was a self-styled elite of ideologically oriented *réfractaires*, a distinct social formation made up of individuals supposedly drawn from different classes and estates and bound together by ideological ties. Although this intelligentsia formed a part of the educated stratum and hailed from different estates, its members served the cause, and identified with the interests, if not the values, of the *narod*—a key symbol of the populist ideology. More often than not, the educated public as a whole was consigned to the bourgeoisie or *meshchanstvo* and contrasted with the "true" intelligentsia. As a term of abuse, *meshchanstvo* was used to signify the way of life marred by spiritual paltriness and stifling parochialism. It conjured up the image of man under whom "the ground, like under the swine, was limited: dung, family, capital, official position, badge, civil rank, God on the icon and Tsar on the throne."[35] In the populist literature, however, the term *meshchanstvo* acquired a distinctly new tinge that foreshadowed a shift from the cultural to the ideological image of *meshchanstvo*. To that extent, this pejorative word differed considerably from Mills' "conglomerated mediocrity," de Tocqueville's *la bourgeoisie moyenne*, or Herzen's faceless crowd of "small shopkeepers." For unlike Herzen, whose aristocratic sensibility made him prone to castigate the middle classes for their vulgar contentment, their alleged lack of regard for individual excellence, and concern for cultural values, the populist authors relegated to *meshchanstvo* the creative intellectuals themselves (distinguished scholars, men of letters, and artists), leaving often the impression that, except for the "true" intelligentsia, all other groups in society were implicated in *meshchanstvo*. To Mikhailovsky, for example, the English historian, Henry Buckle, was a "pure-blooded bourgeois in the political sense" despite his "irreproachable personal integrity" and commitment to the "cause of science."[36] Not even the reflective view of life that the intellectuals might have thought out for themselves could rescue them from the morass of *meshchanstvo* as long as they lacked the "system of truth in the form of program" and "political morality" consonant with the "social ideal."[37] It was one of the impudent claims of the intelligentsia—both the populist and the Marxian— that the individuals without the "system of truth" or ideology were socially irresponsible and morally contemptible men. Mikhailovsky himself dismissed such ideologically uncommitted individuals as swines, even if he conceded that they upheld in word and deed high standards of individual morality and possessed a reflective view of life.

The historical significance of the populist conception of intelligentsia would be hard to exaggerate. It left a lasting mark on the whole controversy over the intelligentsia; it also influenced many Russian writers on the subject, including those (Berdiaev, Potresov, Tugan-Baranovsky, and others) who found it unacceptable on historical or ideological grounds. The characteristic elements of this conception often have been included in the standard definition of the Russian intelligentsia. With some shift in the emphasis, Ivanov-Razumnik's elaborate definition of the intelligentsia amounted in effect to an updated version of the populist view of "true" intelligentsia. His claim that the intelligentsia was "ethically" opposed to *meshchanstvo* and pertained "sociologically" to all estates and to no class can readily be traced to populist sources.[38] More important, perhaps, the populist debate on the intelligentsia and *narod* left a rich heritage against which the Marxian intelligentsia sought to define its relationship to the proletarian class.

The Marxian Debate: Intelligentsia and the Proletariat

From the Marxian controversy over the intelligentsia, one basic problem can be singled out as having broken the sharpest lances of the Russian Marxists: the proper role of the intelligentsia in the working-class movement. In the solution of this problem, however, the Russian Marxists, except for Lenin, were neither groundbreakers nor pacemakers, but rather muted reflections of the German Social Democrats. The first point on their agenda was the removal of the intelligentsia from the unanchored position in the class structure of society. The Russian Marxists accomplished this feat by a wholesale transfer of West European, notably German, controversy over the role of intellectuals in the socialist movement.

The Western Marxists, it may be noted parenthetically, failed to reach agreement among themselves on the social position of the intellectuals. Not a few of them viewed the intellectuals as part and parcel of the bourgeoisie, among whom the socialists would search in vain for "examples of civic courage and moral dignity."[39] Debased as they were by all the vices of the bourgeois society, they were inferior even to those "little bourgeois of 1830 and 1848 who at least knew the smell of gunpowder."[40] Basically unreliable and lacking in "professional class consciousness," they embraced socialist ideas one day, but could easily be swayed in another direction the next. Any reliance on such "imbeciles" would necessitate postponing the "triumph of socialism not to the year 2000 but to the end of the world."[41] At best:

> These intellectuals who for years have had it for their duty to wear out trousers on the benches of the university that they might become experts on exercises, polishers of phrases, philosophers or doctors, imagine one can improvise himself into a master of the socialist theory by attending one lecture or by the careless reading of one pamphlet.[42]

Others regarded the intellectuals as an integral part of every ruling class and, following Marx, relegated them to the status of "conceptive ideologists, who make the perfecting of the illusion of the class about itself their chief source of livelihood."[43] Still other Marxists conceived of the intellectuals as an intermediate stratum in the process of *Verlumpung.* Steadily approaching the economic level of the proletarian masses, the intellectuals should be a rich source of recruitment into the socialist camp. To be sure, this view of the downward mobility of the "bourgeois intelligentsia" and of its inexorable transformation into the proletarian one ("eines Offizierkorps der Arbeiterpartei") was not generally accepted. For as one of them noted with contempt:

> And to fill these "dissipated geniuses," the most incapable, rotting also—socialists, whose greatest deeds consist in debating triumphs, with the delusion that they are called upon to play a "historic role" would mean to augment not only their vanity, which is already quite boundless, but also their incompetence and even harmfulness (my translation).[44]

Finally, some Western socialists considered the intellectuals as a newly rising middle class or stratum bound together by professional and cultural interests. Unlike other classes, however, this new middle class was not a fully constituted class, since its members—the intellectuals—possessed neither "common class interests" nor "class consciousness."[45]

Like their Western tutors, the Russian Marxists placed the intelligentsia in all and sundry classes: in the bourgeois and proletarian classes, in every social class as its leader and/or servant (Lenin, Meshcheriakov, Polonsky), and, finally, in the ambiguous position of a stratum merging either with the petty bourgeois or the proletarian class (Bulkharin, Lunacharsky, Plekhanov, Potresov, Trotsky, Wolfson).[46] To some, the intelligentsia constituted a part of the petty bourgeois class "by nature," even though individual members of the intelligentsia were promised salvation from their unenviable position provided they joined the proletarian camp.[47] To others, the intelligentsia, if looked at from an economic standpoint, belonged to the working class. Unlike the workers, however, who sold only their hands to the exploiting classes, the *intelligenty* sold also a "part of their soul."[48] For this reason, they were inferior to the workers, and resembled more closely the *Lumpenproletariat* infected by bourgeois prejudices and ready to serve any master. On the other hand, the proponents of *Makhaev-shchina* conceived of the intelligentsia as a separate and privileged social class with its own class interests opposed to the interests of other classes.[49] Still others argued with Alfred Weber, who was admittedly unable to grasp the "plain fact," long ago understood by them, that the intelligentsia neither stood above economic interests nor led the class struggle, but—like Lagardelle's intellectuals—assisted in systematizing the nascent socialist ideology.[50]

The bulk of Marxian analysts, however, assigned the intelligentsia to an intermediate stratum, internally divided and merging on the one hand with the bourgeoisie and on the other with the proletariat. This precarious social position attributed to the intelligentsia stemmed partly from the Marxian insistence that the intelligentsia as a group was incapable of acting as an independent force in any society torn by class struggle, and, therefore, could only become an adjunct of one of the existing social classes. Equally important here is the fact that the Russian Marxists used the term *intelligentsia* to denote, in Maurice Baring's phrase, anyone "who tucks in his shirt, which is equivalent in English to wearing a collar."[51] By using the word in this inclusive fashion and by grouping under it the educated and semi-educated public, a category sufficiently broad to take in scholars, scientists, men of letters, professional people, students, and even minor officials, they very often created the impression of being inconsistent in their view of the intelligentsia. Lenin extolled the intelligentsia—all these "steadfast and uncompromising fighters"—for their fanatical dedication to the cause, but yet he also condemned these "educated traitors of the Russian Revolution."[52] He assured Gorky that he intended neither "to drive away the intelligentsia" nor deny its "indispensability for the working class movement,"[53] but he also looked at the intelligentsia as *meshchanstvo* incarnate—"dead," "stupid," "wretched," "democratic," "backward," "pitifully unreliable," and "God-forsaken" *meshchanstvo*. Lenin's many references to the intelligentsia are interspersed with such terms of opprobrium—many untranslatable—as "slaves," "servants," "traitors," and "cretins." As a rule, he qualified the term by distinguishing "revolutionary" and "socialist" from "bourgeois," "liberal," "opportunist," "idea-chopping," or "mystic" intelligentsia.[54]

No single unqualified statement can sum up the attitude of the Russian Marxists toward the intelligentsia. But if we inquire into their attitude toward the people of the liberal professions—doctors, lawyers, professors, and the literati—we find that it ranged from outright hatred and contempt to suspicion and uneasy tolerance. This tolerant—albeit suspicious—attitude, closely resembling that of some German Marxists, was especially noticeable among the Mensheviks: Akselrod, Martov, Potresov. Lenin and his followers approached the intelligentsia by taking this amorphous category as a whole and then tearing it apart. Yet, no single part of it, any more than the unwieldy whole, which he considered on occasions to be *"kith and kin* of the Russian bureaucracy,"[55] seemed an altogether trustworthy vehicle of the proletarian cause. The professional people, like lawyers, were collectively relegated to the growing horde of career seekers and mercenaries of the bourgeoisie. Professors and scholars were chastised for their refusal to instill the "revolutionary bacilli" into the minds of students. But most appalling to Lenin was the penchant of "analytical professors," and the "academic stratum" in general, to fabricate all kinds of deviant ideas, thereby contributing to the growth of "theoretical chaos" and "eclecticism" among the intelligentsia.

> ... have you heard the fact (asked Lenin) long ago noted, that it was precisely the extensive participation of the academic stratum in the socialist movement in recent years that has secured the rapid spread of Bernsteinism.[56]

In a series of articles he wrote on the intelligentsia—from the "mystical idealists" and "analytical professors" to "bourgeois socialists"—Lenin found none of them fit to serve the cause of socialism. Nor did he find anything praiseworthy among the "radical imbeciles" intent on spreading the "revolutionary bacilli" among the masses. "Everyone knows," he observed, "how easy it is in Holy Russia for a radical intellectual or socialist intellectual to become transformed into a *chinovnik* of imperial government."[57] On the whole, Lenin tended to dismiss them as

> ... a wrathful bourgeois intelligentsia which has understood nothing, forgotten nothing, learned nothing, at best—in rare best circumstances— distracted, despairing, groaning, repeating old prejudices, frightened and frightening itself.[58]

Lenin's social world was thus hopelessly torn into two parts: on one side, there were his steadfast, iron-hardened fighters united with the working class and selflessly serving the socialist cause; on the other, the mass of humanity—the "crude in spirit"—steeped in bourgeois prejudices and opportunism. Lenin referred to these fighters by such names as the "Marxian intelligentsia," "revolutionists," "ideologists," "conscious leaders," "tribunes of the people," "consistent proletarians," "party men," or even Jacobins "inseparably connected with the proletarian organization" and conscious of their "class interests."[59]

The critics of these fighters disparaged them as "doctrinaires," "Blanquists," "Bonapartists," "Papal Nuncios," "mystifiers," or simply "Jacobins." But whatever name one may accord to these fighters, the significant fact is that Lenin consistently separated them from other groups in society, which he identified by such blanket terms as "petty bourgeoisie," *meshchane, obyvateli* (philistines), or "mighty fists of hundred fools."

Who were these "tribunes of the people" or "class-conscious fighters" whose ideological and organizational identity Lenin so consistently defended? In the fashion of their populist predecessors, the tribunes constituted a distinct social formation coextensive neither with the intelligentsia, i.e., the educated stratum, nor with any particular class. They formed a separate organization that recruited its members from among the various professions, occupational groupings, and social classes. Like the "true" intelligentsia of the populists, the tribunes transcended classes and estates, although both aimed at establishing some kind of link with either the *narod* or the proletariat. What placed the tribunes above all societal formations was the exclusive character of their organization, which precluded them from multiple group participation and segmented loyalties. In this sense, then, the tribunes were direct descendants of the populist intelligentsia, even if they were harnessed by the party to the proletarian class instead of to *narod*. It is not without good reason that at least one Marxian author, Polonsky, in a series of articles written about the Revolution of 1917, attributed the name of intelligentsia to Lenin's tribunes, relegating professional people, scholars, and men of letters to educated *obyvateli*.[60]

On the whole, it is fair to say, the Russian Marxists displayed a distrustful, if not hostile, attitude toward the intelligentsia, i.e., toward the educated public. And it was in no small measure due to them that the word *intelligentsia,* from being originally a eulogism, came to acquire a derisive coloration. Yet this seeming difference between the populist and the Marxian evaluation of the intelligentsia resulted from two diverse usages of the same term: the specific (normative) and the general (denotative). The populists, too, looked at the intelligentsia (scholars, writers, professional people) as part and parcel of that morally naked world of *meshchanstvo*. If they praised the intelligentsia, it was because this term signified to them the "true" intelligentsia. And it was in this specific sense that Belinsky's "enlightened individuals," Chernyshevsky's and Dobroliubov's "pure people" or "new men," Mikhailovsky's "true intelligentsia," Lavrov's "critically thinking individuals," Shelgunov's "men of thought," Tkachev's "enlightened minority," Lenin's "tribunes of the people," and Polonsky's "intelligentsia" are basically different variations on the same theme. This theme centered around the search for a group of people hostile to the existing social order, united exclusively by ideological bonds, and ready to lead and serve the masses (proletariat or *narod*) in the total reconstruction of Russian society.

Is the Intelligentsia Unique?

Writing in 1905, during the revolutionary upheaval, Merezhkovsky refused to dwell on the nature of the intelligentsia. He was at a loss "to decide whether the Russian intelligentsia is a miracle or a monster."[61] At the same time, he was convinced that the intelligentsia represented something "unique in modern European culture."[62] In what sense, then, was the Russian intelligentsia *sui generis*? Did this uniqueness lie in its socially marginal position, in its ideologically motivated disparagement of the traditional social order, in its persistent attempts to swing over the masses to the revolutionary cause, or in the fact that it was a group bound by ideas and estranged from the society at large?

In the West, too, we find individuals who sought to shake off the "yoke of authority and tradition" in order to establish the "laws of reason,"[63] and many of them believed that they were on the verge of achieving this self-assigned goal. Marmontel was convinced that the *philosophes* had already replaced a decaying clergy in its noble role, that of "preaching from the rooftops the truths that are too rarely told to sovereigns."[64] Duclos declared that of all the "empires, that of the intellectuals, though invisible, is the widest spread. Those in power command but the intellectuals govern, because in the end they form public opinion, which sooner or later subdues or upsets all despotisms."[65] Duclos' empire, of course, was not inhabited by artists, scholars, or scientists, but rather by the "men of letters," by the professional moralists, by truly enlightened *lumières.*

In his reminiscences of Boerne, Heine portrayed "Vaterlandsretter mit Tabakspfeifen im Maule" who pertinaciously pursued him in Paris forcing him to listen to their "patriotic exaltations."[66] Once Boerne woke Heine at midnight, in the midst of a "sweet dream," and chattered the whole hour about the sufferings of the German *Volk.* Like other members of the "Society of Outlaws" *(Bund der Geaechteten)*, Boerne was determined to liberate this *Volk* from the shackles of tradition and ignorance:

> We must seek to free the *Volk*, which does not know the reason for its suffering, from prejudice and ignorance, from indifference and slavish mentality, and arm it against fraud, deception, and sophism. We must make it aware of its true interests, so that the power of conviction brings about an enthusiasm which will express itself in a series of revolutions resulting finally in complete liberation.[67]

Although even these few examples of footloose intellectuals who used to congregate in the cafés of Paris suggest that the Russian intelligentsia need not have been something unique on the European scene, there lurks behind it a more serious problem, one that cannot be overcome by resorting to historical analogies. It involves a difficulty as yet unresolved: that of the very vocabulary of social history. The difficulty remains with us even if we do not assent to the view that the "terminology of social science is, from the historical point of view, necessarily defective, because it is born out of an effort to generalize."[68] Yet what is significant historically is not so much facile similarities as salient differences that lie hidden by our vague terms. The literature on the Russian intelligentsia suffers from a basic failure to delimit the object of study in a way that would make it possible to develop a more rigorous analysis. This difficulty is not confined solely to the intelligentsia. There exists evidence to suggest that historical research has made it necessary to redefine within more precise limits such broad terms as *feudalism, bourgeoisie, peasantry,* and *nobility.* If we ever transcend the fashionable practice of studying the intelligentsia in general, and begin providing a more pointed analysis, a similar fate may befall the concept of intelligentsia. There is no denying the "essential contestability" of this concept not only among the students of the intelligentsia but also among the members of the intelligentsia themselves.[69] It is this contestable nature of the concept that renders elusive the very identity of the intelligentsia and generates divergent views on its origin, continuity, and role in society.

This study hopes to contribute to the comprehension of a historical particular—the Russian intelligentsia. Its main purpose, however, is not so much to present another history of the intelligentsia, as it is to come to grips with the ideologization of Russian intellectual life. It is within the context of this problem that the intelligentsia as a distinct type of social group will be treated here.

Notes

1. A. Blok, *Rossiia i Intelligentsiia* (Berlin, 1920), pp. 16–22.
2. Jan Kucharzewski, *The Origins of Modern Russia* (New York: Polish Institute of Arts and Sciences in America, 1948), p. 88.
3. A. Yakovlevich, "What is the Russian Intelligentsia," *Russian Review* 4 (1918): 73–74.
4. Ibid., p. 73.
5. B. Nazarevsky, *Biurokratiia i Intelligentsiia* (Moscow, 1906), p. 4.
6. M.O. Gershenzon, "Tvorcheskoe Samopoznanie," *Vekhi, Sbornik Statei o Russkoi Intelligentsii,* 5th ed. (Moscow, 1910), p. 80; *see also* A. Peshekhonov, "Na Ocherednye Temy: Novyi Pokhod Protiv Intelligentsii," *Russkoe Bogatstvo* (April 1909), pp. 100–26.
7. D. Merezhkovsky, "Meshchanstvo i Russkaia Intelligentsiia," *Poliarnaia Zvezda,* no. 1 (1905), p. 41.
8. Maxim Gorky, *Culture and the People* (New York: International Publishers, 1939), p. 121.
9. G.P. Fedotov, *Novyi. Grad* (New York, 1952), p. 13; for a similar view of the intelligentsia voiced more recently, *see* Tibor Szamuely, *The Russian Tradition* (New York: McGraw-Hill, 1974), p. 143.
10. Sergius Bulgakov, "Heroism and Service," *Russian Review* 3 (1914): 15.
11. D.N. Ovsianiko-Kulikovsky, *Istoriia Russkoi Intelligentsii* in *Sobranie Sochinenii* (St. Petersburg, 1910), VII, p. 5.
12. N. Oransky, "Narodnyi Vopros: V Nashem Obshchestve i Literature," *Russkoe Bogatstvo* (May 1880), p. 6.
13. *See* E.U. Vorozheikin et al., *Sovetskaia Intelligentsiia: Istoriia Formirovaniia i Rosta 1917–1965 g. g.* (Moscow, 1968), p. 430.

14. It is historically misleading to assert, as George Fischer has done, that the intelligentsia signified originally a "missionary order of educated theory-oriented men—men dedicated to Russian material and spiritual salvation" and that only by the "1890's the term 'intelligentsia' embraced all the professions." *See* George Fischer, *Russian Liberalism: From Gentry to Intelligentsia* (Cambridge: Harvard University Press, 1958), p. 51.

15. I. Turgenev, *The Novels and Stories of Ivan Turgenieff*, trans. Isabell F. Hapgood (New York: Charles Scribner's Sons, 1904), XIV, p. 244.

16. N.K. Mikhailovsky, *Polnoe Sobranie Sochinenii* (St. Petersburg, 1909), VII, p. 681.

17. Ibid.

18. On the use of various adjectives with the term *intelligentsia, see* Michael Confino, "On Intellectuals and Intellectual Traditions in Eighteenth- and Nineteenth-Century Russia," *Daedalus* (Spring 1972), p. 138.

19. *See* N.V. Shelgunov, *Sochineniia* (St. Petersburg, 1904), V, p. 576; N.K. Mikhailovsky, *Sochineniia* (St. Petersburg, 1896), V, p. 509.

20. For a comprehensive analysis of the various usages of the term *intelligentsia, see* Otto W. Mueller, *Intelligencija: Untersuchungen zur Geschichte eines Politischen Schlagwortes* in *Frankfurther Abhandlungen zur Slavistik*, XVII (Frankfurt: Athenaeum Verlag, 1971).

21. Quoted in Ivanov-Razumnik, *Istoriia Russkoi Obshchestvennoi Mysli* (St. Petersburg, 1914), I, p. 8.

22. P. Lavrov, *Istoricheskie Pisma*, 2d ed. (St. Petersburg, 1905), p. 101.

23. Ibid.

24. Ivanov-Razumnik, *Istoriia*, I, p. 9.

25. S. Elpatievsky, "Po Povodu Razgovorov o Russkoi Intelligentsii" *Russkoe Bogatstvo* (March 1905), p. 60.

26. Lev A. Tikhomirov, *Russia, Political and Social*, trans. Edward Aveling (London: Lowry Co., 1888), II, p. 75.

27. Ibid., pp. 25–26.

28. Mikhailovsky, *Sochineniia*, IV, p. 405.

29. Lavrov, *Istoricheskie Pisma*, p. 284.

30. Ibid., p. 144.

31. Ibid., p. 147.

32. Ibid., p. 144.

33. Ibid., p. 151.

34. Ibid., p. 152.

35. Blok, *Rossiia*, pp. 21–22.

36. Mikhailovsky, *Sochineniia*, IV, p. 390.

37. Ibid., pp. 389–90.

38. Ivanov-Razumnik, *Chto Takoe Intelligentsiia?* (Berlin, 1920), p. 17.

39. Paul Lafargue, *Socialism and the Intellectuals* (Chicago: C.H. Kerr Co., 1900), p. 12.

40. Ibid., p. 17.

41. Ibid., p. 11.

42. Ibid., p. 18.

43. Karl Marx and Friedrich Engels, *The German Ideology*, ed. R. Pascal (New York: International Publishers, 1947), pp. 39–40.

44. "Die proletarische Intelligenz und der Sozialismus," *Die Neue Zeit* 13, no. 19 (1894–1895), p. 591.

45. *See* Max Adler, *Der Sozialismus und die Intellektuellen* (Vienna: Ignaz Brand Co., 1910), p. 5; Hendrik De Man, *Die Intellektuellen und der Sozialismus* (Jena, 1926), p. 7.

46. *See* N. Bukharin, "Sudba Russkoi Intelligentsii," *Pechat' i Revoliutsiia*, no. 3 (1925), pp. 1–10; A.V. Lunacharsky, ed., *Ob Intelligentsii: Sbornik Statei* (Moscow, 1923), pp. 9–10; V. Polonsky, *Ukhodiashchaia Rus'* (Moscow, 1924), p. 96; M.A. Reisner, "Intelligentsiia kak Predmet Izucheniia v Plane Nauchnoi Raboty," *Pechat' i Revoliutsiia*, no. 1 (1922), pp. 93–106; S. Ia. Wolfson, "Intelligentsiia kak Sotsialno-Ekonomicheskaia Kategoriia," *Krasnaia Nov*, no. 6 (1925), pp. 121–62.

47. A. V. Lunacharsky, "Meshchanstvo i Individualizm," *Ocherki Kollektivizma* (St. Petersburg, 1909), I, p. 297.

48. Quoted in V. Polonsky, "Zametki ob Intelligentsii," *Krasnaia Nov*, no. 1 (1924), p. 192.

49. E. Lozinsky, *Chto Zhe Takoe, Nakonets, Intelligentsiia?* (St. Petersburg, 1907), p. 167.

50. N. Meshcheriakov, "O Polozhenii Germanskoi Intelligentsia" *Pechat' i Revoliutsiia*, no. 1 (1924), p. 36; *see also* H. Lagardelle, "Intelligentsiia i Proletariat," *Krasnoe Znamia*, no. 2 (1906), pp. 81–82.

51. W. H. Bruford, *Chekhov and His Russia: A Sociological Study* (New York: Oxford University Press, 1947), p. 142.

52. V. I. Lenin, *Sochineniia*, 4th ed. (Leningrad, 1952), XI, p. 220.

53. L. B. Kamenev, ed., *Leninskii Sbornik* (Moscow-Leningrad, 1924), I, p. 88.

54. L. Voitolovsky, "Lenin ob Intelligentsii," *Pechat' i Revoliutsiia*, no. 2 (1925), p. 10.

55. V. I. Lenin, *Selected Works*, ed. J. Fineberg (New York: International Publishers, 1943), I, p. 380.

56. V. I. Lenin, *Collected Works*, trans. J. Fineberg (New York: International Publishers, 1929), IV, p. 98.

57. Lenin, *Selected Works*, I, p. 380.

58. Lenin, *Sochineniia*, XXXV, p. 98.

59. Lenin, *Selected Works*, II, p. 433.

60. Polonsky, *Ukhodiashchaia Rus'*, p. 16.

61. Merezhkovsky, *Poliarnaia Zvezda*, no. 1 (1905), p. 35; *see also* Dmitri Merejkovski, *The Menace of the Mob*, trans. Bernard G. Guerney (New York: Nicholas L. Brown, 1931), p. 59.

62. Merezhkovsky, *Poliarnaia Zvezda*, no. 1 (1905), p. 35.

63. D. Diderot, "The Encyclopedia," *"Romeau's Nephew" and Other Works*, trans. Jacques Barzun and Ralph H. Bowen (New York: Doubleday, 1956), p. 301.

64. Quoted in M. Roustan, *The Pioneers of the French Revolution*, trans. F. Whyte (London: Ernest Benn, 1926), p. 262.

65. Ibid., p. 265.

66. Heinrich Heine, *Saemmtliche Werke*, 8th ed. (Philadelphia, 1880), VII, p. 110.

67. Wermuth and Stieber, *Die Communisten-Verschwoerungen des Neunzehnten Jahrhunderts* (Berlin, 1853), p. 193; quoted in Peter C. Ludz, "Ideology, Intellectuals, and Organization: The Question of Their Interrelation in Early 19th Century Society," *Social Research* 64 (Summer 1977): 290.

68. Charles Seignobos, *Etudes de politique et d'histoire* (Paris, 1934), p. 22; quoted in Alfred Cobban, "The Vocabulary of Social History," *Political Science Quarterly* 66 (March 1956): 13.

69. On the "contestability" of social concepts, *see* Alasdair MacIntyre, "The Essential Contestability of Some Social Concepts," *Ethics: An International Journal of Social, Political and Legal Philosophy* 84 (October 1973): 1–9.

2 Formation of the Cultural Elite in Russia

Until the eighteenth century, Russian intellectual life was religious in character. It was largely confined to the monasteries and preempted by those ordained to serve God and Church, and under the political conditions in Russia, the vice-regent of God, the Tsar. The sacerdotal dominance over intellectual and cultural life in general was reflected in the closure—both ideological and ritual—of the Muscovite society, with its isolation from, and attendant distrust of, the West and all things foreign. Of some 142 writers in pre-Petrine Russia, no more than a dozen were laymen—boyars or princes—all others belonged to the clergy.[1] This conspicuous dearth of secular writers and scholars led Shchapov to suggest that Muscovy was ill fit to produce such men of learning, but instead abounded with men of "strong muscles," conquerors of other lands and people, and "rebels-demagogues."[2]

With the expansion of Russia by military conquests and annexation, with "new windows" opening on to the West, and with the establishment of more enduring contacts with the countries "beyond the seas," the Muscovite tsardom came increasingly under the secular influence of Western Europe. Until the end of the seventeenth century, however, this influence remained too circumscribed in scope to extend beyond the court, as Muscovy lacked, except for the Ukraine, even elementary institutions of learning that would provide for the transmission of secular thought and learning. In the instructions of 1663, for example, Tsar Alexis ordered his representatives in Poland to buy seven books of secular content. Some of these books were, in turn, translated and, to use the Russian phrase, "handed over to the top," that is, the court.[3] The translators of these books were court scribes, recruited for the most part, as their names testify, from Russified foreigners: Kasper Ivanov, Iushka Vichentov, Lukash, son of Magnus, Antsa Andreev, Westermann, Roman Boldwin, Roman Beckmann, Ivan Gelms.[4] During the reign of Alexis, there were at the court over 120 such translators of books, interpreters, and guides. Their contribution to the growth of secular literature in Russia might well be measured by the number of books (94) published in the second half of the seventeenth century. With the exception of those dealing with religious subjects (28), they were translations of Western works of history (14), astronomy and mathematics (12), geography (7), medicine (5), and other sciences.[5]

These early contacts with the secular culture of the West were considerably enlarged during the reign of Peter the Great. His policy of forced Westernization led to extensive cultural borrowings and left Muscovy fully exposed to Western influences in the fields of technical knowledge and science. In Peter's reign alone over 150 young Muscovites were sent abroad to study "all kinds of sciences" and "military disciplines."[6] Like all other Muscovites who traveled "beyond the seas," they were ill-prepared to comprehend Western secular culture, let alone serve as the agents of its transmission. Unfamiliar with foreign languages and lacking in elementary knowledge of history, geography, and secular culture in general, they turned their attention to Western "tricks and wonders"[7] by reporting monotonously on "big cities" with "many artisans and merchants," "big fortifications," "big palaces," "high-towered churches," "big apothecaries," "big orphanages," "big orchards," and other "big" accomplishments in the sphere of material culture.[8] Some of them failed to record correctly the names of towns they passed through on their travels in the West. Thus, Rotterdam, they named "Rostrodam;" Amsterdam, "Ostrodam" or "Strodam;" Mainz, "Amensk" or "Meli;" Augsburg, "Vospourg;" Duesseldorf, "Kouzluk," and so on.[9] The literary protagonists of these Muscovite travelers displayed an equally deplorable knowledge of geography. Some of them covered the distance from Moscow to Paris in a few days, traveled from Vienna to Florence by sea and from England to Egypt by land; in Egypt one of them mounted a horse and "rode straight to Malta."[10]

It was not only an inadequate knowledge of the West, but the failure of the Muscovites to relate meaningfully to Western culture and life that made them unable to make sense of the many wonders they so readily noted. Since the ideational aspect of culture was beyond their capacity to grasp and, as some of them confessed, too difficult to assimilate, the world of appearance— the surface of things and events—came to engage their childlike fancy. In Rotterdam, for example, one of them saw "the figure of a famous man, cast in brass, holding a brass book, and when the clock struck twelve, this figure's hand turned over one sheet—his name was Erasmus."[11] In Genoa, while describing "big fountains" in the garden of a notable, the same Russian traveler had this to record about Michelangelo's sculpture: "... three giant horses mounted by a man; the horse in the middle pouring water from his tongue, the other two from their nostrils. Sitting around them are children made of marble who drink water; below them are twelve eagles made of stone, at their feet are birds and other creatures emitting water."[12]

What attracted the attention of Russian travelers were those aspects of Western social life that contrasted sharply with the *moeurs moscovites.* Some of them noticed, for example, the humane treatment of school children, the cleanliness of table covers, and the involvement of women in public life.[13] In some instances, they made invidious comparisons of Russia with the West and even ventured to draw appropriate conclusions from them, as can be seen from the comment of one on the carnival in Venice:

> Many amuse themselves ... others devise all kinds of entertainment—they play music in their gondolas and wooden barges—and always enjoy themselves without remorse and fear of anyone and anything, as everyone does what he feels like doing. This freedom has always prevailed in Venice, since Venetians live in peace, without fear, without offending anyone, and without burdensome taxes.[14]

The only sphere of Western culture that the Muscovites related to with a relative ease, as well as showed considerable acquaintance with, was religion: religious holidays, ceremonies and processions, the stories of miracles and religious legends, and the lives of saints and the relics of their bodies.

Learning and the Gentry

The introduction of secular learning and thought in Russia required their defense, an explanation of their meaning and value. What were the arguments advanced by Peter the Great and his "Learned Guard" for the defense of science and its bearers and what stratum of society was it addressed to? Although Peter the Great was not without curiosity and appreciation of knowledge, he valued chiefly the practical utility of science and learning. Not unlike Western statesmen of the time, he appreciated knowledge to the extent that it helped to build ships, construct fortresses and canals, and justify his policies and wars.

Inasmuch as science and learning were evaluated from the standpoint of their utility to the state, the gentry—that is, the stratum whose members were charged with serving the state—was urged to acquire education. Peter the Great continually reminded the *shlakhta* that it was through education and service that they could acquire a noble mark and hence distinguish themselves from the mean folk. Likewise, his "nestling" Tatishchev, while speaking in defense of secular learning in his *Discussion of Two Friends Concerning the Usefulness of the Sciences and of Schooling,* had the children of the gentry primarily in mind. He criticized the Academy of Sciences founded by Peter the Great for its failure to provide them with such "noble disciplines" as "fighting with swords, horseback riding, dancing and painting."[15] And although he was not opposed to having "intelligent and learned" peasants, it sufficed on the whole if they knew how to obey their masters.

Yet the reliance on the gentry as the principal bearer of Western scientific culture proved to be a failure. As it turned out, it was the stratum of society least disposed for this role. Not only did some "old believers" among the gentry continue to cling to the idea that their forefathers had lived happily without learning, but they sought refuge in monasteries in order to circumvent the Tsar's order to study abroad. As befits aspiring noblemen, they appeared unwilling to act without the spur of fame and worldly success. Science required from its practitioners the cultivation of personal disinterestedness, dedication, and that respect for discipline of which Bayle, Fontenelle, and other Western men of learning spoke. Russian fictional heroes and historical writers, however, viewed learning quite differently, even if they conceded its value. For them the humanistic quest for knowledge—the purely intellectual aspects of science—was never the *ultima ratio.* Learning was a means for a career of service and fame to be achieved both at home and "beyond the seas." Without learning, argued the Russian cavalier Alexander, one of those fictional men of learning, he would not only have nothing to boast about, but would not even feel justified in calling himself a nobleman.[16] Another such fictional man of learning, the sailor Vasilii Koriotskoi, accomplished, of course, nothing in science, but his "sharp mind" and "learning" enabled him to acquire superior rank (including that of the "King of Florence") and fame in whatever company he found himself.[17] An unknown author, although enjoining his son to study languages, mathematics, architecture, and fortification, tried hard to dissuade him from becoming an expert engineer or architect. He was advised instead to study all these subjects for the subsequent supervision of foreign experts. To paraphrase one more of those heroes, the nobles were not born to become men of science and, according to the eighteenth century observer from the Ukraine, followed the maxim: "nos nobiles sumus, rationem non curamus."[18] In Novikov's satirical periodical *Zhivopisets,* the young gentleman appraised scientific disciplines in this cavalier fashion:

> Mathematics—will it contribute to my income? No! To the hell with it! Physics—will it discover new secrets of nature useful to my adornment? No! Then it is unfit for anything! Geography—will it aid me in becoming more lovable? No! Then it is unworthy of my attention![19]

Significantly, the art of versifying remained the one subject worthy of his attention. Yet the young gentleman was in need of it only during moments of poetic inspiration when he felt like composing a madrigal.

As a result of this kind of attitude toward learning, science and men of science themselves were held in rather low esteem. The leading Russian eighteenth century playwright, Fonvizin, almost like some of his heroes, entertained a low opinion of those learned men who were masters of "useless curiosity" and abstract theorizing. In one of his letters from Leipzig, he appraised scientists and scholars as follows:

> I found this city filled with learned men. Some of them see their own and others' dignity in the fact that they can speak Latin, although it is known that in Cicero's time this language had been spoken by five-year old children; others raising their thoughts to heaven, fail to see what is taking place on earth; still others, possessing the knowledge of artificial logic, know little about the natural one.[20]

From the very outset of Peter's reforms, the gentry displayed its predilection for subjects that fit best with its station in life and were more compatible with its emerging value-orientation. The subject matter of one of the first books published in Peter's reign was far removed from astronomy or navigation. As its lengthy title discloses, it was a guide to manners: *Manual of Letter Writing. How Compliments Are Used in German by the One Ruler to Another; Congratulations, Condolences, etc., Correspondence between Relatives and Friends. Translated into Russian from the German.* Another book on the same theme, *The True Mirror of Youth or Instructions in Etiquette,* met with a huge success and ran quickly through three editions in Peter's reign alone. These translated books presented information on etiquette to be learned by those bent on becoming refined gentlemen and courtiers. They were expected to affect the unaffected manners of the Muscovites rather than enlighten them with the knowledge of sciences. According to the *True Mirror,* the young gentleman was supposedly the man who mastered several languages, horseback riding, and fencing. The knowledge of languages was not intended ultimately for the hard work of translation—after all, it was evident that Russified foreigners and commoners were able to do that—but rather as a mark of social status, a useful device by means of which well-bred gentlemen would be easily recognized among common people.

> Young men should always speak in a foreign language to one another in order to get practice, but especially when they discuss personal matters, so that their servants may not understand the conversation. Moreover, by the use of foreign languages they would distinguish themselves from various numbskulls....[21]

They were also advised to read some books, not too many, which would facilitate their participation in a refined society. Russian eighteenth-century letters abound with this new type of refined gentlemen. Thus, the nobleman Alexander, the hero of the facetiae referred to above, although versed in "philosophy and all other sciences," preferred the amusement of high society to scientific work "in solitude." He went, therefore, to Paris to see the "beauty of this world" rather than learn about "sciences that flourish in the academies," which he came to detest after three years of studying.[22] On his return from Paris, Fonvizin's Ivanushka dismissed the nonsense of all those pedants who think that human heads should be embellished from the inside. For the "devil only knows," he concluded, "what is hidden inside, whereas everyone can see what is outside."[23] Yet, Ivanushka prided himself of knowing how to live "dans le grande monde."[24]

In the course of the eighteenth century, this orientation of the Russian gentlemen—no doubt depicted somewhat exaggeratedly by the Russian writers—acquired much more serious character. Whereas in the *True Mirror,* for example, the young gentlemen were advised to refrain from reading too many books, since the contact with "two or three intelligent people" was more rewarding than the reading of books "for three days,"[25] a couple of decades later an anonymous author dismissed "empty, aimless chatter" and expressed his preference for books.

> Let empty heads suspect you (books) and learning but we shall never forget that you teach the people good morals and humane attitude. You are not for those who are weak in judgement and without authority. You are not for the mean and those blinded by their ignorance.[26]

Despite Peter's recurrent instructions to translate the works whose subject matter dealt with "deeds," that is practical topics, the Russian gentlemen were much more predisposed to read amusing and fond stories, to acquire affected manners and conversational skill *de rebus omnibus*. The aspiring gentlemen in the Cadet Corps, as Table 2.1 discloses, studied not only dancing, fencing, horsemanship, and other "noble disciplines," but also languages, history, literature, and other humanistic subjects. By Catherine's time, the grandsons of the midshipmen whom Peter had sent abroad to study navigation found their way into the most exclusive salons of Paris. In their manners and style of life, they were almost indistinguishable from the French aristocrats of the time, and resembled but little their uncouth grandfathers, who admittedly behaved *comme des sauvages.*[27] Within a short span of three generations, Peter's ideal of the Dutch dockyard thus gave way before the ideals of Versailles.

It was by no means accidental that the Cadet Corps, this university of the nobility, was the very institution that furnished the first Russian-educated men of letters: Elagin, Nartov, Olsufiev, Poroshkin, Shishkin, Sumarokov. As early as the fourth decade of the eighteenth century, young sons of the gentry of the Cadet Corps met together discussing letters and thus "spending usefully their leisure time."[28] Some of these literature-oriented coteries undertook the publication of literary magazines. An unknown author of one of such magazines, *Evenings*, wrote in its first issue: "We all compose a society and this society purports to show that a noble person can forego ombre and other games once a week and devote five hours to literature."[29]

All of them were, in effect, avocational writers, interested in letters, as was Kantemir several decades before, only in leisure hours. The very titles of their

Table 2.1 Subjects Studied by Young Cadets in 1733*

Subject	Number of Students	Subject	Number of Students
German	237	Drawing	34
Dancing	110	History	28
French	51	Horsemanship	20
Fencing	47	Russian	18
Music	39	Geography	17
Geometry	36	Latin	15

*Source: "Raport Minikha o Kadetskom Korpuse," *Chteniia v Imperatorskom Obshchestve Istorii i Drevnostei Rossiiskikh pri Moskovskom Universitete,* No. 1 (1862), 66.

publications shed light on their attitude toward, and the character of, the literary activity: *Evenings, Free Time Turned into Usefulness, Useful Amusement, Free Times,* and *Innocent Exercise.* These first literary practitioners continued to uphold *vita activa* and served more or less successfully the Tsar and the Muse. The generation of the Decembrists and some Decembrists themselves were still typical representatives of such writers of divided loyalty.

The corollary of this avocational interest in literature is readily apparent. With the evaporation of youthful enthusiasm, the incipient literary coteries and magazines disappeared and their members and contributors abandoned their side-line occupation of writers for service and military careers. Some of them terminated the publication of magazines because the contributors decided to take vacation, others because of war activities, still others because of official transfer and other service duties. It is, therefore, important to emphasize that the precarious existence of the first literary undertakings in Russia are not to be accounted for so much by the oppressive policy of autocracy or even by the dearth of a reading public, as by the character of the social stratum that appropriated the literary activity. This stratum was the gentry, which at that time had aimed primarily at a post in the service of the state.

Social Origin and Composition of the Russian Cultural, Military, and Religious Elites

Statistical studies of the growth of the social and national composition of the Russian cultural elite hardly exist. Our findings on this problem are sufficiently comprehensive to shed light on some of the unsettled issues bearing on the social character of the Russian intelligentsia. We have traced and compared on the basis of various sources the social origin of over 2,200 Russian scholars, men of letters, professional people (doctors, artists, actors), and members of the military and religious elites born between 1750 and 1849. At this point in our analysis, we present only that portion of our findings that pertains to those born in the second half of the eighteenth century.

The data presented in Table 2.2 permit a series of important observations on the relative share of the various social strata in the shaping of the cultural life in Russia. First, they confirm a long recognized fact about the conspicuous absence and insignificant role of the so-called middle classes in the cultural life of Russia. Second, they provide a more realistic perspective on the cultural role of the nobility in the eighteenth-century Russia. Most certainly, these data do not confirm the view that the "seedbed" of the Russian intelligentsia was the nobility or that its "first generation ... stemmed largely from the nobility,"[30] unless one equates the intelligentsia with the men of letters. Nor do these data favor the view that the literary craft in Russia attracted the individuals of "most diverse classes and social strata"[31] since the second half of the eighteenth century. Rather, they disclose the tendency on the part of the nobility, clergy, and the commoners to appropriate particular spheres of cultural life. Whereas the gentry, for example, tended to preempt literary and military pursuits, a disproportionately high number of individuals of clerical origin or, as they have come to be known, seminarists, entered scholarly and professional occupations. In this sense, literature in Russia received an aristocratic foundation, whereas scholarly and professional occupations were relegated to the toiler of the lower social order. Over half (53.3 percent) of Russian scholars (excluding foreigners) and 57.9 percent of doctors born between 1750 and 1799 came from the clergy. The religious elite was well-nigh completely preempted by the sons of the clergy, and formed a status group increasingly isolated from the emergent secular culture and its bearers. Finally, the Russian peasant hardly strayed from the place assigned to him by serfdom. His best opportunity for cultural expression and advancement was in the fields of art (painters, sculptors, musicians) and theatre (actors, singers).[32]

It is important to note that the paramount role of the nobility in Russian letters continued for over a century. If we consider those writers who contributed for a short period to satirical magazines—a fashionable literary activity initiated by the Empress Catherine—they consisted of four commoners, twenty-six from the gentry, two counts, one princess, and, of course, leading them all, the "wise Minerva" herself, Catherine. The paramount role of the nobility in Russian letters remained virtually unimpaired until the middle of the last century. Of some 120 writers born between 1800 and 1825, 85 (70.9 percent) of them stemmed from the gentry. The well-known salonnière, Madame de Staël, referred to this preeminence of the gentry in literature when she wrote in 1811: "En Russie quelques gentilshommes se sont occupés de littérature."[33]

It is manifest that it was not so much the literary stratum whose members hailed from diverse ranks of society, but the scholarly and professional groups, the very groups so much despised by the intelligentsia. What is more, their membership comprised a high proportion of the "spiteful" sons of priests and other commoners who, according to a prevalent hypothesis, were responsible for the radical orientation of the intelligentsia. How are we to account, then, for this widely held view of the men of letters as drawn from all strata and ranks of society? By taking the literati alone, of course, in isolation from the scholarly and professional groupings, one can readily point to Trediakovsky, Kostrov, Petrov, Polevoi, Belinsky, and other individual commoners. Furthermore, it can also be argued that the predominance of the gentry among the men of letters reflected the social composition of the educated public in Russia. Such an interpretation, however, runs counter to the fact that the ratio of commoners to gentry among the scholars and the professionals born between 1750 and 1799 was 5.5 and 8.9 respectively. On the other hand, the ratio of commoners to gentry among the literati born between 1750 and 1799 was 0.38. The predominance of commoners among the scholars and doctors remained so throughout the greater part of the nineteenth century. Of the 166 Russian scholars born in the first half of the nineteenth century, only 46 (27.7 percent) were of gentry origin. These differences are even more suggestive in view of the fact that the literary calling did not necessarily require an academic degree, as did the scholarly and professional

Table 2.2 Social Origin of Members of Cultural, Military, and Religious Elites, Born 1750–1799*

Social and occupational status of father	Literati		Artists Actors		Scholars		Doctors		Religious Elite		Military Elite	
	No.	%	No.	%	No.	%	No.	%	No.	%	No.	%
Nobility	92	71.3	6	5.5	22	10.1	12	6.4	1	1.1	315	78.0
Minor officials & Military	3	2.3	28	25.5	15	6.9	10	5.3	3	3.3	24	5.9
Clergy	19	14.7	2	1.8	64	29.4	62	33.0	85	94.5	2	.5
Burghers & Merchants	8	6.2	10	9.1	2	.9	14	7.5	1	1.1	4	1.0
Professionals	1	.8	10	9.1	15	6.9	9	4.8	–	–	10	2.5
Peasants	4	3.1	23	20.9	2	.9	–	–	–	–	–	–
Foreigners	2	1.6	31	28.2	98	45.0	81	43.1	–	–	49	12.1
Total	129		110		218		188		90		404	

*Source: *Russkii Biograficheskii Slovar* (St. Petersburg, 1896–1918), 25 vols.; A. V. Arsebev, *Slovar Pisatelei Sredniago i Novago Periodov Russkoi Literatury XVII–XIX Veka* (St. Petersburg, 1887); S. A. Vengerov (ed.), *Kritiko-Biograficheskii Slovar Russkikh Pisatelei i Uchenykh* (St. Petersburg, 1889–1904), 6 vols.

occupations, and consequently was accessible to talented individuals without formal training.

Education, conceived initially by Peter the Great as preparation for state service, had come to be looked on by the gentry as training for social refinement and conversational skill, and as a preparation for amateur literary activity. The establishment of boarding schools for gentry and Catherine's educational measures aimed at providing "humanistic" education that would emphasize all-round cultural development, strengthened even more the literary orientation of the gentry. The hero of Herzen's novel *Who Is to Blame,* Beltov, represented the climax of this development. Almost like Baudelaire's creation, the Dandy, this young squire frowned on every useful activity.[34] Professional work—medicine, for example—which he looked at as prosaic routine work, he simply abandoned for the sake of art. Indeed, professional and scholarly pursuits were not in keeping with the dignity of the gentleman. Whereas educated sons of nobles, some of them bent on early retirement, founded literary coteries, the sons of the clergy and other commoners viewed education as the major avenue for advancement in the official hierarchy and as a basis for a professional career. So apparent was this separation of scientific and literary spheres along social lines that Russian teachers and doctors were for long equated with seminarists and Ukrainians. When reminiscing on his studies at the University of Moscow during the 1830s, Herzen pointed out that some of the faculties were well-nigh monopolized by commoners.

> Thus, for instance, the medical section, which was on the other side of the garden, was not so closely united with us as the other

faculties: moreover, the majority of the medical students consisted of seminarists and Germans ...[35]

What we witness here is a lag in the assimilation, by educated common-ers, of the values and sentiments of the Russian gentlemen-littérateurs. It was only toward the middle of the nineteenth century that they "caught up" with the high valuation of literary activity and with the hallmark of prestige conferred on it by its noble practitioners. There is no gainsaying the fact, therefore, that for over a century the Russian men of letters formed socially one of the most homogeneous and, except for the military, the most gentry-dominated status group.

During the period under consideration, Russian scholars and professional people were socially and ethnically considerably more diversified. Those few of them recruited from the gentry came mainly from the Ukraine. It was there, as Poletika noted, that scientific and medical professions were not considered below the dignity of the gentry.[36] Of the thirty-one professors of gentry origin who taught at the University of Moscow between 1755 and 1855, twelve were Ukrainians and four Poles.[37] This presence of many ethnics among Russian scholars and doctors is worthy of note here. The first distinguished Russian mathematicians, for example, Buniakovsky and Ostrogradsky, were of Ukrainian origin. A "stubborn khokhol" (derogatory for Ukrainian), Poletika, was the first Russian professor in a European university (Kiel). Another Ukrainian, Desnitsky, educated at the University of Edinburgh, was the "forefather" of Russian legal scholarship. The distinguished mathema-tician Lobachevsky, was most likely of Polish origin, since his father was Catholic and came to Russia from Poland. Another Pole, Senkovsky, was one of the first linguists-orientalists in Russia. The first Russian distinguished doc-tors and professors of medicine were almost exclusively Ukrainians.

Despite the high proportion of non-Russian ethnics among scholars and professional people, Russian scholarship was nurtured for over a century by the West. And, although this fact is being played down, if not altogether ignored, in the Soviet Union today, foreigners dominated Russian scholarship and professional occupations for over a century. It is only since the middle of the nineteenth century that Russian science has stood on its own feet. Of the 107 members of the Academy of Sciences in the eighteenth century, only 26.2 percent were Russians.[38] As late as 1855 the majority of its members were foreigners. Close to half (45.0 percent) of the Russian scholars born between 1750 and 1799 were foreigners (excluding those of foreign parentage). Out of fifty-six professors who taught at the University of Moscow during the second half of the eighteenth century (1755–1800), only seventeen (30.4 percent) of them were ethnically Russians, twenty-nine (51.8 percent) were foreigners, and ten (17.8 percent) were Ukrainians.[39] Even more dominated by foreigners was the field of medicine. Of some 500 doctors who practiced medicine in Russia during the eighteenth century, 410 were foreigners or of foreign origin and only 16 were Russians (53 Ukrainians, 15 Poles, and 6 unknown).[40]

The diverse ethnic and cultural background of the scholars and professional people in Russia, the negligible number among them, as the historian Karamzin regretfully observed, of individuals recruited from the upper stratum of society, left their stamp on these emerging groupings and adversely affected their status in Russian society. Until the reign of Alexander I, hardly any scholar in Russia was able to advance above the rank of collegiate councillor in the service hierarchy, even though repeated petitions for advancement began with Lomonosov.[41] In contrast to the West, where educational institutions and scholarly and professional occupations antedated the rise of modern polities, scholarship and learning in Russia were created, as it were, by the will of the Tsar and by the work of displaced foreigners. They were thus called to life by the state itself in order to serve its needs. Two subgroups—foreigners of diverse national backgrounds and indigenous elements (many of them recruited from non-Russian ethnic groups)—were brought together and commanded to develop science and secular culture in Russia. For understandable reasons, they could neither evolve a corporate solidarity nor assert their intellectual independence from the state. Internally divided, they fell prey to official whims and long availed themselves of the political arbiter in settling their own internal differences and conflicts. Although the history of the relationship of foreign and Russian scholars is still to be written, there is no doubt that this foreign-versus-Russian conflict continued to reappear until the second half of the nineteenth century. Herzen's appraisal of this relationship at the University of Moscow seems to have been typical:

> The professors consisted of two groups or classes who placidly hated each other. One group was composed exclusively of Germans, the other of non-Germans. The Germans, among whom were good-natured men such as Loder, Fischer, Hildebrand, and Heym himself, were as a rule distinguished by their ignorance of the Russian language and disinclination to learn it.... The non-Germans, for their part knew not a single living language except Russian, were servile in their patriotism. The Germans for the most part hailed from Goettingen and the non-Germans were sons of priests.[42]

The echoes of this strife between German and Russian scholars were still heard as late as 1855. At the election of the secretary of the academy, for example, there existed two or even three hostile factions. Prior to the election, the Russian faction circulated a note, endorsed by a highly placed official, in which the Russian Davidov was proposed for the post of the secretary. Commenting on this electoral procedure, one of the members of the academy, Nikitenko, wrote:

> Any German could have stood up and said: "Respected gentlemen, why do you worry? Everyone is allowed to vote.... Please cast your votes and

the balloting shall show whom the Academy prefers. Why these devious methods? We should all adhere to the rules, but you somehow introduce strange electoral procedures."[43]

Finally, the "clever *khokhol*" (Ukrainian), the mathematician Ostrogradsky, represented still another faction, which "silently laughed at both the Germans and the Russians."[44]

These politically inspired recriminations began with the first generation of Russian scholars, as Lomonosov's feuds with his foreign colleagues so tellingly exemplify. Refusing to distinguish, as Mueller complained, a "panegyrical speech" from "historical dissertation,"[45] he flooded the senate and his patrons with letters denouncing his foreign colleagues, the founders of the Russian historiography, for expressing in their works "much nonsense, derogatory of Russia" and for intentionally selecting "black spots" from her history.[46] Another Russian scholar, P. Krekshin, appropriated Mueller's notes and refused to return them on the ground that they contained "defamatory, false and shameful matters."[47] As if to add insult to injury, he went on to suggest that Mueller should not only be forbidden to write but also to think.[48] Ironically enough, Lomonosov and other Russian scholars branded their foreign colleagues as "persecutors" of the sciences. Lomonosov himself, it may be noted in passing, conceived of historical research as series of edifying stories that would remind the world of the "glorious deeds of our Tsars."[49] He accomplished this feat for the most part through the medium of odes.

Anticipating such difficulties, the philosopher Wolff, the father of the German *Aufklaerung,* refused to join the academy in 1722, and explained his decision not solely on the grounds of such considerations as different climate and food but also as follows:

In addition one more principal problem. Shall I be induced to express my scientific ideas only to the extent to which they are convenient for the present-day Russians? Were this the case, I should be deprived of accomplishing that which is feasible here under my present conditions.[50]

Faced with the hostility of Russian colleagues and with the suspicion of political patrons, several distinguished Western scholars left the academy, that "corps phantasque," as the astronomer Delisle called it, and never returned to Russia.[51] The less fortunate ones were forbidden to publish and even to continue their research. At least one scholar, Professor Mellmann, was accused of harboring "subversive ideas" and was dismissed from his teaching position. Since Mellmann refused to repent, he was decreed "mentally deranged" and ordered to leave Russia.[52] Others continued to teach and to pursue their scholarly activities, under conditions in which not only historical facts but astronomical observations were at one time considered as state secrets.

Notes

1. A. P. Shchapov, *Sochineniia* (St. Petersburg, 1906), II, p. 528.
2. Ibid., p. 521.
3. Ibid., p. 531.
4. P. Pekarsky, *Nauka i Literatura v Rossii pri Petre Velikom* (St. Petersburg, 1862), I, p. 267.
5. P. Miliukov, *Ocherki po Istorii Russkoi Kultury* (Paris, 1930), III, pp. 130–31.
6. L. I. Beskrovnyi, M. M. Shtrange, and P. I. Iakovleva, eds., *Mezhdunarodnye Sviazi Rossii v XVII–XVIII vv.* (Moscow, 1966), p. 307.
7. "Posolstvo Likhacheva v Florentsiiu," *Drevniaia Rossiiskaia Bibliotika*, ed. N. Novikov (Moscow, 1788), IV, p. 351.
8. Ibid., pp. 353–59; *see also* "Putishestvie Stolnika P. A. Tolstago," *Russkii Arkhiv* 26 (1888): 519; "Stateinoi Spisok Posolstva Borisa Petrovicha Sheremeteva," *Drevniaia Rossiiskaia Bibliotika*, V, p. 349.
9. "Zhurnal Puteshestviia po Germanii, Gollandii i Italii 1697–1699 gg.," *Russkaia Starina* 25 (May 1879): 116; *see also* A. Brueckner, *Beitraege zur Kulturgeschichte Russlands im XVIII Jahrhundert* (Leipzig: Verlag von B. Elischer, 1887), pp. 164–65.
10. "Povest o Rossiiskom Kavalere Aleksandre," *Russkie Povesti Pervoi Treti 18 Veka*, ed. G. N. Moiseeva (Moscow, 1965), p. 270.
11. "Zhurnal Puteshestviia," *Russkaia Starina* 25 (May 1879): 112–13.
12. Ibid., p. 127.
13. P. Pekarsky, "Poezdka Grafa Matveeva v Parizh v 1705 Godu," *Sovremennik*, no. 6 (1856), pp. 60–63.
14. "Putishestvie…P. A. Tolstago," *Russkii Arkhiv* 26 (1888): 547.
15. V. N. Tatishchev, "Razgavor o Poize Nauk i Uchilishch," *Chteniia v Imperatorskom Obshchestve Istorii i Drevnostei Rossiiskikh pri Moskovskom Universitete*, Book 1 (1887), p. 112.
16. Quoted in G. V. Plekhanov, *History of Russian Social Thought* (New York: Howard Fertig, 1967), p. 26.
17. "Historiia o Rossiiskom Matrose Vasilii Koriotskom i o Prekresnoi Korolevne Irakli Florenskoi Zemli," *Russkie Povesti*, p. 210.
18. I. F. Timkavsky, "Zapiski Illi Feodorovicha Timkavskogo," *Russkii Arkhiv* 11 (1873): 1415.
19. P. N. Berkov, ed., *Satiricheskie Zhurnaly N. I. Novikova* (Moscow, 1951), p. 289.
20. D. I. Fonvizin, *Sochineniia*, 2d ed. (St. Petersburg, 1846), p. 271.
21. V. Desnitsky, "Reforma Petra I i Russkaia Literatura XVIII v.," *Izbrannye Stati po Russkoi Literature XVIII–XIX vv.* (Moscow-Leningrad, 1958), p. 20.
22. *Russkie Povesti*, p. 97.
23. D. I. Fonvizin, *Pesy: Brigadir-Nedorosl'* (Moscow-Leningrad, 1945), p. 17.
24. Ibid., p. 32.
25. Miliukov, *Ocherki*, III, p. 179.
26. P. N. Berkov, *Istoriia Russkoi Zhurnalistiki XVIII Veka* (Moscow-Leningrad, 1952), p. 125.
27. *See* Dimitri S. von Mohrenschildt, *Russia in the Intellectual Life of Eighteenth Century France* (New York: Octagon Books, 1972), p. 52.
28. Berkov, *Istoriia Russkoi Zhurnalistiki*, p. 291.
29. Ibid.
30. Marc Raeff, *Origins of the Russian Intelligentsia* (New York: Harcourt, Brace & World, Inc., 1966), p. 9; for a "democratic" (non-noble) makeup of the eighteenth century intelligentsia, *see* M. M. Shtrange, *Demokraticheskaia Intelligentsiia Rossii v XVIII Veke* (Moscow, 1965).
31. *See* S. L. Peshtich, *Russkaia Istoriografiia XVIII Veka* (Leningrad, 1965), p. 11.

32. E. Leshkova, "Krepostnaia Intelligentsiia," *Otechestvennye Zapiski* (November 1883), pp. 157–98.
33. A. S. Pushkin, *Polnoe Sobranie Sochinenii* (Moscow, 1958), X, p. 607; with some few exceptions, all the contributors to *Poliarnaia Zvezda*, published between 1823 and 1825, were of noble origin: Boratynsky, Bestuzhev, Batiushkov, Prince Viazemsky, Voeikov, Glinka, Gnedich, Grigoriev, Davydov, Count Delvig, Dmitriev, Zhukovsky, Izmailov, Kniazhevich, Norov, Panaev, Rodzianko, Khvostov, Khomiakov, Prince Shakhovsky, Senkovsky. *See* M. I. Semevsky, "Almanakh *Zvezdochka* na 1826 God," *Russkii Arkhiv* 7 (1869): 55–56.
34. A. I. Herzen, *Kto Vinovat* (Moscow, 1948), p. 108.
35. A. I. Herzen, *My Past and Thoughts: The Memoirs of Alexander Herzen*, trans. Constance Garnett (New York: Alfred A. Knopf, 1924), I, p. 121.
36. P. I. Poletika, "Vospominaniia Petra Ivanovicha Poletika," *Russkii Arkhiv* 23 (1885): 307.
37. *Biograficheskii Slovar Professorov i Prepodavatelei Imperatorskogo Moskovskogo Universiteta: 1755–1855* (Moscow, 1855), 2 vols.
38. J. D. Duff, ed., *Russian Realities and Problems* (Cambridge: Cambridge University Press, 1917), p. 113; *see also* "Lichnyi Sostav Imperatorskoi Akademii Nauk," *Zapiski Imperatorskoi Akademii Nauk* 1 (September 1862): 66–78.
39. *Biograficheskii Slovar Professorov.*
40. Compiled on the basis of biographical sketches found in the works of Ia. Chistovich, *Istoriia Pervykh Meditsinskikh Shkol v Rossii* (St. Petersburg, 1883); L. F. Zmeev, *Russkie Vrachi-Pisateli* (St. Petersburg, 1886), 5 vols.
41. *See* Lomonosov's letter to Count Razumovsky in M. V. Lomonosov, *Polnoe Sobranie Sochinenii* (Moscow, 1957), X, p. 458; S. Ashevksy, "Iz Istorii Moskovskogo Universiteta," *Mir Bozhii* (February 1905), p. 2.
42. Herzen, *My Past*, I, p. 136.
43. A. V. Nikitenko, *Zapiski i Dnevnik* (St. Petersburg, 1893), II, p. 7.
44. Ibid., p. 6; *see also* Bulgakov, "Nemetskaia Partiia v Russkoi Akademii," *Russkii Vestnik* 4 (1881): 421–31.
45. Lomonosov, *Polnoe*, VI, p. 67; *see also* "Lomonosov i Peterburgskaia Akademiia Nauk," *Chteniia v Imperatorskom Obshchestve Istorii i Drevnostei pri Moskovskom Universitete*, I (1865): 47.
46. Lomonosov, *Polnoe*, VI, p. 21; *see also* A. N. Pypin, *Istoriia Russkoi Literatury* (St. Petersburg, 1911), III, p. 510.
47. *See* Peshtich, *Russkaia Istoriografiia*, p. 172.
48. Ibid.
49. "Lomonosov kak Istorik," *Russkii Arkhiv* 49 (1911): 564.
50. Pypin, *Istoriia Russkoi*, III, p. 509.
51. P. Pekarsky, *Istoriia Imperatorskoi Akademii Nauk* (St. Petersburg, 1870), II, p. 39.
52. Ashevsky, *Mir Bozhii*, p. 3.

3   Men of Letters: The Birth of the Intelligentsia

Western and Russian authors alike have expressed divergent views concerning the emergence of the intelligentsia as a distinct social group. Some of them trace the appearance of the intelligentsia to Peter the Great and, in fact, conceive of him as the first Russian *intelligent;*[1] others claim that the "type of the Russian intelligentsia was established by its first member Radishchev,"[2] that is, during Catherine's reign; still others date the origin of the intelligentsia from either the forties or the sixties of the last century. There is little doubt that underlying this disagreement over the origin of the intelligentsia are competing definitions of the term itself.

But regardless of the explicit definitions offered by many authors, the image of the intelligentsia was essentially a literary one. The literary historian Pypin, for example, defined the intelligentsia as the leading scholars and writers. Yet, in his enumeration of the "flower of the intellectual forces of the country,"[3] Pypin referred only to the men of letters—to Lomonosov (the literary image of Lomonosov), Radishchev, Novikov, Belinsky, Dobroliubov—and not at all to the distinguished mathematicians Lobachevsky, Buniakovsky, Ostrogradsky, or to the historians Mueller, Solovev, Kostomarov, or to the leading linguists Sreznevsky and Lazarevsky. Similarly, Miliukov defined the term *intelligentsia* as the "inner circle," the creative segment of the educated public, but again he confined the "inner circle" of creative individuals to the men of letters.[4] We find this inadvertent equation of the intelligentsia with the men of letters in the works of many contemporary European and American authors. This divergence between the explicitly formulated and implicitly held conceptions of the intelligentsia indicates that formal definitions are hardly useful in coming to grips with our problem. Obviously such terms as scholars, verse-composers, rhymesters, *literatory,* writers, poets, *bumago-marateli* (scribblers), and literary critics antedate the usage of the term *intelligentsia* in Russia. It was only in the seventies of the last century that the word acquired wide usage. To contend that it was introduced for the sole purpose of subsuming under one name all the poets, writers, and literary critics is hardly convincing. Such generic terms as *literatory* could have served the same purpose. Historically, the introduction of the term *intelligentsia* coincided with the appearance in Russia of ideologically oriented men of letters.

It is with these last, with their rise to preeminence on the Russian cultural scene, that the present study is primarily concerned.

The Writer-Official: Court-Bard and Ode-Writer

The first generation of Russian men of letters found employment in chancelleries as secretaries and copyists, or were attached to newly established state institutions of learning (the Academy of Sciences and the University of Moscow) as official scribes and translators, or, if more successful, to the court as its official bards and entertainers. In an attempt to evolve a proper measure of display, the Russian court had maintained for almost a century the literary retainers who wrote odes and epistles to make known to the world the "glorious deeds" of the Tsars as well as provide other literary bagatelle for *les menus plaisirs* of court dignitaries. Almost all Russian writers of the eighteenth century commenced their literary careers by composing odes and epistles. Some of them, like Perepichin, confined their entire careers to the cultivation of this literary genre, as if to underscore the fact that their talents as well as interest in letters hardly went beyond edifying verses.

Throughout the eighteenth century, writing remained a diversion to be indulged in only when there were no urgent matters of service, and plays, poems, and other amateur diffusions were a matter of secondary concern. To serve the court and the state seemed more honorable than to wield the pen in the name of the Muses. The first men of letters in Russia were thus primarily officials and were writers only in their idleness. Inasmuch as they acquired titles and honors sometimes through service and sometimes through literary work, the two pursuits became sufficiently interwoven to be viewed as complementary aspects of one service to the state. This close interrelationship between service, *chin* (rank), and literary activity can be seen from the career of Kheraskov, so poignantly related by his own wife:

> During the coronation M.M. (Mikhailo M. Kheraskov) was granted the rank of councillor of state, after the coronation, on the occasion of the second arrival of Catherine, M.M. wrote the Epistle, which she liked, and, as a result, she gave him the golden snuff-box filled with *chervontsi.* Later on, for the ode written by him, Catherine granted him 2000 rubles, and again, after the lapse of several years, another snuff-box with diamonds ... During the reign of Paul he received the rank of secret councillor, 600 souls and the order of St. Anne.... With the coming to the throne of Alexander I he became the Curator of the University for the second time and also received another snuff-box with diamonds. During the coronation he was given the ring-solitaire and I was granted the order of St. Catherine.[5]

To be sure, not all writers of the eighteenth century were able to combine so effectively service in the official hierarchy with literary work. The careers of Derzhavin, Dmitriev, and Bogdanovich, however, resembled that of Kheraskov. Like all crafty flatterers, they intermittently turned to extolling their own masters and were granted in return "human souls" and snuff-boxes filled with *chervontsi*; at the very most, they were appointed to high positions in the government or even promoted by the court to the status of "official bards."

The first Russian men of letters experienced a difficulty in their attempts to bestow a semblance of respectability on their literary activities, more formidable, for example, than that faced by Molière or Racine, due to the utter novelty of the literary vocation in the Russian society of that time. It is of little surprise, therefore, that they proclaimed themselves indispensable to the state by making their literary pursuits assume the role of another state service—one that would provide the court and its "supreme authority," the Tsar, with "eternal fame." Within two generations, the Russian Parnassus came to be inhabited by a company of luminaries who promoted each other with little qualm to Homer (Kheraskov), Pindar and Virgil (Lomonosov), Horace (Derzhavin), Racine and Voltaire (Sumarokov), and La Fontaine (Dmitriev).[6] The "northern Racine," Sumarokov, was both conceited and naive enough to appraise his literary achievements in these exaggerated words:

> Whatever Athens and Paris had accomplished and, after a long time, Russia accomplished it by my own labor.... You need not be ashamed any longer either of my plays or of my actors. What many a poet in Germany was unable to achieve, I have accomplished with my own pen, under conditions in which not only literature but the literary language itself were in their infancy. Leipzig and Paris, you can testify how much honor has accrued to me through the translation of one tragedy of mine! The scholarly society of Leipzig has accepted me for its member, and in Paris my name has been mentioned in a foreign journal.[7]

Such sporadic outbursts of pride reflected not so much a high regard for the Muses as the indignation of frustrated men who were treated more often than not as court wits rather than as useful servants of the state. Some court notables, indeed, expounded the view that the writers were "unfit for any useful work" and, as if to add insult to injury, proposed to commit these "superfluous people" to a madhouse.[8] It was no other than Empress Catherine, however, who advised Derzhavin, who seemed to be unable to retain any official position for long, to forego service and devote himself instead to literary pursuits.[9] For determined, as most of them were, on official careers and the acquisition of *chins,* they could not but become exasperated by the fact that favors and honors were more readily granted to scribes and paramours than to self-appointed Homers and Racines. Clinging to the idea of state service and turning to the Muses, in Derzhavin's phrase, only "on occasions free of service,"[10] they were unwillingly pushed into identifying themselves with the men of letters. As late as the 1780s, the leading playwright Fonvizin implored Catherine II to employ all writers in official work in order "to enable us, while serving the Russian Muses in idleness, to devote our lives to the service of Your Majesty."[11] This was necessary, he continued, because some highly placed dignitaries considered the literary vocation a "criminal activity" and had therefore secretly agreed: (1) not to employ any of the writers, and (2) to discharge those of the writers who were employed at present.[12]

Behind the facade of conceit there often existed literary flatterers with fanciful titles whose obeisance to the court and its dignitaries was only too transparent. Sumarokov boasted of the fact that he devoted his whole life to the amusement of the court;[13] Trediakovsky and Lomonosov were only too conscious of their honorific titles of "official bards" and, indeed, seemed to have taken this jestful recognition for a measure of their literary excellence; Derzhavin reminded himself and all who would listen of being "Her Majesty's personal author;"[14] and court rhymester Petrov proudly bore the title of the "pocket poet of Her Majesty."[15] The behavior of Fonvizin shows beyond doubt that this leading playwright of Catherine's reign considered writing at one time as a means of joining the court entourage and himself as little more than its entertainer. On completion of his first play, *Brigadir,* Fonvizin ran from one mansion to another, from one notable to another, amusing them with the readings of his work.

Throughout the greater part of the eighteenth century the social position of writers in Russia was that of favorites, depending on the benevolence and the whims of court patrons. As protégés of courtiers, they learned from harsh experience that not only honors and titles but material security and advancement in the official hierarchy were ultimately dependent on favors. Despite Lomonosov's boastful claim that he would not become another "fool to worldly rulers," he sensed only too well that his own personal dignity was contingent on these same rulers, as his complaint addressed to Count Shuvalov makes quite clear: "On my visits to the office, I am forced to humble myself before every office scribe. This makes me all the more so ashamed because of your patronage."[16] If Sumarokov believed at times that an individual of "distinguished ancestry, with *chins* and honors, and renown all over Europe" would not be forgotten and let "wander in the world or freeze in the street,"[17] on other occasions, he was also capable of asking in despair: "What for do I need the honor of a distinguished writer if there is nothing to drink and to eat?"[18] Far from being a hyperbole, this pathetic passage of Sumarokov faithfully reflected his own life: abandoned by court patrons, without official position and financial security, he ended his literary career as a dipsomaniac and died in misery, forgotten by all, including his literary colleagues. Even less enviable was the literary career of Sumarokov's contemporary, Trediakovsky, whose image of himself as a "wise man" and "prophet" betrayed a servile jester trained to crawl on his knees before the throne of Empress Anna only to be greeted by a slap in the face. Barred from publishing in the only existing magazine and deprived of position in the academy, Trediakovsky too was left without a "single penny at home, without a slice of bread and firewood"[19] and ended his life in wretched circumstances. Moreover, despite his title of an "official bard," Trediakovsky was subjected to physical punishment—that time-honored custom of Muscovy—for writing an epigram that seemed to have offended a highly placed notable. His attempt to find redress brought more of the same: he was placed under arrest and nearly flogged to death.

While reflecting on his literary predecessors, the eighteenth century men of letters, Pushkin compared them to court jesters.

> Sumarokov was a clown to all lords: to Shuvalov, to Panin, and to others. They incited and teased him for their own amusement. Fonvizin entertained dignitaries and flattered Panin ... Derzhavin wrote satires on Sumarokov and delighted himself, in the presence of dignitaries, with his sullen behavior.[20]

Pushkin's harsh reference to the buffoonery of his predecessors is borne out by evidence available from other sources. It is supported by the testimony of patrons, like Count Shuvalov, who witnessed many an encounter of "incensed versifiers."

> In their squabbles, the more angered Sumarokov was, the more Lomonosov tried to tease him. And if both of them were not entirely sober the squabble broke out into abuse of each other. Whenever Lomonosov expressed his grievances I usually called for Sumarokov. Sumarokov, hearing at the door of Lomonosov's presence, either departed or ran in, exclaiming: "Do not trust him, Your Excellency, he is a habitual liar! I wonder how you can patronize such a drunkard and scoundrel." "You are yourself a scoundrel, drunkard and ignoramus," retorted Lomonosov, "all the scenes in your plays have been stolen."[21]

Catherine's venture into literature, her initiative in publishing a satirical periodical, her expressed belief that many "legitimate and illegitimate children" (including the miscreants) would follow suit, and her fondness for poetry, which admittedly equaled that for the "lemonade in summer time,"[22] could not but enhance the self-image of court flatterers. So too, Catherine's encouragement of the writers to take on the function of social critics, combined with her "permission to speak freely," helped to secure for the writers a semblance of public recognition they had hitherto lacked. Writers were thus advised not only to amuse society and celebrate "thundering victories" in verse but also to become secular moralizers who should "defend virtue" and "combat vice." Among the first to respond to this "offer of freedom to the Russian minds" was Novikov, who thanked Catherine for "opening up the path he alone would have feared to tread."[23] One decade later, Fonvizin's Starodum still harkened back to the challenge of Catherine when he called on writers to turn into the guardians of the commonweal.

The satirical ire of Catherine's "children" was directed against unwelcome intermediaries and competitors from the officialdom who acquired *chins* and titles at the expense of enlightened and "decent men." But the chief target of their animus was the petty official on whom the satirists heaped sundry charges until he emerged as vice incarnate. Far more circumspect, however, was the treatment accorded highly placed dignitaries and court favorites. In his ode, *Felicia,* for example, Derzhavin satirized court favorites (Potemkin) only to wax lyrical in praise of Catherine, as if to make the empyrean light of her Majesty shine even more so brightly against the shady background of her favorites.

More important, perhaps, the emergent enmity between the writer and the *chinovnik* (official) heralded a disengagement of the former from the service, which ended ultimately in complete estrangement from the official *ordo.* At the time when *chin* served as the prime source of status in society, indeed, defined the personal worth of an individual, the Russian writers were the first to voice their preference for fame rather than *chin.*[24] Originally formulated by Kniazhnin, this change in the conception of the writer's relationship to office was shared by his contemporaries, including Fonvizin's Starodum who addressed the authors in these lofty words:

And thus Russian writers! What a wide field of work has been open to your talents! If some timid soul, dwelling in a distinguished dignitary, turns against you from fear as well as from trying to avoid suffering from your accusation, your pen can easily expose him before the throne, before the country and the world. I think that this freedom to write that we Russians enjoy endows a gifted individual with the role of watchman of the commonweal. In those countries that grant the writer the privilege of freedom the writers are duty-bound to raise loudly their voice against all abuses and prejudices detrimental to the country. An able individual, sitting in his room with pen in hand, can be a useful adviser to the Tsar and at times a saviour of the citizens and the country.[25]

Whereas Kniazhnin still thought of the *chin* as a useful "adjunct to talent,"[26] Fonvizin's Starodum showed a willingness to forego an active service career and devote himself to the task of a professional moralist with nothing but a pen in his hand. Although no longer engrossed in office work, as the champion of the commonweal he was determined to retain the right of criticizing the *chinovniki,* seemingly unperturbed that, except for such individual patrons as Shuvalov, Panin, and Vorontsov, there was neither a community of writers nor any social group and public opinion that would support his crusade on behalf of the commonweal. To be sure, he still entertained hopes that the Tsar and the court would accept his good advice and might even grant him rewards for his work. But this hope came to naught, since the *chinovnik* retained the confidence of Tsars and Starodum's descendents turned into critics of both.

The Gentleman-Littérateur

The disappearance of the *chin*-oriented writers and court bards from the cultural scene must be viewed against the background of the emancipation of the gentry estate from compulsory state service. This emancipatory process began as early as 1730, with Anna's accession to the throne, and culminated in Catherine's Charter of 1785, which granted the gentry corporate status as well as exclusive domination over peasant serfs.

As a result of these reforms there evolved a privileged status group in society whose members had relinquished service as their primary occupation and followed instead a life of diversion, which suited them because by tradition and education few of them were fit for land cultivation. The seasonal change in residence—moving to Moscow for the winter time and returning to the countryside in early spring—testified to the emergence of a new pattern of life among the nobility. As one witness of this annual spectacle observed:

> Moscow is being deserted: one encounters every minute long lines of coaches and wagons queued up—some depart with their masters for, others arrive to take them to, the country. Soon there will remain in Moscow only her permanent residents: people who serve, the officials, merchants, foreigners and our own brethren, the estate of students. My uncle informs me that one more group of people will not depart from Moscow—the group of debtors, as the creditors will not allow them to leave. Strangely enough, only one part of Moscow continues to be inhabited during the summer time, the German settlement, which remains unaffected throughout the year.[27]

On the whole, these early representatives of "superfluous people" preferred dissipation to disciplined life, but a growing number of them turned into intellectual dilettanti, by shifting with time their interests to art, literature, and theatre. Their styles of life have been depicted in literature in terms of their extravagance and frivolity, their predisposition toward aristocratically tinged bohemianism, with nights turned into days and with several salons (houses without windows) adapted for this purpose. *Les femmes du monde* followed the lead of their companions, performing such complementary roles as flirting, reading French romances in bed (Tolstoy's "recumbent ladies"), or even emulated those who were unashamed of anything but shame (Fonvizin's Princess Khaldina).

Sociologically, this was the aristocratic period in the history of Russian letters: most of the men of letters came from the privileged estate of the gentry, and the social milieu in which the men of letters found encouragement and established their reputations was confined mainly, if not exclusively, to the beau monde and its institution of the salon. This bestowed upon literature an aristocratic halo and, at the same time, helped to elevate the writer from the former subservient position of office scribe and flatterer. Many Russian men of letters, to mention only Zhukovsky, Viazemsky, and Pushkin, were acutely aware of the importance of this fact. In a letter to his friend, Pushkin noted that:

> ... our literature, although lagging behind others with respect to the number of talents, is free of slavish degradation. Foreigners are bewildered ... they do not understand how this came about. The cause is clear. Among us the writers are recruited from the highest stratum of society. With them aristocratic pride is linked with their literary ambition. We do not want to be patronized by equals. That is what the rascal Vorontsov does not understand. He imagines the Russian poet appearing in his anteroom with a dedicatory poem or ode, but this poet appears with a lineage of six hundred years and with a demand for respect—there is a devilish difference.[28]

The revolt against the servility of court bards and flatterers was closely associated with this aristocratization of literature and its practitioners. Fonvizin, toward the close of his life, satirized "court-grammar" and defined it as "an art of clever flattering by oral and written means."[29] And to the question, "What does it mean to flatter cleverly?" he replied: "It means to speak and write such lies that would be pleasant to the dignitaries and useful to the flatterer."[30] The court-bards were referred to as "parrots" locked up in "court-cages" or simply sleeping in the "open air."[31] This was said of the very bards who built so many "temples of glory" that were it possible to place them on this earth, a "city larger than Peking or Rome would have been built."[32] Even the "personal author" of Catherine, Derzhavin himself, deemed it proper to reappraise his literary career and, while brooding in retirement, addressed the following verse to his friend:

> *A slave cannot praise,*
> *He can only flatter.*
> *Forgive me, my friend,*
> *If, at times, I flattered too.*[33]

More significant was the fact that aristocratic society and its salons furnished the social basis for the formation of *la république des lettres,* an autonomous cultural sphere. This was tantamount to the emergence of a separate cultural elite in a society characterized by universal service to the state. One finds often in the writings of Karamzin, Zhukovsky, Pushkin, and others such expressions as "literary republic," "ideal republic," and "republic of the word." What preoccupied their attention was not the relationship of writers to service, the theme that so much worried Derzhavin, Kniazhnin, Fonvizin, Bogdanovich, and other authors of the preceding generation. If they dwelt on this problem as Karamzin did, it was only to bemoan the fact that rank continued to determine "everything in the country" and fame offered but "little attraction" to the young people.[34] Karamzin traced the dearth of "talented authors" in Russia to her tradition of service, which he found still strong enough to lure young people from the gentry no less than from the middle estate. Moreover, the "pursuit of *chins*," argued Karamzian, did not preclude a dissipated style of life—the attendance of "balls, lavish parties, and festivities"—whereas the "life of an author" entailed solitude and dedicated work necessary for the development of his talent.[35]

What concerned Karamzin, Zhukovsky, and others of their generation was the apparent lack of affinity between a style of life evolved by the higher society and that required of writers, who had to spend a portion of their lives in solitude. Zhuhovsky discerned three main difficulties that might stand in the way of writers' success in higher society: attachment to their craft, egotism, and limited economic means. With Karamzin and others, he proposed a compromise: intermittent participation in higher society, necessary for the acquisition of "discerning taste," complemented by intense involvement in the sphere of privacy—the limited circle of friends and the family, which were "more important to the writer than to anyone else."[36] Service and *chins* were altogether ignored by him and writing in solitude, combined with refined sociability (higher society) and intimate friendship and the family, remained the spheres worthy of the writer's attachment.

> To him (the writer) human society should be divided into two circles: the first, the inclusive circle, he enters occasionally and with strong determination to remain there in the role of an onlooker who is composed, reserved, and without undue demands and anticipations. In the second, the narrow circle, he finds happiness, since within it he loves and is loved by his friends and the family.[37]

The participation of the writers in high society was contingent on still other considerations than the cultivation of "discerning taste" and sociability: high society at that time (the turn of the eighteenth century) provided an audience appreciative of literature and a major forum, the salon, within which aspiring littérateurs were accorded respect and given recognition for their literary works. Literature itself, in fact, became a fashionable pursuit in high society—*occupation élégante et aristocratique*.[38] The literary societies at the opening of the last century, like Beseda and Arzamas, had among their members many individuals of the titled aristocracy, and close to one third of those present at Beseda's regular meetings were either counts or princes.[39] So determined was the first titled metromaniac in Russia, Count Khvostov, to become renowned as a writer that he took his literary wares to the streets of Moscow to share them with the passing strangers. "Rich and distinguished gentlemen, all those privileged citizens of fashionable salons," observed Belinsky, "made desparate attempts to publish their verses in order to acquire the title of a poet."[40] Among young people of that time, the interest in letters was general as well as intense enough to resemble a craze. "In almost all schools," according to Pushkin, "young people are engaged in writing and found literary societies; some of them succeed in publishing their compositions in periodicals."[41] Even some elderly society ladies, as the plays inform us, following the prevailing fashion, channeled their idleness into literary pursuits.[42] The former Maecenases, as it were, decided to follow the paths of their former entertainers in order to acquire the renown of men of letters.

From Office to Salon

To the extent that the first men of letters in Russia were officials, there was no separate status group of writers; there were only men of various ranks interested in literature and attached to the state and its institutions or to the court retinue as secretaries, translators, and entertainers. Since writers had no publicly acknowledged status, they were primarily officials, and writers only by avocation. In the absence of a cultural community and under the social conditions in which all served, neither an open forum for the exchange of opinions, the French "esprit de conversation," nor intellectual controversy was feasible. And it is of great interest that the "Russian Voltaire," Sumarokov, conceived of controversy as something of which to be ashamed. In his ideal society of universal service, as envisaged by him in a dream, very little was argued and even less written."[43] Some of them claimed that "controversy helps neither to eliminate vices ... nor to arrive at truth."[44] Even more, it beclouds the truth, "multiplies diverse opinions and helps to develop a technique whereby lie is defended with the same success as truth."[45]

A fruitful exchange of ideas presupposed a community of equal partners, stripped of official ranks. Otherwise—and this was precisely the case—critical views and conflicting opinions had to be channeled through an official hierarchy in the form of secret petitions addressed to superiors. Ultimately they were resolved on the basis of authority rather than in light of the merit of the respective arguments. At times, they turned into personal denunciations, as was the case with Lomonosov and Sumarokov, Sumarokov and Trediakovsky, and Fonvizin and Lukin, and referred to a notable superior for possible reconciliation. Such denunciations abounded with abusive language that ranged from expressions like "fools" and "drunkards" to "liars" and "thieves." The blunt statement of the Western-educated Radishchev that "truth would be robbed of its strong foundation" if "difference of opinions and controversies" were forbidden, found little public support.[46] Commenting on Radishchev's arrest, Lopukhin asserted that every loyal "son of the country, if he feels duty-bound to express his views to the Tsar, should do it directly and secretly ... and not at all by publication of a book which may adversely affect the public peace."[47] Even more hostile was the response of Derzhavin. On receiving from Radishchev a copy of his book, Derzhavin annotated its "offensive" passages and promptly submitted it to Empress Catherine.

The fate of the public discussion between Catherine and her "illegitimate children," despite her one-time espousal of the view that mere words were not a crime, illustrates well the state of freedom of speech and the true role of the "watchman of the commonweal." Fonvizin's question, "Why fools ... jesters did not have *chins* in former times?" was interpreted by Catherine as an abuse of free speech. As an obedient subject, Fonvizin responded promptly by declaring that he despised free speech with "all his soul" and even promised to forego taking up the pen again.[48] When Kapnist wrote the *Ode to Slavery* to protest the enserfdom of Ukrainian peasants, Catherine silenced him with this brief rebuff: "You stand for the destruction of serfdom. None of your business!"[49] Frightened Kapnist retired to his village Obukhovka to reside there for the rest of his life.

Such critics were but individual voices of dissent easily eliminated by arrests, as were Novikov and Radishchev, by threats, as were Kapnist and Fonvizin, or simply by refusal to bestow ranks and honors. They were too dependent on the favors of the court notables, whose changing fortunes they often shared, and too weak numerically to have interests and ideals of their own. With few exceptions, notably Kapnist and Radishchev, they displayed the characteristics of obedient servants enmeshed in state institutions and fully conscious of belonging to them.

It is against the background presented above that the appropriation of literature by higher society can be fully appreciated. For it was within this aristocratic milieu and its institution of the salon that the status of the writer first became fully recognized and the desire for independence was effectively asserted. Without this independence, argued Viazemsky, literature would become "a state service, a branch of the police, or what is even worse, merely a department of the Ministry of Education."[50] The institution of the salon also served as a basis for the allocation of positions of prestige, since it allowed writers to rise to their full stature irrespective of rank in the official hierarchy. The salon of Mme. Karamzina was one of them:

> In order to achieve fame in higher society, it was necessary to enter the salon of Mme. Karamzina, the widow of the historian. There were issued the diplomas for literary talents. This was a genuine society salon with rigid selectivity ... all our known poets deemed it advisable to write epistles to her....[51]

By the first decade of the last century young authors of St. Petersburg could have taken part in the literary gatherings at the salons of various notables on a weekly basis. According to Zhikharev, their regular habitué:

> All literati without exception, once introduced by their acquaintances, have the right to take part in them. Above all, invitations are extended to young people who have achieved some literary success or have shown

promise, since the evenings are held mainly for the sake of making known their works. [52]

In the 1830s and 1840s, enterprising writers of Moscow could have attended the literary drawing-rooms almost daily, going from Mme. Elagina to Princess Golitsina, Count Tolstoy, and other titled hosts. Some writers, in fact, availed themselves fully of this opportunity and "went from one salon to the other reading their works. The crowd of worshipers increased with every new reading."[53] And as regards the writers, Pushkin observed, "Personne ne songeant à retirer d'autre de ses ouvrages que des triomphes de société...."[54]

The Russian society salons, unlike the distinguished French ones, were not the product of the fortunate synchronization of gifted women and an exceptional supply of *philosophes*. The French salons of Mme. Geoffrin, Mme. du Deffand, Julie de Lespinasse, Mme. Necker, or even the salon of Mme. Recamier of Berlin, Henriette Herz, required probably little more than charming hostesses and a few intellectual lions who could be relied on for regular attendance. Russian high society was preeminently an aristocratic community, and the salon one of its institutions embodying the behavior patterns of the aristocratic style of life. The aristocratic character of the salon was reflected, among other things, in the fact that quite a few gentlemen-littérateurs were not eager to identify themselves with professional men of letters. Count Sollogub, encouraged by his literary success, "undertook to write a new novel and often appeared among writers, but he somehow felt uneasy in their company."[55] What he did in fact was to pride himself "in the high society of his literary pursuits and in the literary circles of his earldom."[56] Zhukovsky himself thanked God that he "was never a professional man of letters."[57] Prince Odoevsky criticized the commercial orientation of those writers who were unable to get as far as the anteroom of high society.[58]

Yet this suspicious attitude toward writing as a profession should not be construed to mean that literature and literary pursuits were not held in high esteem by the gentlemen-littérateurs. It was precisely during this period in the cultural history of Russia that literature found its first devoted practitioners. But as literature was preempted by gentlemen and became closely related with their style of life, professional writers were viewed as money-makers bent on debasing the Muses.

By virtue of this aristocratic background of many men of letters and their intimate entanglement in polite society, many Russian salons resembled more closely the nonliterary aristocratic salons in France. They were, as Duclos informs us, those brilliant "societies of *le bon ton*" from which "every important question, every sensible opinion" was excluded, and whose dandies displayed the "greatest wit in saying agreeable nothings."[59] In some Russian salons, indeed, there was scarcely any mention of literature, and, as a result, literary evenings resembled more "literary orgies."[60] The very number of habitués, sometimes more than eighty, and their varied backgrounds and interests, precluded a more serious concern with literary problems. Dancing, drinking, card games and gossip were intermingled with the readings of literary works and with conversation on such sundry topics as military expeditions, politics, astrology, magic, Chinese culture, and social life.

In part, the Russian *saloniers* were responsible for the amorphous character of their salons. Except for Prince Odoevsky, Mme. Elagina, and Chaadaev, they were much less sensitive hosts than their French teachers. When Mme. Geoffrin, for example, the *Czarina de Paris*, noticed that the artists tended to draw apart at her receptions, she arranged a weekly dinner for them on Monday. She even separated her guests by sex: only men were present at the Monday and Wednesday dinners, but "women were admitted to the *petits soupers*."[61] The Russian salons, by contrast, included old and young, men of the world and women of the world, lovers of letters and men of letters, "people who were half gendarmes and half literary men, others who were wholly gendarmes and not at all literary men,"[62] retired generals and high officials, a few professors and academicians, and even some enlightened members of the clergy.

Despite this, however, one important feature characterized many Russian salons: the atmosphere of "freedom and fluidity of relations and habits that had not been reduced to a rigid tradition...."[63] In the salon of Count Tolstoy, for example, "there was no pretension, no limitation, full freedom for those who entered this happy house, well-nigh patriarchal simplicity, sincerity and satisfaction of the host."[64] In such an atmosphere, it was possible, at least during the reign of Alexander I when it was widely believed, as Karazin noted, that the young ruler looked with indifference at the "exclamations of poetry, which shamelessly adapts itself to all the Tsars,"[65] to talk of everything in heaven and earth. And it is known that in the salon presided over by Mme. Golitsyna, the main subject of discussion was politics, even though the hostess shared political views of official conservatives. In this very salon, Pushkin, the alleged "glorifier" of foreign countries and "persistent detractor" of his own,[66] could let off steam without fear of betrayal or espionage. Moreover, Pushkin dared to send her his *Ode to Liberty*, remarking a few years later that for him, Mme. Golitsyna, "Constitutionnelle ou anticonstitutionnelle," was "toujours adorable comme la liberté."[67]

Notes

1. Merezhkovsky, "Meshchanstvo i Russkaia Intelligentsiia," *Poliarnaia Zvezda*, no. 1 (1905), p. 39.
2. S. Kucherov, "The Soviet Union Is Not a Socialist Society: In Defense of V. M. Molotov," *Political Science Quarterly* 71 (June 1956): 196.
3. A. N. Pypin, "Narodnichestvo," *Vestnik Evropy* 105 (February 1884): 725.
4. I. I. Petrunkevich, ed., *Intelligentsiia v Rossii* (St. Petersburg, 1910), p. 94.
5. Kheraskova's letter to Count D. I. Khvostov. *Russkaia Starina* 66 (June 1890): 674.
6. G. A. Gukovsky, "Russkaia Literaturno-Kriticheskaia Mysi' v 1730–1750-e Gody," *XVIII Vek: Sbornik*, ed. P. N. Berkov (Moscow-Leningrad, 1958), V, p. 106.

7. A. P. Sumarokov, *Polnoe Sobranie Vsekh Sochinenii v Stikhakh i Proze*, ed. N. Novikov (Moscow, 1781), VI, pp. 391–92.
8. S. P. Zhikharev, *Zapiski Sovremennika* (Moscow-Leningrad, 1955), p. 370; *see also* V. F. Khodasevich, *Derzhavin* (Paris, 1931), p. 123.
9. G. R. Derzhavin, "Pisma i Ordera Derzhavina Raznym Litsam," *Russkaia Starina* 136 (December 1908): 646.
10. Quoted in D. D. Blagoi, *Istoriia Russkoi Literatury XVIII Veka*, 4th ed. (Moscow, 1960), p. 407.
11. D. I. Fonvizin, *Sochineniia*, 2d ed. (St. Petersburg, 1846), p. 686.
12. Ibid.
13. Sumarokov, *Polnoe Sobranie*, p. 394.
14. N. Firsov, "G. R. Derzhavin, kak Vyrazitel Nastroeniia Rossiiskogo Dvorianstva v Ekaterinskuiu Epokhu," *Izvestiia Severno-Vostochnogo Arkheologicheskogo i Etnograficheskogo Instituta v Gorode Kazane*, I (1920): 114; D. Maslov, "Derzhavin-Grazhdanin," *Vremia* 5 (1861): 145.
15. Khodasevich, *Derzhavin*, p. 107.
16. M. V. Lomonosov, *Sochineniia*, ed. A. A. Morozova (Moscow, 1957), pp. 482, 500.
17. N. Bulich, *Sumarokov i Sovremennaia Emu Kritika* (St. Petersburg, 1854), p. 80.
18. Ibid., p. 124.
19. Blagoi, *Istroiia Russkoi*, p. 122.
20. A. S. Pushkin, *Polnoe Sobranie Sochinenii* (Moscow, 1958), VII, p. 283.
21. I. F. Timkavsky, "Zapiski Illi Feodorovicha Timkavskogo," *Russkii Arkhiv* 11 (1873): 1453.
22. V. Ia. Stoiunin, "Kniazhnin-Pisatel'," *Istoricheskii Vestnik* 5 (1881): 430.
23. P. N. Berkov, ed., *Satiricheskie Zhurnaly N. I. Novikova* (Moscow, 1951), p. 284.
24. Stoiunin, *Istoricheskii Vestnik*, p. 446.
25. Fonvizin, *Sochineniia*, p. 534.
26. Ia. Kniazhnin, *Sobranie Sochinenii* (Moscow, 1802), IV, p. 156.
27. Zhikharev, *Zapiski*, pp. 60–61.
28. Pushkin, *Polnoe*, X, pp. 146–47.
29. Fonvizin, *Sochineniia*, p. 546.
30. Ibid., p. 547.
31. I. A. Krylov, *Polnoe Sobranie Sochinenii* (Moscow, 1945), I, pp. 347–49.
32. Ibid.
33. N. Barsukov, ed., *Dnevnik A. V. Khrapovetskogo: 1782–1793* (St. Petersburg, 1874), Introduction, p. XVIII.
34. H. M. Karamzin, *Izbrannye Sochineniia* (Moscow-Leningrad, 1964), II, p. 146.
35. Ibid., p. 186.
36. V. A. Zhukovsky, *Sochineniia*, 8th ed. (St. Petersburg, 1885), V, p. 275.
37. V. A. Zhukovsky, *Sobranie Sochinenii v Chetyrekh Tomakh* (Moscow-Leningrad, 1959), IV, pp. 400–401.
38. Pushkin, *Polnoe*, X, p. 607.
39. Compiled on the basis of the attendance of the society's meetings. *See* V. Desnitsky, pp. 92–130. "Reforma Petra I i Russkaia Literatura XVIII v.," *Izbrannye Stati po Russkoi Literature XVIII–XIX vv.* (Moscow-Leningrad, 1958), pp. 92–130.
40. V. G. Belinsky, *Polnoe Sobranie Sochinenii*, ed. V. S. Vengerov (St. Petersburg, 1900), II, p. 492.
41. Pushkin, *Polnoe*, VII, p. 47.
42. M. N. Zagoskin, *Sobranie Sochinenii* (Moscow, 1902), III, pp. 44–60.
43. Sumarokov, *Polnoe Sobranie*, p. 387.
44. I. Boltin, *Primechaniia na Istoriiu Drevniia i Nyneshniia Rossii g. Leklerka* (St. Petersburg, 1788), II, pp. 354–55.

45. Ibid.
46. A. N. Radishchev, *Putishestvie iz Peterburga v Moskvu* (St. Petersburg, 1905), p. 175.
47. Quoted in G. V. Plekhanov, *Istoriia Russkoi Obshchestvennoi Mysli* (Moscow, 1915), III, p. 273.
48. Fonvizin, *Sochineniia*, p. 666.
49. D. S. Babkin, "V. V. Kapnist i A. N. Radishchev," *XVIII Vek: Sbornik*, IV, p. 272.
50. Quoted in Gunther Wytrzens, *Pjotr Andreevich Vjazemskij* (Vienna, 1961), pp. 115–16.
51. I. I. Panaev, *Literaturnye Vospominaniia* (Leningrad, 1928), p. 144.
52. Zhikharev, *Zapiski*, p. 341.
53. Panaev, *Literaturnye*, p. 69.
54. Pushkin, *Polnoe*, X, p. 607.
55. Panaev, *Literaturnye*, p. 213.
56. A. Panaeva, *Vospominaniia* (Leningrad, 1928), p. 120.
57. A. V. Nikitenko, *Zapiski i Dnevnik* (St. Petersburg, 1893), I, p. 213.
58. V. F. Odoevsky, "O Napadeniiakh Peterburgskikh Zhurnalov na Russkogo Poeta," *Russkii Arkhiv* 2 (1864): 1015–1022.
59. Charles Duclos, *Considerations sur les Moeurs*, ed. F. C. Green (Cambridge: University Press, 1939), pp. 102–3.
60. Panaev, *Literaturnye*, p. 132.
61. G. P. Gooch, "Four French Salons," *Catherine the Great and Other Studies* (London: Longmans, Green and Co., 1954), p. 133.
62. A. I. Herzen, *My Past and Thoughts: The Memoirs of Alexander Herzen*, trans. Constance Garnett (New York: Alfred A. Knopf, 1924), II, p. 131; *see also* Zhikharev, *Zapiski*, p. 370.
63. Herzen, *My Past*, II, p. 281.
64. Panaev, *Literaturnye*, p. 167.
65. A. I. Herzen, *Sochineniia* (St. Petersburg, 1905–1906), V, p. 419.
66. "Pushkin," *Biblioteka Velikikh Pisatelei*, ed. S. A. Vengerov (St. Petersburg, 1907), I, p. 441.
67. Ibid., p. 522.

4   Men of Ideas: Freelance Literati

The oppressive regime of Nicholas I witnessed the rise of freelance literati in Russia who gave up service to the state and instead turned their youthful energies and talents into intellectual pursuits. The members of the generation of the "remarkable decade" represented the crowning point of this emancipatory development. While contrasting the cultured Moscow before 1812 with that which he left in 1847, Herzen's heart throbbed with joy and satisfaction:

> We have made tremendous strides forward. In those days there was a society of the discontented—that is, of those who have been left out, dismissed or laid on the shelf; now there is a society of independent people. The lions of those days were capricious oligarchs, such as Count A. G. Orlov and Ostermann, "a society of shadows," as Miss Wilmont says, a society of political men who had died fifteen years before in Petersburg but went on powdering their heads, putting on their ribbons, and appearing at dinners and at festivities in Moscow; sulking, giving themselves airs of consequence, and having neither influence nor significance. After 1825 the lions of Moscow were Pushkin, M. Orlov, Chaadaev, Yermolov. In the earlier days society had flocked with cringing servility to the house of Count Orlov, "ladies in other people's diamonds," gentlemen who dared not sit down without permission.... Forty years later I saw the same society crowding around the platform of one of the lecture-rooms of the Moscow University; the daughters of those ladies in other people's jewels, the sons of the men who had not dared to sit down, were, with passionate sympathy, following the profound, vigorous words of Granovsky, greeting with outbursts of applause sentences that went straight to the heart from their boldness and nobility. [1]

An interest in cultural matters became fashionable in polite society and the former *femmes du monde*, former readers of French romances and madrigals, began to "converse on historical topics and cite philosophical works."[2] The young historian Granovsky was even requested by them, although he politely refused, to deliver a series of lectures to a select audience of Moscow society ladies.[3] The members of the generation of the "recumbent ladies" read boring articles, listened attentively until late at night to long arguments, and waited impatiently for the end in order "to see which of the matadors would dispatch the other and how he would be dispatched himself...."[4] They were not those "well-educated" ladies, like Madame Manilova of Gogol's *Dead Souls,* versed in three principal subjects, "the French tongue, which is indispensable to family happiness; the piano-forte, to afford pleasant moments to a husband; and lastly, the sphere of domestic management—the knitting of purses, and other surprises."[5] In short, these were the salons in which, not the retired generals, counts, the daring guard officers of 1812 or even those of 1825, the men of sword and pen, who served, wrote, and revolted, reigned supreme, but those who sought no rank in the political and military hierarchies and cared for "books and ideas." Unlike the aristocrat Chatsky of Griboedov's comedy, *Woe from Wit,* the heroes of the salons of the forties were neither ready to serve nor willing to become subservient. These were the salons in which, truly, the first Russian adventurers of the spirit came to the fore.

> (The salons)... in which Khomiakov argued from nine in the evening until four o'clock in the morning; in which K. S. Aksakov with a *murmolka* in his hand fiercely defended Moscow though no one had attacked it, and never took a glass of champagne in his hand without repeating a prayer and a toast which every one knew; in which Redkin logically deduced a personal God *at majorem gloriam Hegelii;* in which Granovsky appeared with his firm but gentle speech; ... in which Chaadaev with his delicate wax-like face, scrupulously dressed, enraged the nonplussed aristocrats and orthodox Slavophiles by biting sarcasm; ... in which A. I. Turgenev, young in spite of his age, gossiped charmingly about all the celebrities of Europe, from Chateaubriand and Recamier to Schelling and Rahel Varnhagen; in which Botkin and Kriukov *pantheistically* enjoyed M. S. Shchepkin's stories; and into which Belinsky sometimes fell like Congreve's rocket, setting fire to everything he touched....[6]

Obviously, these salons, as Belinsky himself conceded, were "no longer content with the chase, luxury, and feasts, not even with dancing and card-playing alone."[7] They were, more exactly, intellectual circles in which philosophical, historical, and literary problems predominated. The leisured segment of the Moscow and Petersburg societies of *le bon ton* furnished, as it were, the physical surroundings and the eager audience more and more transcending the former interest in romances and madrigals. It is worthy of mention that this period in the cultural life of Russia coincided with the appearance of almost all the leading nineteenth-century Russian poets and novelists—Lermontov, Gogol, Turgenev, Goncharov, and Dostoevsky—and, what was no less significant, with the initiation of the intellectual controversy led by the generation of the "remarkable decade." This fact alone is sufficient for the rehabilitation of the "superfluous gentlemen" subsumed by Dobroliubov under one sweeping and derogatory title of *oblomovshchina.*

Cultural Community: First Freelance Literati

There is a tendency on the part of many historians to conceive of the organizational setting of the literati of that period as a series of small circles bound by ideas and isolated from society at large. This view, exemplified, as a rule, by the circles of Stankevich and Ogarev, requires careful scrutiny and reappraisal. At that time, as Belinsky somewhat exaggeratedly but with discernment emphasized, literature and intellectual preoccupation, "in drawing people of different estates closer together in bonds of taste and aspirations towards a noble enjoyment of life, transformed the *estates* into *society*."[8] Belinsky, of course, did not intend to convey the view that literature transformed the estate-like and rigidly stratified Russian society as a whole. He was only too painfully aware of the fact that in Russia each of the social estates possessed "specific traits of its own—its dress and its manners, its way of life and customs, and even its own language."[9] To be convinced of this it sufficed, according to Belinsky, "to spend an evening in the chance company of a government official, a military man, a landowner, a merchant, a burgess, a barrister, a clergyman, a student, a seminarist...."[10] And "seeing yourself in such a company," concluded Belinsky, "you might think you were present at the distribution of tongues."[11] What he meant primarily was the formation of the small community in the two capitals of Russia, not based on official rank, title, or social origin, but bound together by intellectual and literary interests. A handful of small circles was thus only one of the organizational forms of this community. For besides them there existed also other institutions—the salons (literary and semi-literary), literary gatherings, clubs, and even cafés littéraires. This community, linked together and permeated by an increasing number of enlightened individuals interested in literature, art, philosophy, and demanding nothing from the government but freedom of thought, was, in our opinion, of singular significance. In the first place, it enabled the emergent group of freelance literati, most of them still of noble origin, to come into contact with people of diverse backgrounds and ages, of different occupations and professions, and even of opposing intellectual and ideological views. Thus, in the salons of Prince Odoevsky, Chaadaev, and Mme. Elagina, the literati met generals, high officials, professors; at the literary parties of Pletnev, the "notorious Skobelev," commandant of the St. Petersburg Fortress, "a certain Vladislavlev, the editor of *Sunrise* ... an equerry in the uniform of a gendarme"... "the translator of *Faust,* Guber, an officer of the Transport Department,"[12] the provincial authors and poets, like Belinsky and Koltsov, "and, last but not least, our most warm hearted and unforgettable Prince Odoevsky";[13] in the literary cafés, in turn, artists, professors, and roving gentlemen. The Moscow café littéraire included among its habitués professors—Granovsky, Rulie, Meshevich, and Artemev—and artists and writers—Gogol, Herzen, Shchepkin, Sadovsky, and, rarely, even Belinsky. True, some of them disliked the informal atmosphere that prevailed in the café among that "strange folk" whose members on the very first encounter tried to become relatives, "either an uncle or a cousin."[14] Yet, these informal and easygoing relations did not prevent some of the title-conscious visitors from frequenting the café. Neither can it be claimed, as Panaev did, that the generation of the "remarkable decade," that is, of the first freelance literati in Russia, displayed aversion toward the salons and the aristocratic style of life. Almost all of them, to mention only Ogarev, Herzen, Granovsky, Turgenev, Annenkov, Stankevich, Aksakov, Kireevsky, Botkin, and Panaev himself, had attended at one time or another aristocratic salons and social occasions. Turgenev prided himself on his acquaintance with aristocratic circles and was ashamed of the fact that some plebeian literati behaved clumsily in the salons in the company of society ladies. "Among new acquaintances," he wrote to Annenkov, "let me mention Grand Duchess Elena Pavlovna ... I am very close to Prince Cherkassky and his wife ... I meet very often Prince D. Obolensky ... Please express my regrets to Prince Viazemsky and visit finally Countess Lambert...."[15] In a letter to his sister, Granovsky wrote: "Je travaille jour et nuit, ce qui ne m'empêche pas d'aller de temps en temps dans le monde...."[16] Even Belinsky, whose attitude, as we shall see, was profoundly ambivalent, could write the following lines:

> As far as we are concerned, we are not men of society and do not visit society; but we do not entertain any philistine prejudice against it....

> Allow me to make another reservation: we do not for a moment confound society ways with aristocratism, though they most often go together. Be you a man of any origin, or of whatever convictions—society life will not spoil you, but only improve. It is said: life in high society is wasted on trifles, the most sacred feelings are sacrificed to worldly interests and the conventions. True, but then is life in the middle circle of society spent only on what is great, and are feeling and reason not sacrificed to worldly interests and conventions? Oh, no, a thousand times no! The only difference between the middle and higher circles consists in the fact that the former is pettier, smugger, more conceited, gives itself greater airs, has more petty ambitions, is more starched and hypocritical. [17]

And one of the reasons why Belinsky did not entertain any "philistine prejudice" against it was his justifiable conviction that it was precisely this stratum, the estate of gentry, which was "preeminently representative of society and preeminently the direct source of all society's education."[18]

Through participation in the emergent semi-bohemian cafés, in literary gatherings, in the society salons and drawing rooms, the literati were offered the opportunity of coming into contact not only with the men of consequence (generals, counts, princes, high officials), but also with professors, with artists and actors (some of them, like Shchepkin, emancipated serfs), and with provincial upstarts, like Koltsov and Belinsky himself. This differentiated community, which, to be certain, was still lodged in an aristocratic milieu, laid the ground for the internal rapprochement of different segments of the cultural elite (scholars and literati) and also provided a base for the formation of freelance literati, within the framework of which the generation of Stankevich, Herzen, Kireevsky, Aksakov, and other "adventurers of the spirit" reasserted themselves. What distinguished them from the gentleman-littérateur of the generation of Zhukovsky, Viazemsky, Sollogub, Odoevsky, and even Pushkin and Lermontov was not so much their social origin, their style of life, their unwillingness "to enjoy luxury and feasts" and to participate in the society of *le bon ton* (for almost all of them did), but their conception of themselves, their sense of independence, their growing estrangement from the official *ordo*, and, consequently, their changed position in it. Unlike Zhukovsky, Odoevsky, Sollogub, and others, they thought of themselves primarily as men of letters. Most of them refused to serve the state, if not the Tsar, and believed, as did Goethe in his old age, that "Wer gerne leben mag und ein entschiedenes Streben in sich fuehlt, einen freien Blick ueber die Welt hat, der muss von einem kleinen Dienst wie vor dem Grabe schaudern."[19] Explaining his decision not to enter state service, I. Kireevsky wrote to his friend, Koshelev, in 1827:

> I can be a man of letters, and is not working for the enlightenment of the people the greatest service I can perform for them? Since the main goal of my whole life has been to educate myself, can I not be a force in literature? [20]

Even more outspoken was young Ogarev, who dispatched to the devil not only state service but all other practical pursuits (industry), and proclaimed art as the only "sphere of activity" in which he felt comfortable. "For this," he concluded, "I bless life and providence."[21] If the younger Aksakov seemed bewildered enough to ask in his *Chinovnik,* "To serve or not to serve, that is the question," it was only to allow the official, one of the dramatis personae, to reply in despair: "I have lived in vain! I have lived in vain!"[22] When Count Perovsky, his superior, reminded Aksakov that a dedicated servant like him "can hardly find free time to engage in literary pursuits without detriment to service,"[23] Aksakov responded in this characteristic fashion:

> I consider both my right and my duty to inform Your Excellency that it is not service that suffers from my literary activities, but, on the contrary, my literary activities, moral and intellectual development, are being sacrificed to service. [24]

Learning and intellectual pursuits were viewed by them neither as a means of advancement in the military and political hierarchies, as was the case with the official-writer, nor as a part of the aristocratic refinement and style of life to be led by the gentleman-littérateur, but rather as the ideal to be aspired to by an enlightened individual. Unlike Sollogub and Pushkin, who prided themselves either on an earldom or on a long genealogical record, or even on close association with the court, as was the case with Zhukovsky, and were still unwilling to admit that they were professional men of letters, the generation of Herzen, Ogarev, Kireevsky, and others proudly bore the title of men of letters, of writers and poets, or simply of "thinking individuals." As such they were accepted by and invited to the aristocratic salons. The gentlemen of leisure, in turn, as Belinsky pointed out with satisfaction, considered it a privilege to be acquainted with the men of letters, listened to their conversations in order to be able to utter a word or two about their works, and looked at them as an adornment of their salons. What this amounted to was the emergence of the status group of freelance literati still related, by their origin and style of life, to the Moscow and Petersburg drawing rooms.

Viewed within this framework, the apparent isolation and the warring spirit of the small circles must be reevaluated. Certainly, those few circles exhausted neither the interests nor the activities of their members. On the contrary, they had other social ties (formal and informal), played different roles and occupied different statuses within diverse social contexts. For example, at social balls and in the aristocratic salons, they led the life of gentlemen of leisure; at literary parties and cafés littéraires, they discussed current literary and artistic events; in the small circles of Stankevich and Herzen, they conversed on abstract philosophical and social topics; and in the English club, they gave themselves to card playing and drinking. Finally, they were still closely related by familial ties to their kinship groupings and through them to their aristocratic and landowning milieux. Many of them shared the values and even the prejudices of their parents. Suffice it to mention that, although they viewed the prevailing system of serfdom critically and sympathized with the oppressed *narod,* all of them—with the exception of Ogarev, and including Samarin, the Aksakovs, the Kireevskys, Koshelev, Turgenev, Kavelin, Chicherin, and even Lev Tolstoy—deemed it inadvisable to put their ideas to the test of practice by freeing the serfs. Moreover, most of them treated their fathers with exemplary filial piety and were far from willing to revolt against the stringent traditions of kinship. Prior to his departure abroad, Stankevich attached to the institutions of the family and Church a kind of sacredness and did not allow anyone in his presence to attack them.[25] Granovsky was convinced that "Les mariages sans l'aveu des parents portent malheur,"[26] and, therefore, resolved to refrain from marrying without his father's permission. Awaiting his father's approval, he complained to his sisters:

> Is it laziness or indifference or a genuine concern with my future which prevents him from writing to me? My God, what I would give to be wrong about him, how I wish that last of those three suppositions were correct (my translation).[27]

The exiled Ogarev, out of respect, followed the directives of his father, who tried hard to plunge his young son into a life of pleasure in the provincial society of Penza. In a letter to Herzen, he explained the motives of his compliant action:

> I have not emancipated myself from the control of my father.... But come over here and look yourself at that old man. Even if I intended to get rid of his guardianship and love—do not forget love—then you would retort: unconscionable.[28]

He, therefore, obediently attended society balls, made visits, roved about aimlessly, and fell in love. The whole life of the brothers Aksakov and Kireevsky was spent under familial protection—in the atmosphere of complaisance of close relatives—without which they seemed unable to envisage their very existence. Even Herzen, who certainly had more reasons to rebel, believed that his *papenka (Vaeterchen)* loved him in his own fashion. If, at times, he failed to respect family life, then at least he had an ample opportunity to learn its values from most of his friends.

To the extent that the kinship ties remained intact, the family met one important need: it served as a shelter from the onslaughts of autocracy, a refuge to which they were banned by the Third Section, as was the case with Ogarev, Kireevsky, Aksakov, Turgenev, and others. Persecuted by the Third Section and arbitrary censorship, they turned to the family, to that realm of privacy most of them valued so highly. Willingly or unwillingly, they followed the advice of Zhukovsky, who had suggested that there were two alternative spheres of participation worthy of the littérateur: the high society salon, which he equated with the "literary republic," and the sphere of privacy—friendship and the family. All other spheres, outside the family (friendship) and salon, were viewed by Zhukovsky as "extraneous," a nebulous world of petty officialdom, unworthy of the attachment of the writer and, indeed, of every "virtuous" and happy man.[29] In defense of this sphere of privacy, Zhukovsky dared to write a letter to the Chief of the Third Section, Count Benkendorf, lecturing him on its significance to the writer:

> In one of the letters Your Excellency expressed displeasure with the fact that Pushkin had read his tragedy in certain circles without official approval. What kind of crime is this? Are there any writers who do not read their works to friends in order to elicit their critical comments? Should a writer disapprove of his work as long as it has not been officially approved? This kind of reading in a circle of friends provides the writer with the greatest of pleasures. All the writers have done so, since they consider it their personal affair, like private conversation or correspondence. To prohibit this would amount to prohibiting to think, to dispose freely of one's own time, and so on.[30]

Pushkin went so far as to declare in a letter to his wife that it was conceivable to live without "political freedom" but impossible without "inviolabilité de la famille."[31] It is noteworthy that the Slavophiles found the prototype of the "ideal society" in the kinship group patriarchally structured and based on close familial attachments. Like their German contemporary, Dahlman, the Slavophiles stood for withdrawal into one's own family, which thereby becomes a "model of the good state" and the seat of an "inviolable realm of freedom."[32] Exiled Herzen, in his moments of resignation, "when dark thoughts of helplessness, of inactivity, of the loss of all hopes" drove him to desperation, fell back on the sphere of calm and appeasement, the "family and two or three friends."[33] It may be added that this return to the sphere of privacy, to the fold of the family, went beyond the confines of the immediate family circle—father, mother, wife, and children—it was of a more primordial nature, an "aristocratic feeling," to cite Herzen again, "of an attachment to the possession of the place," the estate with a mansion that recalled different phases of happy country life, a "tree under which I sat as a child, a road on which I pursued the village beauty...."[34] Ogarev spoke of the same attachment when he wrote to Herzen from Berlin:

I miss the steppes and the troika, the birch-trees, the nightingale and the snowy glade: that romantic feeling which I have not been able to find anywhere else. It is a matter of attachment to one's childhood, to the past, and to the graves of one's ancestors. Peace unto you, my grandfathers![35]

Obviously, these young men remained in touch with their social and historical origins. It is not only that they were dependent economically on their parents, as was Herzen, the Kireevskys, the Aksakovs, and Stankevich, indebted to them for their education, as was Turgenev, Ogarev, Samarin, Annenkov, and others, as well as for their contact with men of consequence. Their interest and attitude toward life, indeed their whole outlook were in many ways affected by the social environment from which they had come. Far from being socially isolated or deprived of an "organic tie with society"[36] (whatever the meaning of this phrase), they were still entrenched economically, socially, and culturally in their social milieu, bound by kinship ties to their families, had friends and a relatively wide acquaintance, and led, for that time, a well-rounded and diversified life. It is, therefore, highly questionable whether the generation of the literati under consideration, usually conceived as the first Russian *intelligenty,* experienced painfully the feeling of their isolation, and, as a result, developed the "moral and intellectual belligerence"[37] that inspired radical attitudes. For no matter how one may misuse this overworked and equally ambiguous term of isolation, by equating it either with physical isolation or with the anonymity of relations, or finally with the lack of a harmonious stream of primary personal contacts, it is evident that they neither were lost in a strange humanity nor lacked personal ties. The mere estrangement from the official *ordo,* as reflected in their unwillingness to serve or be subservient, should not be confused with social isolation.

The Sphere of Intimacy and Freedom: Friendship Groups

The atmosphere of Moscow and, to a lesser extent, Petersburg drawing rooms changed considerably in the forties of the last century. It resembled more the France of Louis XV and Louis XVI, in which men of letters turned to history, philosophy, and even science, than the France of Richelieu and Colbert, in which they busied themselves with *belles-lettres*. All leading contemporaries of that period emphasized the rising interest in philosophy, in the writings of Fichte, Schelling, and Hegel. "There is almost no man," wrote Kireevsky, "who would not converse in philosophical terms, no youth who would not discuss Hegel, and no book and journal article in which there would be unnoticeable the influence of German thinking; ten year old boys speak of concrete objectivity."[38]

Basically, the circles, as this discussion will show, were neither anti-government conspiracies (coteries of *révolté* young men bent on developing "revolutionary principles," the view repeated ad nauseam in the Soviet hagiography), nor tiny groups of young people bound together by identical ideological convictions. They were primarily friendship groups founded in the university milieu and, therefore, based on an acquaintance that went beyond the confines of kinship and transcended social estates. By necessity, of course, they were homogeneous with respect to age and might be viewed as age groupings. If we look, in turn, at their social composition, the circles consisted predominantly of, and were led by, young men of noble origin. What was important, however, was the fact that they were the first groupings of young literati in Russia that allowed for the assimilation and the rapprochement of individuals on an informal and personal footing, regardless of their social background. In this sense, the circles served as a mediating link between the students' milieu and the literary community, at that time still preempted by the gentleman-littérateur. Their success ought to be carefully assessed. We may remark in passing that Belinsky remained an unassimilable outsider.

The extent to which the circles were primarily friendship groupings can be seen from the character of their internal relations. Certainly, the mutual attachment of their members was not solely based on and limited to interest in the philosophy of Fichte and Hegel, or preoccupation with French socialists. This is to say, Herzen, Granovsky, Ogarev, Stankevich, Turgenev, and others liked each other and were attached to each other not because of the fact that they shared Hegelian philosophy, or Fourier's utopia, but because they were primarily long and tested friends who enjoyed similar things and led a similar pattern of life. Inasmuch as the circles were sustained by friendship sentiments, conflicting views did not stand in the way of their remaining members. That is why Granovsky, despite momentary disagreements with Ogarev and Herzen, valued highly their friendship and believed firmly that they would remain friends and "come as close to each other as was the case during the best years of our friendship."[39] Herzen hastened to add "that if time proved that we could think differently, could fail to understand and could wound each other, time has also proved with redoubled force later on that we could neither part nor cease to be friends, that even death could not divide us."[40] That is why Kavelin declared in a letter to Herzen: "Uns verbindet jenes Band, dass nie reisst, wenn auch die Ansichten auseinandergehen."[41] Even at the height of disagreement, Kavelin could still write to Herzen:

> I love you even now just as I did earlier, although you are unfair to me, unfair to an extent that would be unwonted in a stranger. Should you reject me, I shall go on loving you just the same, since a friendship is not an old shoe: you cannot throw it out of the window at your whim (my translation).[42]

And on another occasion he specified the nature of his attachment to Herzen in these words (my translation): "it is not the kind of love we feel for great and remarkable individuals, but rather that personal love which embraces the other's whole being as it is with all its qualities."[43]

At the same time they retained friendly ties with Kireevsky, Aksakov, and other Slavophiles "regardless of the fact that they held opposite views."[44] That is why Herzen, Granovsky, and Botkin met with them frequently, read to them their articles and asked for their criticism. "A few days ago," recorded Herzen in his *Diary,* "I read to Kireevsky and Khomiakov my fourth article—great effect and praise."[45] During his stay in the village of Sokolovo, Granovsky half-jokingly begged Herzen and other Westerners to let him go to Moscow to see his friends, the Slavophiles. "I need it," remarked Granovsky, "in order to avoid getting completely rude—you have succeeded in depriving me of the immortality of the soul."[46] Young Korsh refused to embrace "on faith any doctrine" and, by weighing carefully the arguments of opponents, remained sufficiently dégagé to be able to shift with ease from one camp to another.[47] The leading Slavophile, Kireevsky, was not even certain who were his actual adversaries—the Westerners or the Slavophiles. Addressing Khomiakov, he asked:

> Who are our opponents? Can it be that you are referring to Granovsky and Co.? If so, are you not also mistaken in me? Perhaps you take me for a damned Slavophile, and for this reason propose the *Muscovite* to me. As far as that is concerned, I must say that I share this Slavophile way of thinking only *in part*, but *another part of it I consider further* from myself than *the most eccentric opinions of Granovsky.*[48]

Linked together by close friendship bonds that cut across ideological convictions, the circles could neither form into two irreconcilable camps nor draw a clear-cut boundary between themselves. The Westerners were even ready to contribute to the Slavophile periodical *Moskvitianin,* and if they refused, as did Granovsky, they justified their refusal in this significant manner:

> I do not wish to enter the company of the majority of the contributors to *Moskvitianin* not because they are Slavs and Orthodox Christians and I am—in their view—the enemy of the Church and Russia, but because I do not respect them as persons.... If the actual editor were known, if your name (Kireevsky's) were on the cover of your journal, I would not hesitate to put my name at your disposal.[49]

On the whole, and this needs emphasis, neither the Westerners nor the Slavophiles made personal questions of differences of opinion. The very atmosphere of urbanity that prevailed in the salons (especially in the salon of Mme. Elagina) precluded the expression of personal rancor and insult, at the same time that it allowed for the unrestrained exchange of ideas. Most of their habitués recognized, as did Granovsky, that it was possible for an "individual to stand above his opinion."[50] Censuring with Granovsky the irreconcilable attitude of Belinsky, Herzen wrote:

> Friendship ought to be indulgent and passionate, it ought to love a person and not an idea; an idea is solely an underlying element of rapprochement, it can only provide a comrade, a fellow believer, but friendship requires an acknowledgement of a person and not his ideas.[51]

His friend, Ogarev, not only agreed with this view of friendship but also went on to insist that:

> It is time to love a concrete human being. Even the most general conception—*die Idee des Menschen*—is not empty and abstract, but comprises a living individual in all his fullness. Even the people who are unknown to you cannot be loved abstractly; as for the individuals who are close to you—*dio santo*—you love them for their personal qualities.[52]

There can be no doubt that these circles arose partly in response to the political conditions existing in Russia. Like the institution of the family, they furnished an intimate milieu, where close personal attachments, mutual confidence, and the unrestrained exchange of ideas were safe from the intrusion of the Third Section. But, to emphasize the point again, the circles did not consist of individuals holding identical ideological views. Indeed, they disagreed on many issues. Speaking of Granovsky, that man, "endowed with a wonderful power of love in his nature," Herzen observed pungently: "With many I was more in agreement in opinion, but to him I was nearer—deep down, somewhere in the soul."[53] And this "deep down, somewhere in the soul" was nothing else but a personal attachment of two friends to each other, an attachment that transcended intellectual views and ideological convictions. Just as the realm of privacy and of personal friendship was neither coterminous with nor exhausted by the small circle, the intellectual interests of its members were neither limited to nor absorbed by the narrow enclosure of several fellow believers. Seen in this light, they did not commit themselves totally either socially or intellectually to the life of the circles. They refused to equate the interests and activities of the circles with the whole of life, as was true of Belinsky, but participated in diverse social contexts and played different roles—those of sons and husbands, sharing many traditional values and conventions of the kinship groupings, those of close friends that went beyond the confines, as has been indicated, of a few fellow believers, those of freelance literati attending semi-bohemian cafés and drawing rooms, those of young gentlemen participating in the leisurely life of high society, and even those of landowners studying new methods of land cultivation. It would be a great injustice to the literati under consideration if we generalized, as did Professor Isaiah Berlin, that the Russian attitude, as contrasted with the French one, was that man is one and could not be divided; "that it is not true that a man is a citizen on the one hand and, quite independently of this, a money-maker on the other, and that these functions can be kept in separate compartments; that a man is one kind of personality as a voter, another as a painter, and a third as a husband. Man is indivisible."[54] Although it is true that at least one Slavophile, I. Kireevsky, defined the "Russian man" in a similar vein,[55] most of the members of the generation of the "remarkable decade," including Kireevsky himself, could still draw a distinction between a friend and a fellow believer, between a littérateur and a gentleman of leisure, between informal and formal relations. That is why they shared not always consistent values and conventions, why they felt equally at home in diverse social situations, and refused to be made *aus einem Guss*.[56] Indeed, they were different things to different people, and were absorbed as much in dogs, horses, society balls, and other diversions as in Fichte, Hegel, and Fourier. It suffices to pursue Herzen's *Diary*, Granovsky's and Ogarev's letters and Turgenev's reminiscences to be convinced of the wide variety of experience and of the numerous spheres of life to which they so eagerly responded. It matters little whether we relate this attitude of mind to the fact that they retained, throughout their life, the manners and customs of their aristocratic background and education, or to their social rootedness and multiple group participation. The root of the problem is that just as they were unwilling and refused to devote themselves wholly to any particular activity, in the same way they refused to commit themselves to any particular "truth," to use a favorite expression of the intelligentsia, or to the service of any single cause.

A glance at the pattern of activities within the circles offers an additional illustration of our point. Most certainly, they did not consist solely of endless discussions of Hegel, of the "accursed Russian reality," but were interspersed with "chat, jests, and wine." Like the ancient sage, they thanked gods who, taking pity of men born to work, have appointed "holy festivals ... and had given them the Muses, and Apollo, the leader of the Muses, and Dionysus, to be companions in their revels."[57] To cite Herzen: "Feasting goes with fullness of life, ascetic people are usually dry, egoistic people, we were not monks, we lived on all sides, and, sitting round the table, gained more in culture and did no less than those fasting toilers who grub in the backyards of science."[58] Yet, this somewhat leisurely atmosphere that prevailed at the gatherings did not remove the discussion of serious problems, "the most rapid exchange of ideas, of news and of knowledge." Only "dull pedants and tedious scholars," in Herzen's phrase, ascribed a frivolous character to their gatherings and saw nothing else but the "meat and the bottles."[59]

They were just "too cultured and independent to be completely lost in Fourierism," Saint Simonism, Hegelianism, and any other *ism*, or to be totally committed to the service of any doctrine or creed. This attitude of mind, this partial aloofness from and participation in, but by no means isolation from, the world at large, this suspicion of total surrender to any Moloch, this desire to "live on all sides," they called scepticism. "I am a sceptic," claimed Botkin, "in the sense that I see in each of the warring camps as much of value as non-sense, and, consequently, I am unable to attach myself to either of them ..."[60] Granovsky expressed a similar sentiment when he defended his "right to scepticism" in a letter to Ogarev:

> I do not agree with your last letter.... You contend that scepticism is in its very nature something cynical—strikes to the right and to the left. This definition is somewhat narrow. It contains (scepticism) as much grief as irony and does not strike always to the right and to the left, but more often looks suspiciously at both sides. You are not right in saying that I entertain an attitude: leave me alone and I shall do the same with respect to you. But there is in me a profound hatred of every intolerance, incapable of respecting specific views which characterize every relatively educated and thinking individual.... At best intolerance can be useful and justifiable in a youth who imagines that he embraced the light of truth only because he had read and heartily accepted a clever and noble book as well as in those people with a limited and uncultivated mind. The more one's mind is limited, the easier he accepts every petty conviction on which he can conveniently sleep.[61]

In response to this letter, Ogarev assured Granovsky that he too valued tolerance, even if he conceded of being less tolerant than his friend.[62]

It was precisely this forbearing orientation marked by the "fullness of life" and accompanied by diffuseness of interest that formed the bridge over which the individual men of letters successfully travelled from one enclosure to the other.

First Intellectual Controversy

The generation of the "remarkable decade," if viewed historically, may be credited with laying the foundations for critical spirit and social thought in

Russia. Moreover, it may also be credited with the initiation of the first genuine intellectual controversy on Russian soil. One should recall the general
character of the debate led by the official-writer and even the gentleman-
littérateur a half century earlier. Both of them still thought of themselves as
obedient servants and loyal advisers, dispatching petitions and letters to the
court and its dignitaries. Clearly, they could readily forego freedom of speech
and, indeed, hate it with all their soul. Novikov himself went so far as to
declare that all those people who write books in any way critical of and detrimental to the autocracy and the country were nothing but "noxious vermin."
The regime, on its part, was willing to tolerate controversy, which often
turned into a series of recriminations and personal reproaches. One reads
with dismay the polemical articles—written by such cultured gentlemen as
Prince Odoevsky—in which he defended Pushkin, for example, by challeng-
ing the social standing of the critics.[63] This failure to formulate conflicting
opinions in sufficiently abstract terms, no doubt, reflected the general state of
intellectual life in Russia. It does not seem too rash to state, therefore, that
controversy was not among men of letters, equal intellectual partners, but
rather among officials of different ranks, among aristocrats of different titles
and diverse genealogical records, and a few parvenus, or as Viazemsky called
them, "lackeys and little boys," trying hard to enter the "literary republic"
located in the Moscow drawing rooms.[64]

Against this background, the debate between the Slavophiles and
the Westerners was a long step forward in the intellectual life of Russia.
Despite its enigmatic character, despite the tendency of the participants to
overstate their respective positions, and despite their slipshod manner of dealing with historical evidence, it was truly the first clash of ideas, not of personalities, the first debate between equal partners that was neither inspired
nor supported by the autocracy. Its participants did not fawn, like Pogodin
and Shevyrev, for the favor of the court and its notables. Most certainly they
were not those men of the pen, as was Bulgarin, ready to execute zealously
"His Majesty the Emperor's will whenever His Majesty may be pleased to use
(their) pen for political articles."[65] When Yazykov, in a play *Our Opponents*,
called Chaadaev a renegade, Granovsky a false teacher corrupting the youth,
and other Westerners traitors to the country, Aksakov branded with indig-
nant disapproval his attack, declaring that their opponents were those very
Slavophiles who played the gendarmes "in the name of Christ." Indeed, the
Westerners and the Slavophiles alike were not only suspected but persecuted
by the regime. As literati ex professo they were neither engaged in exposing
their opponents before the throne, nor interested in becoming the watchmen
of official *ordo* by turning into official moralists, historiographers, or simply
informers, but in establishing the autonomy of the cultural community and
freedom of opinion, necessary for the successful operation of the man of ideas.
It is assuredly no coincidence that it was at precisely that time that a clear-cut
distinction was drawn between the state and society, power and knowledge.
Suffice it to note here that the generation of the gentleman-littérateur, and

Zhukovsky was one of them, had tended to equate society with the beau monde and defended "freedom of expression" within the confines of privacy—friendship and the family. The members of the generation of the "remarkable decade," in turn, spoke of society composed of individuals drawn together from different estates, who, like the officials and the generals in the political and the military spheres, respectively, should reign supreme in the "Republic of the Word." To secure this they asked little more from the government than the freedom to voice their views and to discuss openly literary, aesthetic, philosophical, and other issues. In this desire for intellectual independence, they all agreed, Slavophiles and Westerners. The Aksakov brothers were the authors of the most passionate defense of the freedom of thought in nineteenth-century Russia. "If you expect the sincerity of the word," wrote Ivan Aksakov, "then everyone should be allowed to speak in his *own* voice even if this voice is uncouth and unpleasant."[66] Freedom of speech, according to him "is an end itself for which we should all strive; it is an express condition of social development; a good which should be continuously planted, caressed, looked after, and cultivated with love...."[67] Similarly, his older brother, Konstantin, opposed the repression of the "spoken and the written word" by arguing that "freedom of speech is an inalienable human right."[68] Herzen, like his Slavophile opponents, proclaimed freedom an end in itself and was willing to sacrifice everything "to human dignity, to free speech."[69] Turgenev was convinced that without freedom in the widest sense of the word—that is, not only in relation to external restraints, but also "in relation to oneself and to one's preconceived ideas and systems—a true artist is unthinkable; without the air, it is impossible to breathe."[70] To cite him again:

> Nothing makes a man so free as knowledge and nowhere is freedom so needed as in art, in poetry.... Can a man "grasp," "catch hold of" what surrounds him if he is all tied up inside? Pushkin felt this deeply; it is not for nothing that he said in his immortal sonnet, a sonnet every young writer ought to learn by heart and remember as a commandment—... by a free road. Go, where your free mind may draw you....[71]

In this sense, they were the first Russian intellectuals, men of ideas, who conceived of creative activity as "fully free" and, consequently, as finding "justification and purpose in itself."[72] The very existence of such groups of people, precarious though it might have been, marks one of the basic distinctions between the Tsarist autocracy and the Soviet dictatorship.

Notes

1. A. I. Herzen, *My Past and Thoughts: The Memoirs of Alexander Herzen*, trans. Constance Garnett (New York: Alfred A. Knopf, 1924), I, pp. 181–82.
2. T. N Granovsky, *T. N. Granovskii i Ego Perepiska*, 2d ed. (Moscow, 1897), II, p. 416.

3. Ibid.
4. Herzen, *My Past*, II, p. 284.
5. N. Gogol, *Dead Souls or Tchitchikoff's Journeys*, trans. J. F. Hapgood (London, 1886), I, p. 31.
6. Herzen, *My Past*, II, p. 280.
7. V. G. Belinsky, *Selected Philosophical Works* (Moscow: Foreign Languages Publishing House, 1948), p. 213.
8. Ibid.
9. Ibid., p. 333.
10. Ibid.
11. Ibid.
12. Ivan Turgenev, *Literary Reminiscences and Autobiographical Fragments*, trans. David Magarshack (New York: Farrar, Straus and Cudahy, 1958), p. 108.
13. Ibid., p. 109.
14. A. D. Galakhov, "Literaturnaia Kofeinia v Moskve," *Russkaia Starina* 50 (April 1886): 83.
15. P. V. Annenkov, *Literaturnye Vospominaniia* (St. Petersburg, 1909), p. 130.
16. Granovsky, *T. N. Granovskii*, II, p. 82.
17. Belinsky, *Selected*, pp. 215–16.
18. Ibid., pp. 213–14.
19. Quoted in Franz Schnabel, *Deutsche Geschichte im Neunzehnten Jahrhundert*, 4th ed. (Freiburg im Breisgau, 1948), I. p. 253.
20. I. V. Kireevsky, *Polnoe Sobranie Sochinenii*, ed. M. Gershenzon (Moscow, 1911), I, p. 10.
21. N. P. Ogarev, *Sotsialno-Politicheskie i Filosofskie Proizvedeniia*, ed. M. Iovchuk and N. Tarakanova (Moscow, 1956), II, p. 309.
22. I. S. Aksakov, *Ivan Sergeevich Aksakov v Ego Pismakh* (Moscow, 1888), I, pp. 3–18.
23. Ibid., II, p. 395.
24. Ibid., p. 396.
25. K. S. Aksakov, *Vospominaniia Studentstva 1832–1835 Godov* (St. Petersburg, 1911), p. 20.
26. Granovsky, *T. N. Granovskii*, II, p. 114.
27. Ibid., I, p. 178.
28. Ogarev, *Sotsialno*, II, pp. 285–86.
29. V. Ia. Stoiunin, "Nasha Semia," *Vestnik Evropy* 105 (February 1884): 482.
30. V. A. Zhukovsky, *Sobranie Sochinenii v Chetyrekh Tomakh* (Moscow-Leningrad, 1959) IV, p. 622.
31. A. S. Pushkin, *Polnoe Sobranie Sochinenii* (Moscow, 1958), X, pp. 487–88.
32. F. C. Dahlmann, *Die Politik, auf den Grund und das Maas der Gegebenen Zustaende zurueckgefuehrt* (Gottingen, 1835), I; quoted in Leonard Krieger, *The German Idea of Freedom: History of Political Tradition* (Boston: Beacon Press, 1957), p. 309.
33. A. I. Herzen, *Sochineniia* (St. Petersburg, 1905–1906), VI, p. 151.
34. Ibid., p. 82.
35. Ogarev, *Sotsialno*, II, p. 367.
36. *See* Martin Malia, *Alexander Herzen and the Birth of Russian Socialism* (New York: Grosset and Dunlap, 1965), p. 86.
37. Herbert E. Bowman, *Vissarion Belinskii 1811–1848: A Study in the Origins of Social Criticism in Russia* (Cambridge: Harvard University Press, 1954), p. 7.
38. Kireevsky, *Polnoe Sobranie*, II, p. 133.
39. Granovsky, *T. N. Granovskii*, II, p. 449.
40. Herzen, *My Past*, II, p. 244.

41. Michail Dragomanov, ed., *Konstantin Kawelins und Iwan Turgenjews social-politischer Briefwechsel mit Alexander Iw. Herzen*, Vol. 4 of *Bibliothek Russischer Denkwuerdigkeiten*, ed. Theodor Schiemann (Stuttgart, 1894), p. 1.
42. Ibid., p. 60.
43. Ibid., p. 9.
44. Granovsky, *T. N. Granovskii*, II, p. 402.
45. Herzen, *Sochineniia*, VI, p. 65.
46. Annenkov, *Literaturnye*, p. 284.
47. F. M. Golovenchenko, ed., *Belinskii v Vospominaniiakh Sovremennikov* (Moscow, 1948), p. 427.
48. Kireevsky, *Polnoe Sobranie*, II, p. 233.
49. Granovsky, *T. N. Granovskii*, II, p. 442.
50. F. F. Nelidov, ed., *Zapadniki 40kh Godov* (Moscow, 1910), p. 240; *see also* K. D. Kavelin, *Sobranie Sochinenii* (St. Petersburg, 1899) III, p. 1120.
51. Herzen, *Sochineniia*, VI, p. 135.
52. Ogarev, *Sotsialno*, II, p. 366.
53. Herzen, *My Past*, II, p. 147.
54. Isaiah Berlin, "A Marvellous Decade," *Encounter* 4 (June 1955): 35.
55. Kireevsky, *Polnoe Sobranie*, II, pp. 210–11.
56. Ogarev, *Sotsialno*, II, p. 343.
57. Plato, *Laws*, II, 653.
58. Herzen, *My Past*, II, p. 230.
59. Ibid., pp. 229–30.
60. Annenkov, *Literaturnye*, p. 313; *see* Herzen's reflections on the same theme in *Sobranie Sochinenii v Tridtsati Tomakh* (Moscow, 1954), XXII, p. 109.
61. Granovsky, *T. N. Granovskii*, II, pp. 448–49.
62. Ogarev, *Sotsialno*, II, p. 392.
63. V. F. Odoevsky, "O Napadeniiakh Peterburgskikh Zhurnalov na Russkogo Poeta," *Russkii Arkhiv* 2 (1864): 1020.
64. For a review of the controversy between "literary aristocrats" and their opponents, *see* Abbot Gleason, *European and Muscovite: Ivan Kireevsky and the Origin of Slavophilism* (Cambridge: Harvard University Press, 1972), pp. 45–74.
65. Quoted in E. Lampert, *Studies in Rebellion* (London: Routledge and Kegan Paul, 1957), p. 41.
66. I. Aksakov, *Sochineniia* (Moscow, 1886), IV. p. 485.
67. Ibid., IV, p. 467.
68. K. Aksakov, "On the Internal State of Russia," in *Russian Intellectual History: An Anthology*, ed. Marc Raeff (New York: Harcourt, Brace and World, Inc., 1966), p. 250.
69. Herzen, *Sochineniia*, V, p. 170.
70. Turgenev, *Literary Reminiscences*, p. 131.
71. Ibid.
72. Aleksei S. Khomiakov, *Polnoe Sobranie Sochinenii*, 4th ed. (Moscow, 1911), III, pp. 418–19.

5 Men of Convictions: First Intelligenty

The friendship circles of the generation of the "remarkable decade" have been traditionally conceived of by Western and Russian authors alike as a "holy union" of fellow believers, a "brotherhood of warriors," bound together by a doctrine and alienated from society at large. Indeed, this conception of the circles has been repeatedly offered as a standard definition of the Russian intelligentsia. We have attempted to show, however, that the circles of the first freelance literati in Russia were neither organized solely on the basis of allegiance to ideological tenets, nor were their members conscious of being alienated from the mass of indifferent humanity. As Herzen phrased it:

> We were not like the emaciated monks of Zurbaran, we did not weep over the sins of the world, we only sympathized with its sufferings, and were ready for a smile for anything and not depressed with forebodings of our sacrifices in the future. Ascetics who are forever austere have always excited my suspicion; if they are not pretending, either their mind or their stomach is out of order.[1]

There was, however, one member of the circles whose total commitment to ideas pouring, as they were, from the West, and whose attitude toward and relations with friends and people in general lend credence to this conception of the intelligentsia and raise a series of issues basic to this study. This man was Belinsky, or, as his friends called him, "Orlando Furioso." Similar observations, however, apply equally to all his spiritual heirs, foremost among whom were Chernyshevsky and Dobroliubov. The unique character of their attachment to "truth," to people—dead and live, men and women, friends and strangers—and the meaning they attributed to "friendship" and to human relations in general cannot but be of engaging psychological interest.

Unlike his friends, Slavophiles and Westerners alike, Belinsky always took his ideas in earnest. He never jested, to cite Turgenev, "with the object of his researches, nor with his readers, nor with himself."[2] Such a humorless seriousness, such a depth of conviction, was at times unbearable to his friends and companions; as Turgenev admitted, "the frivolity of youth asserted itself, I wanted to have a rest, I was thinking of going for a walk, of having dinner...."[3] Belinsky, however, led a full life when he was carried away by ideas and convictions; in the "heat of disputation and having forgotten myself, I saw one truth which engaged me even then, when all the others had gathered in the reception room crowding around the piano and singing together."[4] If no one objected to his views and he was not irritated, Belinsky failed even to converse well, but when his cherished convictions were touched on, or worse, questioned, then the discussion "would often end in blood which flowed from his sick man's throat; pale, gasping, with his eyes fixed on the man ... he would lift his handkerchief to his mouth with shaking hand and stop, deeply mortified, crushed."[5] It was as if Belinsky would never think without feeling and feel without thinking. For him, as he readily confessed, to think, to feel, to understand, and to suffer were one and the same thing. He was, according to Turgenev's diagnosis, a "central nature" staking his whole personality on the ideological issues involved. He believed in those theories and ideas, Herzen observed, and did not flinch before any considerations—those of moral propriety or the opinion of others.[6] In other words, Belinsky did not accept and expound ideas because they were valid and followed logically from known facts, but because they elicited the response of his mind, will, emotion, of his whole personality, because, in short, he loved them. It is safe to assume that, had Belinsky been asked to explain his attitude, he would have failed to make explicit the various reasons for it. Almost in the manner of personal attachment, Belinsky either liked ideas or did not, and, in doing this, he either liked or resented people. Indeed, he loved ideas as if they were persons and loved persons, in turn, as if they were nothing but "concrete expressions" of ideas. His thought was no doubt emotive, was charged with affectivity, and involved the commitment of his whole personality.

> You do know my nature: it always takes an extreme position and never hits the center of an idea. I depart from the old idea with difficulty and pain and go over to the new one with all the fanaticism of a proselyte. I have now reached a new extreme, that is the idea of *socialism* which has become for me the idea of ideas, the existence of existence, the question of questions, the alpha and omega of belief and knowledge. Everything from it, for it, and toward it. It is the question and the solution of the question. For me it has absorbed history, religion, and philosophy, and that is why I explain in its terms my life, your life, and the life of all those whom I meet on the road of life.[7]

These and similar statements, recurring frequently in his correspondence, indicate clearly that Belinsky was on the lookout for a special kind of ideas. He was on the lookout for those ideas that would not so much provide him the material for an exercise in dialectics and the tools for abstract theorizing but furnish a stable foothold from which he could attribute meaning to his own existence, to relate himself meaningfully to his friends and society at large. "People like me," he wrote to Bakunin's sisters, "remain most unfortunate as long as they do not find in religious convictions a solid point of support for their lives and a firm rational base for their ties and relations with other people."[8] Ideas, in this sense, constituted the "way of ways of living." At one and the same time, ideals because he aspired to, and identified with them; moral norms because he attempted to conform to them; social bonds because he related himself to other people in terms of them; and explanatory principles because he interpreted the social universe in the light of them. They permeated the very tissues of his being and were accepted in his conscience. As such, they evoked in Belinsky the typical attitude that was a mixture of pathos, obligation, and devotion. Certainly, they were much more than scientific theories, rules of scientific method, cognitive, aesthetic, and technical norms. Scientists and artists may consider these norms to be "true" and "right," but they are true primarily for relations among ideas, percepts, and physical operations. Belinsky, however, did not conceive of ideas as the objects of cognitive or appreciative orientation, but as principles of action, as the properties of individuals and social bonds. They were "true" for relations among individuals and groups. That ideas to Belinsky were not the tools for a detached analysis and understanding of reality can be seen from the fact that he "smelled blood" in them, that he committed himself totally to them and passionately believed in them, and that he departed from them with pain and fell on new ones with the fanaticism of a proselyte.

To appreciate the unique character of Belinsky's intense attachment to ideas, it is sufficient to contrast it with that of his friends and contemporaries. When Khomiakov, for example, that Slavophile "duellist of dialectics," was engaged in debate, it was difficult at times to recognize whether he argued from an artistic pleasure in argument or from depth of convictions. Indeed, he had no difficulty in making people laugh at their convictions and theories. People like Khomiakov, Botkin, Herzen, Turgenev, and Korsh, not to mention the gentlemen-littérateurs, like Pushkin and Lermontov, easily made fun of and referred jokingly to theories, convictions, and learning itself. There was an element of play, of leisurely exercise in dialectics, of pleasure in intellectual conviviality in the whole controversy between the Slavophiles and the Westerners.

According to Samarin, the Slavophiles and the Westerners continued to meet in the heat of the controversy, "were on friendly terms and composed, as it were, one society; felt the need for one another and were attracted by mutual sympathy based on the same intellectual interests and reciprocal respect."[9] True enough, Herzen, Botkin, Granovsky, and others disagreed with the Slavophiles, but they were not "Slavophobes" and were able to distinguish the Slavophile ideas from their individual bearers. They eagerly sought the company of Kireevsky and Aksakov and gladly invited them to parties and celebrations. It was at such informal friendly gatherings that they could engage in intellectual contemplation while sniffing the "fragrance of Turkey" and listening to the "songs of Schubert."[10] In Herzen's phrase, his friends were too cultured and independent to be consumed by any one set of ideas. Any *ism,* according to him, attracted only those "tired people" who begged almost "with tears for Truth to take them in her arms and lull them to sleep."[11] In short, they were far from willing to give up their personalities for the sake of solving all the "cursed questions," for getting rid of hesitation and uncertainty. They conceived of life and human beings as too complex to be rendered meaningful by any one abstract formula. Although Herzen, Granovsky, and their friends did become enthusiastic about particular theories and ideas, certainly ideas neither animated the whole of their lives, nor became the alpha and omega of their very existence. Only people of "limited and uncultivated minds," to recall the remark of Granovsky, committed themselves totally to every "petty conviction" on which they could conveniently sleep.

The Sphere of "Truth": Ideological Bonds

To elucidate fully this attitude of intensely concentrated attachment to ideas, we shall shift the emphasis of our analysis somewhat and approach it in terms of the effect on the nature of relations to friends and people. This approach, hitherto completely overlooked, will help to put into sharp relief the character of the ties that bound Belinsky to Herzen, Aksakov, and Botkin, and Chernyshevsky to Dobroliubov, Nekrasov, and others.

The bonds that linked the members of the first circles of the generation of the "remarkable decade" were basically those of diffuse affective attachment. They were deeply attracted to Granovsky because he was first and foremost their friend, a "loving," "serene," "indulgent spirit," because of his "positive moral influence" and the "purity of his character," and because his love was deep and free from "unconcerned indifference." They liked Herzen because there was never a trace of anything false in him, because of his gentle, amiable, almost feminine character, and because of his charm and delicacy. They were all attached to Stankevich because of his warm understanding, his sympathetic and friendly disposition, and because of his artistic, musical, and contemplative nature. They liked the Slavophile, Kireevsky, because of his "broad, noble nature which cannot be narrowed by any opinion."[12] In short, they responded warmly to the friendly dispositions and to the personal qualities of their friends. That is why they could remain friends and appreciate friendship, despite momentary ideological conflicts. It is of interest to note what personal quality they all perceived in Belinsky—precisely what they all lacked—the attitude of total commitment and intense attachment to ideas, that is, the quality they inadvertently ascribed to uncultivated and limited minds.

The striking difference between Belinsky and his friends becomes at once apparent from his conception of the nature of relations with his friends. It was, according to him, a "holy union" based on the striving toward truth, a union subsequently exemplified by the relationship of Chernyshevsky and Dobroliubov, "full agreement upon, one can say full identity of theoretical and political views, their uncompromising ... defense."[13] Chernyshevsky, as the Soviet author rightly noted, "could not admit of any other kind of friendship."[14] This kind of friendship, according to Dobroliubov himself, was not based on personal bonds—changeable and unreliable as they were—but on the unity of commonly held ideas and aspirations. As early as 1836, Belinsky was convinced that it was not an individual's personality, the "immediate attributes of a human being" that "form the bonds of friendship,"[15] but similar beliefs and convictions. In 1842, in one of his letters to Bakunin's younger brother, he expressed it unequivocally in this way: "Only one conviction can at present both separate me from and bind me to other people."[16] Belinsky thus approached his future friend Bakunin by responding first to his "lively aspiration" to truth: "I saw you assiduously reading Fichte and becoming excited by it; this elevated you only more in my eyes."[17] It was this consideration, concluded Belinsky, that "more and more made me view you as my friend."[18] To another of his friends, Botkin, to whom Belinsky wrote long and tiring letters, pledging his love and friendship, he suddenly admitted:

> Botkin, I departed from you very coolly, and in Petersburg you became to me an abstract conception and cold reminiscence. You have done much to me, I saw it, but I was not in the least worried, as if this did not concern me at all. I conceive of friendship as a cold feeling, an exchange of vanity, a result of habit, idleness, and egoism. More than that, I hated friendship and I could not avoid the feeling of satisfaction for being unable to see you and others.[19]

But this was true not only of Botkin. On one other occasion he readily let his friends know that they were of no interest to him; that insofar as he was concerned, they had never existed and did not now exist. Yet it sufficed for Belinsky to become acquainted with Botkin's article in which German Hegelians were referred to approvingly to elicit anew his "love" and "friendship" to Botkin. "After the dinner Panaev read aloud your article.... This is the way it should be written! Whatever it is I clearly recognize now that I loved none as much as you and do not want to be as close to anyone as to you."[20] When Herzen, another of his friends, refused to share the view that "might is right" and to become enthusiastic over the "sacred quality" of the Tsarist autocracy, Belinsky responded in this characteristic fashion (to be sure, Belinsky was consistent in his conception of friendship): "Herzen should not pity me—I spit at him."[21] Having thus embraced one "little truth," Belinsky did not hesitate to spit at his friend. Again, a few years later, after his discovery that socialism was the alpha and omega of life, Belinsky vented his spleen on other friends. Herzen became a noble person—"there are very few such persons in the world"[22]—and the Kireevskys, the Aksakovs, became his foremost enemies. He declared, therefore, with the same ease: "I spit in the face of all Khomiakovs [implying, of course, that he spits in the face of Aksakov,

Kireevsky, and others] and let that man be cursed who would censure me for that."[23] Moreover, he sent to Herzen and other Westerners threatening dispatches, excommunicating and anathematizing all those who continued to fraternize with his ideological enemies. As a man with the "Tsar in his head" and a "Jew by nature," Belinsky detected in Herzen and Granovsky the symptoms of "moderation, that is, of decay and corruption."[24]

Belinsky's strange ties that bound him to his friends, disguised, as they were, under the terms of "love" and "friendship," merit a careful scrutiny. Clearly enough, they allowed for rapidly shifting attitudes. He wrote, for example, that the "more I know Aksakov, the more I love him; he is one of those scarce families of the sons of God,"[25] or "his sympathy evokes tears in me,"[26] yet he did not hesitate to spit in Aksakov's face and to proclaim him a fool. He wrote in 1838 that his heart burned with love for Bakunin, yet two years later he began to hurl abuses at the same friend. In 1843 he again reversed his attitude toward Bakunin and informed Botkin: "After you, I love this man more than any other."[27] He called Herzen a "noble person," viewed Botkin as the only individual he ever loved, yet he also spit in Herzen's face, conceived of Botkin as a mere abstraction, and cursed Granovsky for his refusal to do the same.

It should be pointed out, however, that Belinsky was indebted in many ways to the same people. It was due to them that he learned many of the "little truths" he so wholeheartedly embraced, and it was due to their disinterested financial help that he was able to survive in Moscow. His letters are interspersed with such admissions as these: "On my return from Priamukhino I borrowed 500 rubles from Botkin, before Easter I took again 500 rubles from him, later on from Aksakov...."[28] "I owe money to Aksakov-father, to his son (and this is a special case which is the more unpleasant because his father knows it)."[29]

Such disinterested assistance was no doubt prompted by a generous and humane response to the needy young friend on the verge of starvation. Yet in return for this, Belinsky spat with ease in their faces. This showed not only a plain lack of decorum, of human gratitude and delicacy, but something much more significant—the very nature of his attachment to people. Clearly, his affection for close friends, like that of Dostoevsky's "Underground Man," was "of a fantastical order which could not possibly have been applied to a human being ..."[30] Belinsky was convinced for long that it was not a concrete person, his kind and sympathetic disposition, the personal qualities of an individual that enter into affective relations, but similar ideological aspirations and convictions. It was the same kind of ideological friendship that Chernyshevsky tolerated and his fellow believer Dobroliubov so highly praised. As if to inform his friends, Belinsky wrote:

Oh, no! Let them interpret your actions as they like, let them fail to comprehend their cause and objective, but if thought and convictions are accessible to you—go forward and be not detracted from that road by calculations of egoism, by the deception of spurious friendship which aims at offering its insignificant gifts at the cost of depriving you of a more valuable treasure—independence of conviction and pure love of truth.[31]

Phrased differently, Belinsky, Chernyshevsky, and Dobroliubov were not attached to people because they were "kind," "gentle," "considerate," "indulgent," in short, because of their friendly dispositions and personal qualities. They failed to recognize that human love goes out neither to ideas nor convictions, but to individual persons. Thus, Dobroliubov avoided the company of the kind, delicate Turgenev, ready to help any young author (this Dobroliubov failed to appreciate) because Turgenev refused to share his convictions. This was enough for him to dismiss Turgenev's company as unworthy of his attention and to declare with pride that poor allies were not allies at all. The personal qualities of their friends were removed into the background, or, more exactly, completely eliminated, and human beings were conceived of as nothing but the bearers of convictions. What they did, in effect, was to shift the attitudes they held toward ideas from ideas to individual persons, and in this way confound convictions with human beings.

Consistent Men: Personal Insensitivity and Rigidity of Behavior

It can be safely stated that, as a result of this orientation, neither Belinsky, nor Chernyshevsky, nor Dobroliubov had personal friends. Belinsky plainly admitted to Botkin that he was nothing but an abstraction and that Botkin's generosity did not concern him in the least. Between Granovsky and Belinsky, wrote Kavelin, there was never an "intimate sympathy and, of course, could not be."[32] Of young Stankevich, who introduced Belinsky to his circle, he said: "I could not consider Stankevich my friend...."[33] When Stankevich died, Belinsky had this to record:

> I am a strange man, Botkin, the death of Stankevich had an insensible effect upon me. I have lost, as it were, not my close friend but a distinguished man.... His death affected me in the same way as the death of Lermontov and Pushkin.[34]

To appreciate the significance of this confession, one should be reminded that Belinsky was never personally acquainted with Pushkin, and that when he met Lermontov for the first time and began to converse excitedly about Voltaire and the encyclopedists, Lermontov laughed at and made fun of both Voltaire and Belinsky. For Lermontov, as he told Satin, Belinsky was a "half-learned *fanfaron* who, having read a few pages of Voltaire, imagines that he swallowed all the wisdom."[35] Despite this, Belinsky experienced the death of Stankevich, one of the friends of whom he could have safely stated, as did Schlegel of Schleiermacher, "Dein eigentlicher Beruf ist die

Freundschaft,"[36] in the same way as the death of Pushkin, whom he never met, and the death of Lermontov, who made jokes about him, calling him a "ponderous windbag."

Belinsky failed to respond to and sympathize with individual human beings, failed to draw a line between a friend and a stranger, between a friend and a fellow believer, and between a person and his convictions, and failed to attach himself to his friends in terms of their personal qualities. Instead of responding to "immediate characteristics" of individual persons, Belinsky, as, indeed, every "belief possessed person," approached them "in the lights of their symbolic rather than personal significance."[37] Apologizing to his friend Aksakov for this kind of attachment, he wrote: "What can I do? I love in my own fashion."[38] It was this peculiar love that allowed Belinsky to love strangers who died long ago, to love Voltaire and Schiller, to love Lermontov who insulted him and Pushkin whom he never met. Indeed, it allowed him to love in the same way his close friends—Stankevich, Botkin, Aksakov—and also the strangers (dead and alive) he read about in books.

One learns with surprise, therefore, of the view of Belinsky as a kind of Russian Kierkegaard, a personalist whose "revolutionary socialism is, in fact, unintelligible without reference to his personalistic ethics."[39] It is true that on several occasions Belinsky professed his attachment to the idea of "human person." Yet, his was not Kierkegaard's revolt against those who have forgotten "in the fit of world-historical absent-mindedness what is meant to be an individual"[40] and, consequently, have lost any sense of themselves as persons. For it is not without significance that, "at his most personalistic," when Belinsky spoke of his "love for the freedom and independence of the human person,"[41] he also exclaimed in the same breath: "I am beginning to love mankind *à la* Marat: to make the least part of it happy I believe I could destroy the rest of it with fire and sword."[42] In the letter to the same friend, he arrived at a no less "personalistic" conclusion: "People are so stupid that you have to drag them to happiness.... In any case, what is the blood of thousands in comparison with the humiliation and sufferings of millions?"[43] Moreover, it was "at his most personalistic" that Belinsky lost any sense of himself as a person and proclaimed with pride: "Person is nothing to me now—conviction is everything."[44]

Viewed within the framework of Belinsky's orientation and state of mind, this same personalism turns out to be profoundly antipersonalist and collectivist. For it allowed him to speak of personalism and at the same time be disposed to implement anti-personalism; to defend the dignity of the human person and, at the same time, to resort to fire and sword to annihilate human beings en masse; to fight autocracy and oppression and at the same time be prepared to become another tyrant.

The truth of the matter is that Belinsky, like his followers Chernyshevsky and Dobroliubov, hardly ever responded to concrete human beings, with their *Einzigartigkeit* and *Eigentumlichkeit*, or sympathized with the plight of individual persons. It is as if they were unable to establish enduring personal bonds with people, as if they were inaccessible to the personal responses of others and hence incapable of sharing in the delights and sufferings of individual human beings. It is for this reason that they were so insensitive to personal relations with other people. As Belinsky boasted:

> God is my witness—I do not have any personal enemies. This is because of my nature (and I can say it without boasting) which stands above personal wrongs. But the enemies of public good—oh, let their intestines be thrown out so that they can hang themselves on them! I am ready to offer them the last service—to prepare the knots and to put them on their necks.[45]

"Nature," wrote Belinsky to Turgenev, "has not given me the ability to hate a man for a personal injustice he has done to me; I am more likely to hate a man for a difference of opinion or for his faults and vices which do not affect me in the least."[46] This kind of displaced sensitivity was exhibited even more strikingly by Chernyshevsky. On his visit to one family in Petersburg, in the home of which he met several young ladies and also one young unhappily married couple, Chernyshevsky made this entry in his *Diary:*

> I sympathize with the woman who married that simpleton, that is, I do not pity her as the individual, but as one of those persons of her kind; not personally her, but as a symbol, as a vessel in which it appeared.... I sympathize finally with the young ladies, that is, again, not personally with those ladies (the daughters of the host—obviously they are amiable), but with all the ladies of their position.[47]

At the same time Chernyshevsky was unable to sympathize with his cousin Lubinka, who was in the same position. "In fact, what foolishness," exclaimed Chernyshevsky, "not to perceive what is taking place around you."[48] It is now understandable why the relationship of Chernyshevsky and Dobroliubov, according to Golovacheva-Panaeva, was unlike that of any other people she was acquainted with. They conversed gladly on "accursed Russian reality," and met frequently, but there was literally nothing resembling personal friendship. Chernyshevsky failed to notice the most pitiful conditions under which sick Dobroliubov lived, the dark, shabby room in which his fellow believer stayed. It was only because of the intervention of Nekrasov and Panaev—who, we may add, were never on close personal terms with Dobroliubov and Chernyshevsky—that Dobroliubov was removed to Panaev's house. Yet one finds in Dobroliubov's *Diary* this significant confession:

> Today I received a letter from V. I. Dobroliubov, in which he informs me of the death of E. P. Zakhareva, who used to take care of my younger sister, Liza.... This worries me a little, but to be truthful, only very little. For almost one month I have been writing my diary and yet I find there

no single reference, no single thought, not a word, not even a hint of my family relations. How much I have become estranged from them....

If intellectual and moral interests diverge, respect for and love of relations weaken and, in the end, vanish altogether. In fact, were Chernyshevsky to die now I would suffer a hundred times as much over his death as over the death of my relative (uncle), were he to pass away, of course.[49]

As we see it, the very nature of such orientation precludes the establishment of personal ties. Belinsky, Chernyshevsky, and Dobroliubov responded to concrete persons, be they friends or relatives, as if they were "vessels" and "symbols." According to Chernyshevsky, neither he nor Dobroliubov were "expansive" people, that is, they were not interested in each other's personal matters. Their relationship was, in a sense, frozen and deprived of sensitivity to each other's feelings and needs. Although they might have exclaimed with Dostoevsky's "Underground Man": "How much love, God! How much love—I used to expend in those dreams, in those yearnings,"[50] they expended it for "truth," for encrusted formulas in terms of which they related themselves to friends and people. That is why they sympathized with a "vessel" and not at all with an unhappy young lady; indeed, that is why they loved people in the fashion of Marat, why they did not hesitate to deceive individual peasants in order to liberate *narod*; that is why to them, as Herzen perceptively observed, and Belinsky proudly proclaimed, an individual person counted for nothing and conviction for everything.

It is only now that Professor Isaiah Berlin's observation that the Russian attitude, as distinguished from the French one, was that man is one and indivisible, acquires quite a different meaning. Of course, this contrast between the French and Russian attitudes is arbitrary and should in no way be related to the national character of the respective people. Considered in the light of our approach, the displaced sensitivity of Belinsky and Chernyshevsky was intimately related with their rigidity of attitude and behavior. As we have emphasized, Herzen, Granovsky, and others were quite aware of the difference between a friend and a fellow believer, between a person and his convictions. To the extent, however, that Belinsky, Chernyshevsky, and Dobroliubov equated individuals with their convictions, thereby endowing them with one "social identity," man to them was one and indivisible. That is why Belinsky refused to admit that people with opposing views could ever be "decent people," let alone friends. On the occasion of his accidental meeting with the Slavophile Aksakov, he wrote to Botkin: "Indeed, I fall into a terrible heresy and begin to think that there can be decent people among Slavophiles."[51] His remark that he experienced life to its utmost when he saw "one truth" at the same time that other young people "gathered around the piano," clearly points to this lack of flexibility—both personal and social. It was not unusual for a gentleman-littérateur, like Lermontov, to make fun of Belinsky, who at their first meeting turned to Voltaire. Having offended Aksakov, by expounding to him one "little truth," Belinsky significantly apologized in this manner: "I see that I behaved improperly. I forgot that one should not appear before everyone in a dressing-gown, that one should appear before some in formal wear, before others in a frockcoat, depending upon the character of the relations."[52] During his solitary broodings and self-reflection, Belinsky came very close to grasping his difficulty. As he expressed it, he loved in moments of abandonment when "I ceased thinking or when I thought on my own, without the influence of authorities or under the influence of revolt against those authorities."[53] Otherwise he let convictions triumph over personal feelings and loved his friends and even women "objectively," instead of "simply" and "subjectively":

> ... simple girls, whose life was love and belief, but *simple* love and belief, stemming from their simple, holy and deep immediacies, not only feel, but know. For them the words of a man they love are true not only because they are actually true, but because they are his; for them the behavior of a man they love is noble, not because it is actually noble, but because it is his. I have derided formerly such a love, declaring with sympathy that Vera Alexandrova cannot love in any other way and that her love could never satisfy me. But now I feel that such love of a woman could satisfy me.[54]

Similarly, Dobroliubov discovered his own humanity and came "to feel like a human being" on his visit to Paris where he stayed briefly with one French family. "Here I begin to see myself," wrote Dobroliubov to Kavelin's wife, "as a human being who has been given the right to live and to avail himself of life, rather than as one who has been called upon to sacrifice his life to the service of humanity."[55] On the other hand, Dobroliubov experienced an unbearable loneliness in Petersburg and remained disconsolate in the midst of people with whom he shared "common ideas and aspirations:"

> Nothing of this kind exists in Paris. Here I found something that I had never experienced anywhere else. I have met people with whom I get along easily and enjoy their company—people who attract me not because they are the representatives of lofty ideas, but for what they are as people, for their sweet and lively personalities.[56]

Chernyshevsky's manner of approaching his future life companion, his wife-to-be, illustrates well the degree to which he depersonalized other human beings and standardized his relationship to them. Having learned that "she is a democrat" and not too religious, he approached her declaring: "My assumption is correct and now I adore you unconditionally ... my love is now unconditional ... I have heard many things about you, but this prompts me to look at you in a special manner ... for such a kind of ideas I cannot but love you."[57] Then he proceeded to introduce himself in a manner no less significant. "The nature of my ideas is such that sooner or later I will be caught."[58] Continuing on the same theme, he elaborated:

> I cannot discard this kind of ideas because they lie in my very character, exasperated and dissatisfied with everything I see around.... In any case, up till now this trend was becoming more and more strengthened, was becoming sharper, colder, penetrating more and more my existence. And thus I await every minute the appearance of the police, and, like a pious Christian, await the Last Day of Judgment. Besides, there will soon be revolt, and when it comes I will unavoidably participate in it.[59]

Such an introduction had, of course, a strange effect on the young lady. But Chernyshevsky was determined to marry.

> I should possess an idea that I do not belong to myself; that I have no right to risk my life. There should be some protection against democratic, revolutionary conviction, and this protection cannot be anything else but the idea of a wife.[60]

Certainly, and the evidence is overwhelming, some kind of personal deficiency rendered Belinsky, Chernyshevsky, and Dobroliubov incapable of experiencing conviviality, love, intimacy, and the personal nuances and incongruities of the relations between individual human beings. It is as if they were psychologically and socially inflexible, and hence unable to respond differently to different situations. To speak metaphorically, they were dressed on all occasions in one and the same attire; as a result, they were bent on playing only one master role—that of men of convictions. Further, they expected other people to respond as if they were nothing but "conviction-possessed" beings. Since it is evident that most Russians, like other people, amused themselves, relaxed, half-jokingly exchanged opinions, and discussed theories at informal gatherings, they could hardly feel comfortable and at ease in their company. Indeed, they utterly failed to mix freely with other people and were literally afraid of them. Determined, as they were, to meet people on their own terms, they were inwardly impelled to alienate everyone around them. An inevitable consequence of this was social isolation and an accompanying feeling of loneliness.

Self-Estrangement: Impoverishment of Personal Ties

One of the most striking characteristics, applying with equal force to Belinsky, Chernyshevsky, and Dobroliubov, was their deep, although subdued, feeling of estrangement from the people. Probably no other nineteenth-century Russian man of letters made so many references to love, repeatedly pledged his affection to friends, as did Belinsky. Yet he was more tormented by "solitude than by love" and was afraid that he might lose his mind, if not die, out of sheer loneliness. One cannot but sympathize with a man whose loneliness prompted him to contemplate buying an animal, a "rabbit or a hedgehog in order to have something to love, something to care for and to caress."[61] One cannot but appreciate the extent to which Chernyshevsky was haunted by loneliness when he failed to have a single friend with whom he would "love to share feelings" and thus avoid speaking "with anyone, even with myself."[62] One cannot but detect Dobroliubov's feeling of isolation from the people when he thanked his "beloved angel"—a prostitute—for responding to his quest for human company and affection. In another intimate verse to the same woman, Dobroliubov again confessed:

Tormented by a passionless longing,
Sick, worn out, estranged from all.
To you alone, my beloved friend,
To you alone I offered love.[63]

One cannot help but discern the depth of Dobroliubov's self-estrangement—ready as he was to escape from himself—when he wrote: "This evening I am willing to sacrifice my mind, knowledge, dignity, noble convicitions for the superficial education, aimless chatter, easygoing manners of the worldly fop."[64] Truly, they found themselves in the same predicament as one of Dostoevsky's heroes. "I had no friends or intimates, and was gradually coming to confine myself more and more to my lodgings."[65]

It was Dostoevsky's genius that so profoundly understood their complex attitude toward love, friendship, and people in general. This attitude was characteristically ambivalent—Belinsky, Chernyshevsky, and Dobroliubov experienced deeply the need for love and longed for affection, and yet were without the capacity for loving in return; they were in need of friendship and human company, and yet were incapable of establishing enduring personal ties. Theirs was not a simple rebellion against the generation of "superfluous men," against the institution of the salon, against the easygoing manners of its habitués. Theirs was not an unquestioned determination to get rid of the "literary republic," lodged, as it was, in the Moscow and Petersburg drawing rooms, a revolt of "revolutionary democrats" determined to annihilate once and for all the traditional social institutions—the views too often repeated by the pre-revolutionary *intelligenty* and expounded obligingly by the present-day Soviet scribes and official myth makers. Like Dostoevsky's "Underground Man," they realized only too painfully that the gentlemen-littérateurs, the "superfluous men," indeed the young aristocrats, were not only authorities on *vornehmer Anstand*, but also the representatives of society, successful in conquering the fair sex, in loving, in establishing ties of friendship—in short, as Belinsky and Chernyshevsky admitted, were "normal," "harmonious," "decent" persons. At the same time they were convinced that these same people represented everything they despised and scorned, everything "superfluous," even sham in society. "It is strange, indeed," recorded Dobroliubov in his *Diary*, "that a few days ago I felt capable of falling in love, and yesterday I was willing to learn how to dance. The devil knows what is happening to me."[66] Such sentiments, he continued, "would amount to the appeasement of society.... But I should not be lulled by these sentiments ... I should not yield to society; on the contrary, I should keep aloof and foster my hatred toward it."[67] Although it is true that Belinsky proudly proclaimed to his readers: "We are not men of society and do not visit society,"[68] in a letter to his brother he boasted with exaggeration of having gained entrée into Moscow society:

> Through the Petrovs I got acquainted with the home of one landowner ... in which I was very politely and lavishly received. In this house there are many ladies; you may surmise why it is with great satisfaction that I spend a lot of time there. On the seventeenth of September I was there on the occasion of a namesday, I danced a little bit, was drunk somewhat ... and was happy. I can say to you that high society in Moscow differs strikingly from that in Chembar by its simplicity, greater freedom of relations and the absence of dull ritual. ... In general, one is less confused here. ... And ladies! Oh, how different from yours! It seemed to me as if I were transferred to some world until now unbeknown to me. ... Do you see how many acquaintances and contacts I have in Moscow.[69]

As is known, however, and as all his contemporaries unanimously agree, Belinsky was utterly lost, not only in the salon but in larger company. Indeed, he was "savagely shy," lost his head in a numerous company, shunned outsiders, and, according to him, "loved like a bear, the solitude of his lodgings."[70] So much was this the case, that he felt lonely and uncomfortable in the company of his close friends. As he readily confessed:

> One thing worries me terribly. My timidity and confusion not only do not subside, but, on the contrary, increase in a monstrous progression. I cannot show myself before people—my face becomes inflamed, voice and legs tremble, I am afraid I may fall down. It is truly the Lord's punishment. This had brought me to the brink of despair.... I am simply afraid of people, society terrifies me.[71]

"No single woman ever did love me," complained Belinsky, "neither noble nor common—and from none I did ever receive the slightest respect. It seems to me that on my face there is something repellent and that because of it no woman can ever fall in love with me."[72] He was ashamed of his relations with women and seemed to be unable to understand why "he should be wasting his time talking about all sorts of disagreeable personal affairs when there were many much more useful and important things to talk about."[73]

Chernyshevsky faced precisely the same difficulty. Reflecting on his presence in the company of young people, he wrote:

> I have noticed in myself diverse results of this evening. First of all, my heart somewhat throbs … because I am dissatisfied with the role I played last evening—a post and nothing else. As a result of it I have learned many things which I refused to learn up till now … it is necessary, before other things, to dance, decisively necessary, in order to be able to establish contacts with young women, in order to open the door to their society. Secondly, it is necessary to play the piano or something else, although this is less necessary.… Finally, it is necessary to speak French and German.[74]

Yet, a few months later, when one of Chernyshevsky's acquaintances wanted to introduce him to a young lady, he made this entry in his diary: "I don't like it, that is, to make acquaintants; it seems to me to be very awkward, it is as if I were put in an inferior position.…"[75] In the same breath, however, he added: "What it is not to participate in the activities of society, not to see women and to turn into a man who is ready to explode upon hearing the name of a woman."[76] Again, having been offered a position as a teacher in the home of one family, Chernyshevsky became excited by unrealistic anticipations:

> The contact with this house should introduce me into a circle of decent people, I think. Maybe it will not, maybe I will continue to live in the solitude of my room. No, I think I will come closer, will become as it should be, will speak French and German after a while, in one word, I will become as it should be.… And thus I anticipate society life, with its brilliance of mind, knowledge, sharp tongue, sharp mind, some prospect of amiable company, a pleasant person with whom I could meet and converse several times a day.[77]

Chernyshevsky's suppressed desire to acquire the bearing of a gentleman took on ludicrous proportions at times. Having bought himself a new fur coat, he exclaimed with childish delight: "Now I am with respect to dress equal to all those gentlemen … and I wear it on all possible occasions."[78] Despite a new fur coat, Chernyshevsky remained, according to his own admission, a "fully dressed seminarist," and failed to establish contact with society, let alone with its young ladies. Like Belinsky and Dobroliubov, however, he longed to fall in love, anxiously anticipated the enjoyment of their company, and tried to find friends in order to cease speaking to himself and to his dead friends. At the same time he was afraid of this association, fled from it, and deeply felt that people got tired of his company. As Dobroliubov stated it, while waiting for his first meeting with a young lady: "Theoretically I am afraid that she is pretty and will entice me, but deep in my soul I should terribly like it to happen."[79]

It was this deeply rooted ambivalence that defined their attitude toward love, friendship, and human association. On the one hand, they tried hard to model themselves in the image of "normal" young men, equally at home in diverse social situations, indeed, looked on themselves with dissatisfaction, if not with loathing; on the other, they resented the same people, were afraid of human association and life itself. "In this manner," Belinsky observed, "there were whole days during which I looked for company, and having found it, I fled from it."[80] If they were alone, as was Belinsky, they turned to their solitary dens and broodings, condemning the world around them, or if they met each other on the road of life, they formed an attachment incomprehensible to their contemporaries. In fact, they established a social group based neither on the diffuse personal ties of two friends, nor on the functionally specific relations of two professional men of letters. It was rather an association of alienated outsiders consumed by convictions and ideas. It was in this sphere, in the sphere of "truth," in the company of the brethren of conviction, that they found a substitute for love, friendship, human affection, and, indeed, felt comfortable and at ease.

Notes

1. A. I. Herzen, *My Past and Thoughts: The Memoirs of Alexander Herzen*, trans. Constance Garnett (New York: Alfred A. Knopf, 1924), II, p. 230.
2. Ivan Turgenev, *Literary Reminiscences and Autobiographical Fragments*, trans. David Magarshack (New York: Farrar, Straus and Cudahy, 1958) p. 139.
3. Ibid., p. 123.
4. A. N. Pypin, *Belinskii: Ego Zhizn i Perepiska* (St. Petersburg, 1876), I, p. 171.
5. Herzen, *My Past*, II, p. 132.
6. Ibid., p. 121
7. V. G. Belinsky, *Izbrannye Pisma* (Moscow, 1955), II, p. 168. Here are some additional statements to the same effect: "One year ago my ideas were diametrically opposed to those I hold now. Indeed, I do not know whether it is fortunate or unfortunate that it is all the same to me to think and to feel, to understand and to suffer. And it is here that one should fear fanaticism. Do you know that at present I hate myself as I was in the past; and if I had power and authority, it would be tragic for all those who are now as I was in the past." Ibid., p. 142; "Oh, my friend, at present I am overwhelmed by an idea which has swallowed and devoured all of me. You know that I am not destined to get into the center of truth, from which I could grasp equally well any point of its circumference—no, I somehow find myself at its edge." Ibid., p. 158.
8. Ibid., p. 214.
9. G. A. Maksimovich, *Uchenie Pervykh Slavianofilov* (Kiev, 1907), p. 26.
10. Herzen, *My Past*, II, p. 230.
11. Ibid., p. 233.
12. T. N. Granovsky, *T N. Granovskii i Ego Perepiska*, 2d ed. (Moscow, 1897), II, p. 259.
13. I. Novich, *Zhizn Chernyshevskogo* (Moscow, 1939), p. 210.
14. Ibid., *see also* V. Zhdanov. *Dobroliubov* (Moscow, 1961), p. 141.
15. Belinsky, *Izbrannye*, I, p. 193.
16. Ibid., II, p. 201.

17. Ibid., I, p. 196.
18. Ibid.
19. Ibid., II, p. 11.
20. Ibid., p. 12.
21. Ibid., p. 75.
22. Ibid., p. 162.
23. Ibid., p. 212; *see also* D. I. Chizhevsky, *Gegel v Rossii* (Paris, 1930), p. 114.
24. Belinsky, *Izbrannye*, II, p. 211.
25. Ibid., I, p. 87.
26. Ibid.
27. Ibid., II, p. 211.
28. Ibid., I, p. 76.
29. Ibid., p. 196; on the financial assistance of the Aksakovs, *see* their correspondence in *Literaturnoe Nasledstvo*, ed. A. M. Egolin et al. (Moscow, 1950), LVI, pp. 128–29.
30. F. Dostoevsky, *Letters from the Underworld*, trans. C. J. Hogarth (London: J. M. Dent and Sons, 1945), p. 65.
31. V. G. Belinsky, *Polnoe Sobranic Soghinenii*, ed. V. S. Vengerov (St. Petersburg, 1900), II, p. 514.
32. F. M. Golovenchenko, ed., *Belinskii v Vospominaniiakh Sovremennikov* (Moscow, 1948), p. 96.
33. Pypin, *Belinskii*, I, p. 408.
34. Ibid., II, p. 150.
35. Golovenchenko *Belinskii*, p. 100.
36. Quoted in Paul Kluckhohn, *Das Ideengut der Deutschen Romantik*, 3d ed. (Tuebingen: Max Niemeyer Verlag, 1953), p. 68.
37. Edward Shils, "Primordial, Personal, Sacred and Civil Ties," *British Journal of Sociology* 7, no. 2 (1957): 143.
38. Belinsky, *Izbrannye*, II, p. 7.
39. E. Lampert, *Studies in Rebellion* (London: Routledge and Kegan Paul, 1957), p. 84.
40. S. Kierkegaard, *Concluding Unscientific Postscript*, trans. D. F. Swanson and W. Lowrie (Princeton: Princeton University Press, 1944), pp. 112–13.
41. V. G. Belinsky, *Selected Philosophical Works* (Moscow: Foreign Languages Publishing House, 1948), p. 158.
42. Ibid.
43. Belinsky, *Izbrannye*, II, pp. 173–74.
44. Ibid., p. 201; Bernhard Schultze has commented on Belinsky's "personalistic" revolt against Hegel as follows: "Merkte es denn Belinskij nicht, dass er nun in gewisser Weise wieder an seinem Ausgangspunkt, der Hegelschen Philosophie, der Lehre vom Allgemeinen, angelangt war, dass er sich eigentlich nur im Kreise bewegt hatte. Er wollte den Einzelmenschen vor dem Moloch des Allgemeinen retten, von dem er Rechenschaft forderte ueber die zahllosen, angeblich von jenem verschlungenen Opfer. Nun wird die Menschheit fuer ihn zum Moloch, zu einem abstrakten, irrealen Allgemeinen." Bernhard Schultze, *Wissarion Grigor-jewitsch Belinskij: Wegbereiter des Revolutionaeren Atheismus in Russland* (Muenchen-Salzburg-Koeln: Verlag Anton Pustet, 1958), pp. 77–78.
45. Belinsky, *Izbrannye*, II, p. 129.
46. Turgenev, *Literary Reminiscences*, p. 155.
47. N. G. Chernyshevsky, *Polnoe Sobranie Sochinenii* (Moscow, 1939), I, p. 212.
48. Ibid.
49. N. A. Dobroliubov, *Sobranie Sochinenii v Deviati Tomakh*, ed. B. E. Bursova et al. (Moscow-Leningrad, 1961–65), VIII, pp. 558–59; *see also* N. A. Dobroliubov, *Dnevniki*, ed. V. Polansky (Moscow, 1932), p. 241.

50. Dostoevsky, *Letters*, p. 65.
51. Belinsky, *Izbrannye*, II, p. 281.
52. Ibid., p. 7.
53. Ibid., I, p. 174.
54. Ibid., p. 173.
55. Dobroliubov, *Sobranie*, IX, p. 454.
56. Ibid., p. 455.
57. Chernyshevsky, *Polnoe*, I, p. 412.
58. Ibid., p. 414.
59. Ibid., p. 318.
60. Ibid., p. 483.
61. Belinsky, *Izbrannye*, I, p. 136.
62. Chernyshevsky, *Polnoe*, I, p. 33; *see also* Ibid., XIV, pp. 198–99.
63. Dobroliubov, *Sobranie*, VIII, p. 67.
64. Ibid., p. 436.
65. Dostoevsky, *Letters*, p. 49.
66. Dobroliubov, *Sobranie*, VIII, p. 508.
67. Ibid.
68. Belinsky, *Selected*, p. 215.
69. Belinsky, *Izbrannye*, I, p. 40.
70. Ibid., II, p. 208.
71. Ibid., p. 68.
72. Ibid., p. 135.
73. Turgenev, *Literary Reminiscences*, p. 150.
74. Chernyshevsky, *Polnoe*, I, pp. 208–9.
75. Ibid., p. 249.
76. Ibid., p. 250.
77. Ibid., pp. 273–74.
78. Ibid., p. 400.
79. Dobroliubov, *Sobranie*, VIII, p. 522.
80. Pypin, *Belinskii*, II, p. 119.

6   Ideas and Their Carriers

The shift in the social habitat of the men of letters from the court and office to the salon and fashionable society went hand in hand, as has been pointed out, with their emancipation from subservience to the official *ordo* and with the reassertion of the autonomy of culture. This development reached a climax in the emergence of the tiny stratum of freelance literati still lodged in the beau monde and its institution—the salon. The generation of the "remarkable decade" marked the crowning point of the manorial culture in Russia. More specifically, it ended the aristocratic period in the history of Russian letters and also heralded the rise, in the person of Belinsky, of a *déraciné intelligent*: on the one hand, unassimilated to the aristocratic milieu that hitherto provided the fertile soil on which Russian literature thrived, and, on the other, pried loose from the social environment from which he had come. It was far from fortuitous that the *intelligenty* of the 1860s drew both a sharp line between themselves and the generation of the "remarkable decade" and also searched hard for spiritual begetters among the people of the same generation. There is no difficulty, of course, in identifying the individual whose personality and writings evoked an eager response among them. This individual, as Aksakov's candid observations testify, was Belinsky—the Pied Piper of the Russian intelligentsia.

> The name of Belinsky is known to every thinking young man, to everyone who is hungry for a breath of fresh air in the reeking bog of provincial life.... If you want to find honest people, people who care about the poor and oppressed, an honest doctor, an honest lawyer not afraid of a fight, you will find them among Belinsky's followers.... Slavophile influence is negligible.... Belinsky's followers increase.[1]

Furthermore, the surviving members of the generation of the "remarkable decade," Slavophiles and Westerners alike, came into conflict with the new men of ideas. The generational rift produced by this conflict marked a truly radical breakdown in the cultural continuity of nineteenth-century Russia. The new men of ideas not only changed the character of the cultural community, but also introduced in their wake different attitudes toward art, literature, and culture in general, different conceptions of themselves and their role in society, and finally, different perspectives on man and society.

Who were, then, these new men of ideas? It has been argued in the preceding chapter that the Russian *intelligenty* represented a particular type of man. The core of their personality was not so much the content of ideas they professed or the nature of collective causes they served—although it is true that certain ideas appealed to them more than others—as it was the mode of their attachment to and orientation toward these ideas. The *intelligenty* were not only sensitive to some ultimate values and symbols, they were also totally committed to and completely identified with them. These ideas absorbed the *intelligenty* to such an extent that, like a lover with his beloved, they did not hesitate to play out their whole lives around them. Having made some single set of ideas their only point of reference, they turned into men of convictions and principles, bent on ideologizing every sphere of their relations to people, including the ties of friendship and marriage. To follow Chernyshevsky's own argument, the *intelligenty* were neither German "high priests" who possessed only enough "strength to express general ideas, but not enough strength to adhere undeviatingly to these principles and to draw all the necessary deductions from them,"[2] nor French "charlatans and phrasemongers" who were "utterly devoid of definite principles ... whatever they believed in, they only half-believed, timidly and pretentiously; whatever they denied they only half-denied."[3] It remained for the Russian intelligentsia to overcome both "abstract thought" of the men of ideas and "unprincipled action" of the men of affairs.

Basic to this view of the *intelligenty* is their cast of mind—the ideological mentality—and the resultant orientation of conviction-inspired intolerance and fanaticism. No conventional distinctions are drawn here between "idealist," "materialist," "positivist," "populist," "socialist," or "Marxist" intelligentsia. Within the context of this approach all such distinctions are considered of little consequence. Moreover, the mere analysis of the content of their ideas, without any reference to their mode of orientation to these ideas, may lead to deceptive and highly dubious conclusions. What is significant, however, is why the Russian *intelligenty*, like Chekhov's hero in *On the Road*, fell on ideas and theories "po-russki" (in the Russian manner), that is, transformed them into causes and, in doing so, terrorized themselves and terrorized others on behalf of them.

The new men of ideas were thus neither "high priests" fastidious with regard to action nor men of affairs devoid of principles, but Russian doctrinaires—the *intelligenty*—determined to ideologize every phase of their encounter with life. The chief vehicle through which they sought to dispense "high truth" was literary criticism—the literary reviews and essays that served as a sounding board for their social and political ideas. If some of them tried their pens at creative writing, they produced at best *romans à thèse*.

Under the guise of literary criticism the intelligentsia made ideological demands on literature and the men of letters themselves. Literature was in fact to become an ideological lever; it was to propagate social and political ideas in order to hasten their triumph in "collective life."[4] Belinsky himself came close to obliterating the boundary between literature and politics when he extolled the poetry of Béranger: "For him politics is poetry and poetry is politics, for him life is poetry and poetry is life. This is the poetry of a Frenchman, he does not know of any other kind."[5] Pisarev drew extreme conclusions from this view when he implored the poets to exchange poetry for political pamphlets. In his attempt to forge a close link between literature and ideology, Chernyshevsky resorted to the following argument:

> Before that time [that is, before Belinsky] only very few of our poets and fiction writers had been able to bring the meaning of their works into harmony with the ideas which seemed right to them. As a rule, stories and poems had very little relation to what is called the author's "world outlook," if, indeed, the author had a "world outlook." By way of example we point to Marlinsky, in whose works the most careful search will fail to reveal the slightest trace of the principle which the author no doubt held dear as a man. As a rule, life and the convictions it aroused on the one hand, and poetry on the other, were each kept in separate compartments, as it were. The connection between the writer and the man was very feeble.[6]

What this demand amounted to in effect was that men of letters subordinate their literary pursuits to the service of a cause. By acting in each and every sphere of life as men of convictions, in brief, by totalizing themselves, they would endow their literary activity with a higher significance: ideological significance.

The overriding issue here is beyond doubt the autonomy of culture. The Russian *intelligenty* displayed an utter inability to appreciate literature and science as autonomous spheres of creative activity. Any detached theorizing was branded by them as useless and, indeed, impermissible. Belinsky despised "abstract thought" and eagerly dispatched to hell speculative theories and ideas.[7] "Abstract thought" suffocated him and made his life unbearable. He preferred instead "the sphere of flaming words and living images."[8] Chernyshevsky disparaged science that was "abstract" and "cold" and voiced preference for one that "loves and hates, pursues and protects."[9] He viewed science, indeed, as a closed doctrine established with finality and his own ideas as "high truths" destined to be translated into *praxis*. Pisarev made anything but ambiguous his scorn for abstract theorizing when he observed of philosophy:

> What, in the final analysis, is this science known as philosophy? Can it be merely medicinal gymnastics for the mind ... an occupation that commences at a whim and ceases when we so will it, without leading anywhere, or solving a single problem, or shattering a single delusion,

or imparting a single living idea in the mind, or causing the heart to beat more rapidly? Can that be philosophy ...? Was it not philosophy that brought about mass movements, shattered the old idols and shook antiquated forms of civic and social life in the past?[10]

It is in this sense that the so-called politicization of the intellectual life in Russia should be interpreted. It entailed not so much a shift of interest from philosophy and literature to social issues and politics, as an attempt to ideologize all the spheres of cultural life and thereby harness them to the service of a cause. To accomplish this, the editors of *Sovremennik* opposed the very existence of literary groups and periodicals devoid of ideological perspectives. "Let those journals be published," declared Chernyshevsky, "around which are organized people with known and definite ideas, as to others ... they should neither have readers nor should they exist."[11] The first to crumble under the onslaught of the intelligentsia was the emergent community of letters, the autonomy of which the literati of the "remarkable decade" and even the gentlemen-littérateurs sought so hard to secure. The literary salons and drawing rooms, the *Gesammtphilosophieren* of the members of the generation of the "remarkable decade"—the institutions whose very survival under the oppressive regime of Nicholas I testified to the emancipation of the men of letters from subservience to the state—fell into abeyance under the reign of Alexander II, only to become replaced by the "holy unions" of zealots ready to subject themselves to a lush crop of new masters: *humanity, narod, class*, and other hypostatized abstractions.

The ascendancy of the new men of ideas and the accompanying breakdown in the style of thought combined to usher in the "age of ideology" in Russia, the uncompromising *isms* of which have continued to plague her cultural life for the past hundred years. One telling expression of this breakdown was the conflict of generations, more commonly known as the revolt of "spiteful sons" against "superfluous fathers." No attempt will be made, nor is it necessary here, to assess the degree of truth in their respective ideas and beliefs—to establish their validity or trace in detail their origin and historical development. Rather, the present study will seek to interpret these ideas *ab extra* by relating them to individuals and groups who were their characteristic bearers. Although such an approach to ideas is problematic and, what is more, may deteriorate into clever unmasking, it remains true that Russian intellectual history provides a compelling example of its merit.

The Slavophile Image of Ideal Society: The Primordial and the Sacred

A quest for the ideal human association of consensual order sanctified by religion and rooted in custom may cogently express the central theme of the Slavophile *Weltanschauung*. In keeping with the romantic tradition, the Slavophiles harked back to the past and discovered it in the surviving village commune, which supposedly approximated

...a moral choir, and just as in the choir a voice is not lost, but follows the general pattern and is heard in the harmony of all voices, so in the commune the individual is not lost, but renounces his exclusiveness in favor of the general accord—and there arises the noble phenomenon of harmonious, joint existence of rational beings (consciousness), there arises a brotherhood, a commune—a triumph of human spirit.[12]

In the Slavophile commune, as indeed in every genuine human association, unity based on the collective conscience (moral consensus) is assumed. The elements of coercion and legal compliance—consulting neither customs nor "sacred traditions"—were considered as unworthy of any society. The Slavophiles thus recoiled from the external, the coercive, the formal-legal, and the contractual, that is, from anything characteristic of the state and civil society. Rather, the commune was characterized by social cohesion (diffuse familial and communal ties) and a high level of consensus regarding values and beliefs. According to Kireevsky, the Russian society of ancient times resembled such a unified whole, albeit formed of juxtaposed segments spread all over the entire country:

> ...a countless multitude of small communities scattered over the face of the Russian land, each of them under the leader who operates with certain limitations, each of them representing its own consensus, its own small world; these microcosms, these tiny accords merge together in other, larger accords, which in turn form territorial and then tribal accords; out of the latter is formed the one vast accord of the entire Russian land.[13]

Of course, the Slavophiles failed and, indeed, refused to concede that the Russian commune was not so much a spontaneously formed institution developing "melodiously and harmoniously" on the Russian soil as an externally imposed "liturgical" association designed primarily to secure the payment of taxes and the recruitment of soldiers. But the validity of their historical claim is scarcely of concern to us. Of significance here is the fact that like the German romantics who believed in a *verlorene Heimat*, a lost home, and who claimed to have discovered an "organic whole" in the medieval *Staendestaat*, the Slavophiles, too, projected their vision of ideal society onto the past (Old Muscovy), which they cast in the image of a "big commune" endowed with a high degree of consensus by virtue of symbolic (sacred) integration. What were its implications? First, the Slavophiles sharply contrasted two "hostile principles" of social order: "natural," as distinguished from "rational"; "organic," as distinguished from "artificial"; "spontaneous," as distinguished from "coercive"; "consensual" (based on convictions), as distinguished from "contractual" (based on interests). In other words, they set up "faith" against "reason," "custom" against "law" and "fashion," "conviction" against "opinion," and "consensus" (basic unanimity or indivisible unity) against "conflict" and "coercion." Obviously, the Slavophiles borrowed almost in toto the imagery of their Western tutors and, in doing so, turned against the West, repeating time and again that the history of the West was one of coercion, law, "sinful individualism," and "external freedom," whereas that of Russia was one of "fraternal love," "communalism," "moral consensus," and "inner freedom."

> The entire private and public life of the West is founded on the concept of separate, individual independence which assumes individual isolation. Hence the sanctity of the external, formal relations, the sanctity of property and of conditional enactments are more important than human personality. Each individual—a private person, a knight, a prince, or a city—*is within his rights,* a despotic unlimited individual, who is the law unto himself. The first step of every man in society is to surround himself with a fortress, from the depth of which he begins to negotiate with other and independent powers.[14]

The Western man, like the Roman citizen, considered himself "as being not merely distinct but different from his fellow men" and could not conceive of any other relationships with them except those "logically deduced from the external circumstances of life."[15] This atomistic condition of Western society (spirit of individual separatism) made an individual virtually unaware of any "possible bond between people save the bond of mutual interest, or any unity save the party unity."[16] For this reason, historical development of the West has been marred by conflict of interests and discord between social classes and estates, religious and political factions, and diverse interest groups. All kinds of factions—"papal parties, imperial parties, city parties, church parties, court, private, governmental, religious, political, folk, middle class, and even metaphysical parties"[17]—were ever fighting in the West determined to undermine the existing state of affairs in order to promote their own particular ends. Medieval societies in the West admittedly exemplified such a fragmented social world devoid of cohesion and consensus.

> Anyone who attempts to visualize Western society in feudal times is bound to see it as a profusion of fortified castles, each inhabited by a noble knight and his family and surrounded by the huts of the lowborn rabble. ... The warring of these individual castles with each other and their relations with the free cities, the king, and the Church form the entire history of the West.[18]

On the other hand, the "vast land of Russia" retained moral consensus (common faith) intact as well as integrity of communal life (*obshchinnoe nachalo*), remaining a "single living organism" even when its "political order became fragmented into petty principalities."[19] In contrast to the West, where the individual and his independence formed a cornerstone of social development, the social order of ancient Russia was constituted on the basis of an "infinite number" of "small communes."[20] Superimposed on these "small communes" were religious institutions—a network of churches, monasteries and hermitages—which continually propagated a "single set of ideas about social and private relationships."[21] These ideas were gradually transformed into "common convictions," and "common convictions," in turn, into "customs," the latter serving as a "substitute for laws."[22] Under the aegis of the Church, there admittedly prevailed throughout the Russian land "one thought, one outlook, one aspiration, and one pattern of life."[23] By virtue of this cultural homogeneity (overall uniformity) and a high level of unity—both moral and communal—Russia was spared the malaise of dissension, since, unlike the West, she experienced neither the struggle of feudal estates over privileges nor modern "class contempt, class hatred, and class envy."[24]

> The princes, the boyars, the clergy, the people, and the troops maintained respectively by the princes, the boyars, the towns, and the rural communities—all these strata and classes of the population were imbued with the same spirit, the same convictions and beliefs, and a like desire for the common weal. There might have been differences of opinion on details, but there was hardly any discord in essential matters.[25]

The Slavophile predilection for a "natural society" based on the authority of custom rather than rational assent betrayed the conservative distrust of any deliberate tampering with the social order. The Slavophiles maintained that, in the "artificial society" found in the West, "every improvement is accomplished in terms of some premeditated plan," whereas in a "society formed naturally from the independent development of its original principles," every sudden change according to a comprehensive plan is tantamount to "sickness, more or less dangerous."[26] The extent to which the Slavophiles abhorred any such change can be seen from Kireevsky's attitude toward the emancipation of the peasantry. Kireevsky's distrust of reform, as he observed in one of the letters to his sister, stemmed not so much from the view that serfdom is "good and useful" and as such deserved to be retained in Russia, or even that it was feasible to do that, as from the conviction that any such "sweeping change will issue only in disturbance, general disorganization, swift increase of immorality."[27] His only desire was that "they leave us alone in the condition in which we are—be it good, or be it bad—they do not disturb us with changes and, what is still more important, with threats of change, which create a moral perturbation worse than the physical one."[28]

These and other statements plead, in effect, for the retention of the status quo; they betray Kireevsky's fear that "premature and vain" changes would not only generate social conflict but would also damage the "cause of indigenous development."[29] Yet, it would be unjust to conclude that the Slavophiles were addicted to the uncritical preservation of everything sanctified by tradition. "If the past was better than the present," argued Kireevsky, "it does not follow that the past would be better at present. What is fitting at one time, in one circumstance, can be unfitting at other times, in other circumstances."[30] The Slavophiles considered history inherently dynamic and the social order a spontaneously unfolding process.

> Everything is in a constant movement; at times this movement is fast and strikes even a slightly perceptive observer; at other times it is slow and can hardly be caught by the most attentive observer. Full stagnation is impossible, movement is necessary.... A correct and successful movement of enlightened society consists of two different but harmonious and congruent forces. One of them is basic and original, belonging to the whole structure, the whole past history of a society—it is a force of life developing from its origins, its organic principles; another one is a rational force of individuals based on the social force and living its life. This latter force neither creates nor aims at creating anything, but is constantly present in the general work of development, preventing it from turning into a blindness of dead instinct or uncritical one-sidedness.[31]

There is no difficulty in deciphering what the Slavophiles meant by "spontaneous development" or "organic principles" in the light of their praise of England and concomitant disdain for France and the United States. On his visit to England, Khomiakov reported:

> Soon I came to know London sufficiently well; I became comfortable, as if at home. I saw the Tower of London with its centuries-old fortifications, saw Westminster Abbey with its hundreds of tombs, a small part of which would be enough for the glory of an entire people, and I saw how the English revere the greatness of their past ... and I understood London: the summits are here, but then the roots are here too.[32]

Despite the fact that the two factions were struggling in England for dominance—the Tories and the Whigs—Khomiakov was delighted to report that "In most cases a Whig is still a little of a Tory, because he is an Englishman."[33] Moreover, the Whig movement had evolved "naturally" from English life and to that extent represented its "legitimate" expression.

> It retained its bonds with the people and with the spiritual essence of the country even when it broke with its traditions and its historical past. An English Whig remains wholly an Englishman; his ways and habits, his spiritual life, even his outward appearance—all are English; he has not yet condemned himself to total social and moral impotence.[34]

England, then, represented a country that succeeded in preserving "the calm and the smiling sanctity of the family circle, the entire poetry, the entire fragrance of life. In England every old oak with its long branches, every bell tower silhouetted from afar against the sky, is a Tory."[35]

Except for Kireevsky, other Slavophiles praised England in equal measure. Aksakov, for example, found in England a happy "combination of a true enlightenment and of a respect for the customs of the entire people, for ancient traditions, for the originality and the peculiarity of the organic development of the people."[36] In short, England represented an epitome of balanced development, "on the one hand, the moral principle in family, society and religion; on the other, respect for the past, and for tradition; there is the source of the calm freedom in England."[37]

The United States and France followed a different path of development—one of material aggrandizement and technical advancement bought at the cost of moral putrescence and spiritual impoverishment. In the absence of conventional constraints (tradition and historical heritage), American society suffered most from this moral and spiritual malaise and was least prepared to cope with it. As a result, the social structure of America resembled a "machine" emptied of all human love and held together solely by "conditional ties" of contract.[38] This same ailment afflicted in varying degrees other European societies, and, most of all, France, which Khomiakov compared to an "aggregation of individuals searching for, but unable to find organic ties."[39] The French Revolution, argued Aksakov, by installing a tyranny of an abstract doctrine, radically undermined the continuity of social life, depriving the people of all roots in the past. It also provided the "most striking application of theory to practice, this immolation of life on the altar of abstract theory ... a Bacchanalia of the despotism of abstract, self-confident thought of separate individuals."[40] Finally, the same Revolution, by annihilating traditional forms of social life, reduced everything to external uniformity, and replaced the concept of a people as an organism by an agglomerate of isolated individuals whose thoughts and wishes are determined by a count of votes.

> History, tradition, popular custom—down with them; all moral factors of the life of a people many centuries old—down with them; instead of quality—quantity; instead of moral truth—external, legal truth; instead of a historical living system—a formally legalistic system; in one word, instead of living personal rule, living, popular, organic union—a state mechanism.[41]

The Slavophile paradigm of the social order may now be formulated as follows: in their search for a society that would resolve the antithesis of individuality and collectivity, "sinful principle" of individualism and "communal principle," the Slavophiles fell back on the Muscovite past and discovered it in the village commune. This commune was fashioned in the image of an enlarged family based on traditional moral ties and spontaneously formed relations by kinsmen and neighbors of long duration. As such it stood opposed to an "artificial" society constituted on rational assent and convenience, devoid of authority of custom, and comprised of individuals whose only social bond was contract.

But although the Slavophiles, like the German romantics, affirmed the primacy of kinship within the social organization, they conceived of ideal society not simply as "eine grosse allumfassende Familie"[42] but also as a confraternity of people united in a common faith. Overlaid on the natural groups of kinsmen was the *congregatio fidelium*—the "higher and true form" of human community.[43] Out of these two dimensions of social life— the primordial and the sacred—the Slavophiles conjured a vision of society devoid of civil order—one which excluded the *civis*, the citizen as such, and admitted only of "kinsmen" and *fideles*, on the one hand, and the Tsar's *kholopy* (bondsmen) and *siroty* (orphans) in need of support and protection, on the other. Convinced that the Old Muscovy represented the historical prototype of this society, the Slavophiles marshaled appropriate evidence to back up the religious cast of mind of their forefathers, seizing especially on the testimony of foreigners to the effect that "Russian people talked only of religious matters, neglecting political conditions."[44] In the words of Aksakov: "The Russian people is not a people concernced with politics, that is to say, it has no aspiration toward self-government, no desire for political rights, and not so much as a trace of lust for power."[45] Rather, the Russian people, as befits all helpless orphans, have always acquiesced in the "absolute power" of the Tsar, preferring his benevolent protection to the rule of law, and sought only "inner" or "communal" freedom, disregarding altogether "external political freedom"[46] admittedly so dear to the people in the West.

The Slavophile critique of social contract, legal authority, and popular sovereignty, including the harangues against the "materialistic" West, followed closely the conservative pattern of thought that can be readily traced to Western sources. The Slavophiles were indebted to the Western romantics for many of their arguments directed against the doctrine of *ius naturalis*. There is, however, only remote affinity between the ideal society of the Slavophiles and the model of *Gemeinschaft* as evolved by their romantic confreres in the West. The Slavophile image of society brooked no variations—whether social or individual—and presupposed instead the "solidarity of resemblance" based on moral consensus and institutional homogeneity. Consonant with this form of solidarity based on likeness was the archaic organization of the Slavophile society. For the commune, as the archetype of this society, constituted a relatively isolated, undifferentiated, and segmentally structured system—a network of kinship groups, economic collectivity with a minimal division of labor, and a moral community.

The Slavophile preference for a society in which unity and common accord prevail and in which conflicting group and individual interests are unifiable, sharply contrasts with the romantic sense for diversity in all forms of social life. Diversity and many-sidedness, including the inequality of rank, were not only preferable to Western romantics, they were deemed indispensable to society, just as discrete and different parts were necessary to an organism. The medieval social order, with its division into estates, corporate groups, and competing jurisdictions, together with its rich variety of cultural life, was viewed as paradigmatic for a society trying to reconcile unity with diversity. All this signified to the Slavophiles the spectacle of discord symptomatic of the social order that had succumbed to the "sinful principle" of individualism, variously dubbed as "egoism," "the source of evil," "the principle of individuality," or "the spirit of individual separatism." But whatever the expression used, the Slavophile opposition to individualism was too comprehensive to be confined to that "frightful book" of ancient Roman law (*Corpus Juris*), which Heine branded as the "Bible of egoism." Except for Koshelev, the Slavophile opposition to individualism extended over the whole spectrum of ideas that postulated the autonomy of man and of personality: from the unbridled pursuit of individual self-interest (economic individualism of Hegel's civil society) and the demand for legal guarantees of individual rights (political liberalism based on inalienable rights of man) to the romantic quest for individual self-fulfillment (humanistic individualism) and "aristocratic individualism" developed in the medieval West.

The antiindividualistic posture of the Slavophiles tallied closely with their conception of society (see Table 6.1), even though it was scarcely consistent with their defense of the freedom of conscience and opinion. It is true that the Slavophiles shared with the early romantics a number of ideas in common, including the notion of organic growth and development, from which arose their interest in the past. They were also opposed to everything that was "mechanical" and "forced" in social life. Unlike the early romantics, however, the Slavophiles were neither inspired by a belief in a worth of the individuality—that *Urspruengliche und Ewige im Menschen*—nor made the individual and his development the leitmotif of their thought. For the Slavophile image of ideal society entailed the absorption of its members in the communal whole; indeed, it required that they surrender

Table 6.1 The Slavophile Conception of Two Societies: Russia and the West

	Russia	*West*
1. Image of Society	Society as an Organism (Natural Society)	Society as a Machine (Artificial Society)
2. Unit of Society	Obshchina Family	Individual Citizen
3. Principle of Social Order	Communal Spirit	Spirit of Individual Separation
4. Type of Social Relations	Fraternal Moral Ties	Formal Concordance of Interests
5. Basis of Normative Order	Sacred Traditions Custom Tradition	Logical Deductions Fashion Law
6. Type of Social Integration	Moral Unity (Organic) Love Faith	Formal Unity (Mechanical) Contract Force
7. Type of Freedom	Inner Communal Freedom	External Political Freedom

their very individualites to this communal whole. If one were to believe Kireevsky:

> The striking peculiarity of the Russian character in this respect was that an individual in his relationship with others, never stressed his personal characteristics as giving him special merit; individual ambition was confined to the desire to be a correct expression of the general spirit of society.[47]

Herzen and the Westerners: The Sphere of Spontaneity and Freedom

In marked contrast to the Slavophiles, whose encomium of the commune (except for Koshelev) was unequivocal, Herzen entertained important reservations concerning it. To be sure, he was convinced, like the Slavophiles, that the commune was opposed to the centralized, externally imposed authority—that is, the state—but he refused to believe (even at his most populistic) that the commune allowed for a free development of the individual. On the contrary, the commune, like the Russian state, by depriving the individual of his autonomy and freedom, left little room for his development.

> The individual at home, ever oppressed, had never made as much as an attempt to get a hearing. Free expression of opinion at home was always regarded as an insolence and independence as sedition. The individual was absorbed in the state; was dissolved in the commune.[48]

On another occasion, reflecting on the reforms of Peter the Great, Herzen discussed this subjection of the individual to the state as follows:

> The revolution effected by Peter I replaced the antiquated landlord rule of Russia by the European bureaucratic system. Everything that could be transferred from the Swedish and German codes was; everything that could be transplanted from Holland, a land of free municipalities, to an autocratic government of rural communes was borrowed. But the unwritten, moral restraints of the government, the instinctive recognition of the rights of individuals, the rights of thought, of truth, could not be transplanted and were not.[49]

Whereas the Slavophiles argued that the Russian society of "harmonious communes" was undermined by the Western spirit and code, Herzen, by contrast, contended that it was due to a superficial and haphazard transfer of Western forms of life, which helped to develop in Russia an autocratic regime with its expanding officialdom. Because of this, the government in Russia was more despotic and unrestrained than that in Turkey or Persia. "There is nothing to restrict it, no traditions of the past; for it has disowned its own past, and has no concern for that of Europe."[50] In the West, as Herzen conceded, "customs and long evolution compensate for some of the absurd theories and laws."[51]

> People here live on the soil fertilized by two civilizations; the path trodden by their ancestors in the course of two and a half thousand years, was not futile, and much that is human has sprung up in spite of externalities and the official system. In the worst days of European history we find some respect for the individual and a certain recognition of his independence, certain rights conceded to talent, to genius ... in this involuntary recognition of the individual lies one of the greatest humanistic principles of life in Europe.[52]

Much more significant than this difference in the interpretation of the Russian and the Western past was Herzen's refusal, as has been pointed out, to find in the Russian commune a ready formula for a harmonious reconciliation of the individual and the collectivity. The Russian commune, as it stood, was in his opinion an unsatisfactory form of human association, precisely because it deprived the individual of his freedom and autonomy. No other nineteenth-century man of letters in Russia upheld so impassionedly the "liberty of the individual" or asserted with such intransigence his supreme worth as did Herzen. "Personal freedom" was to him a "magnificent thing; *by it and by it alone* can a nation achieve true freedom. Man must respect and honor his freedom in himself no less than in his neighbor or in the people at large."[53] For this reason alone it would be an injustice to Herzen to conceive of him as simply the prophet of populism. For he was first and foremost an uncompromising individualist willing to stake everything on behalf of man thwarted in the struggle for self-assertion. In opposition to the Slavophiles' "harmonious commune," Herzen, as well as Ogarev, Turgenev, and Granovsky, affirmed the individual—his dignity and freedom—as the supreme value of their *Weltanschauung*.

The disagreement between the Slavophiles and the Westerners thus reflected a significant shift of emphasis: one focusing on the symphysis of the individual and the collectivity, the other on the autonomous and free individual; one bent on adapting the needs of the individual to a solidary group (the commune), the other on finding the group that would meet the needs of a freely developing personality; one sidetracking the individual for the sake of a collective whole, the other refusing to assume any point of reference outside of the individual. It is this shift of emphasis from the commune as the basic unit of society to the "autonomous individual" following his own inclination, the *Eigenwuechsigkeit* that Goethe so much admired, and not so much a diverse evaluation of the Russian and the Western past, that marks, in our opinion, a real difference between such Slavophiles as Aksakov, Khomiakov, and Kireevsky, and the Westerners like Herzen, Ogarev, Turgenev, and Granovsky. As if addressing the Russian detractors of individualism, Herzen asked:

What is the meaning of those harangues against egotism, individualism? What is egotism? What is brotherhood? What is individualism? And what is love of mankind?

People are egotists, of course, because they are personalities. How can a man be himself without an acute consciousness of his personality? To deprive him of his consciousness means to break him down completely, to destroy his backbone, to make him insipid, stereotyped, amorphous. We are egoists and for that reason struggle for independence and prosperity, for recognition of our rights. And for that very reason we crave love, seek activity and, therefore, cannot deny the same to others without falling into hopeless contradictions.

The moralists speak of egoism as if it were a bad habit, without questioning whether a man can remain a man if he has lost a keen awareness of his personality, without saying what compensation awaits him in "brotherhood" and "love of mankind," without even explaining why he should be on a fraternal footing with everybody, and why he should love everyone on earth.[54]

Herzen realized only too well that there is an egoism that is "narrow, bestial, and unclean, just as there is love which is unclean, bestial, and narrow."[55] But the point at issue, he argued, was not so much to destroy egoism and eulogize brotherhood and love of mankind, as to combine them on the basis of freely consenting individuals. Committed, as he was, to the freedom of the individual *hic et nunc*, Herzen was far more careful than were the Slavophiles in venerating the "calm freedom" of English society. Yet, despite the fact that he dismissed England on one occasion as that "European China called Britain," he was able to appreciate the "two cornerstones of English life—individual liberty and inherited tradition."[56] On the same occasion, while contrasting France with England, Herzen spoke the language of his romantic tutors:

The world of self-government and decentralization, an independent capricious growth, seems so barbarous and incomprehensible to the Frenchman, that, however long he lives in England, he never understands her political and civil life, her laws and judicial system. He loses his way in the uncoordinated variety of English laws, as if he were entangled in a dark forest; he altogether fails to notice the tall majestic oaks which compose it, and how much charm, poetry and good sense can be found in this variety. He hankers after a little code with neatly swept paths, lopped trees and policemen-gardeners in every avenue.[57]

Herzen was not an exponent of the liberty that allowed the state to go on eradicating all the traditional immunities, historically formed social differences, in fact making the whole of the individual's life vulnerable to subjection. What offended him most about Russia was not so much social inequality or the economic plight of the people as the lack of effective safe-guards of individual freedom and independence.[58] Social variety, that roman-tic *Reichtum in der Mannigfaltigkeit*, and equality among individuals with specific and recognized rights were more preferable to Herzen than general-ized sameness and egalitarian leveling. Accordingly, the rise of the estates was a "tremendous step forward, for it meant enlightenment, the end of animal uniformity, the division of labor."[59] Herzen looked with no less suspicion at the "animal uniformity" of remote ages than he did at the "crowd uniform-ity" of the emergent society of his day, with its tyranny of opinion, ruthless leveling of sensibilities, and the resultant effacement of individual personality. Like so many of his counterparts in Orleanist France—the literary detractors of the bourgeoisie—Herzen evinced intense distaste for a society composed of "small shopkeepers."

> Everything withers and dwindles to pigmy size on the exhausted soil; there is no talent, no creative work, no power of thought, no power of will. Life has grown more coarse, less elegant and gracious. All have come to live like small shopkeepers.[60]

Whereas this society of "small shopkeepers" represented to Herzen something impersonal—even more so, inhuman—the "development of an independent personality" constituted the "whole charm in which everything free, talented and strong crystallized."[61] Because social differentiation and traditional insti-tutions such as the family, private ownership, or even religion were "tremen-dous educational forms of human emancipation and development,"[62] any wholesale refutation of them would be simply senseless. "Property, particu-larly the ownership of land, has represented to the man in the West his eman-cipation, his independence, his dignity, and constituted an element of the highest civic importance."[63] The same observation, claimed Herzen, applied equally to the institution of inheritance.

> Except for celibate fanatics such as monks, Raskolniki, or Icarians, no large group of people will consent to renounce their right to leave part of their property to their heirs. I know no argument which would coun-teract this form of love, be the ties selective or of blood, this desire to transmit objects which were our tools, together with life, with traits of character.... Perhaps this can be renounced in the name of forced univer-sal *fraternity* and love for the whole world. The poorest *muzhik* deprived of his right to make his will is sure to take up a stick and go to defend his own property, his family, and his liberty.[64]

Even if it is granted that the old world must be dealt a blow, this does not mean that everything that is different and original, should be rooted out wholesale. "Woe to that revolution, so poor in spirit and in artistic sense, which will reduce all the past and all that has been accumulated into a dull workshop."[65] This alleged revolutionary could hardly believe that "people who prefer destruction and brute force to evolution and amicable agreements are really serious."[66] The French Revolution, added Herzen with a half-ironical suavity, had put down enough "statues, pictures and monuments for us to be able to dispense with playing at iconoclasm."[67]

Concerned, as he was, with the defense of the individual, Herzen not only refused to sacrifice him to a stagnant Arcadia rescued from the Russian past, but he also refused to sacrifice him—and this alone is sufficient to differentiate Herzen sharply from the intelligentsia of the sixties—to the Arcadia of the future that would have to be ushered in probably by the corps of "socialist gendarmes." Should we proceed, asked Herzen, "to establish the new order, the new form of emancipation by resorting to a massacre?"[68] His view of history, his aristocratic insistence on remaining oneself and on doing nothing under duress, made him averse to any such sacrifice of individuals to the Arcadia of the future. By proclaiming, in the fashion of Goethe, that the purpose of life is life itself and that the goal of every generation is the generation itself, Herzen vehemently opposed any attempt to turn morally free human beings into puppets, into means for attaining a future felicity.

> If progress is the goal, then what is it we are working for? What is this Moloch who, as the toilers approach him, recedes instead of rewarding them; who, to console the exhausted and doomed crowds greeting him *morituri te salutant*, can only reply with the ironic promise that after their death life on earth will be splendid. Can it be that you, too, doom the people of today to the sad destiny of the caryatids supporting the balcony on which others will dance some day? Or assign them to the role of those unfortunate workers who, knee-deep in mud, are to drag along the bark with the mysterious golden fleece in her hold and the meek inscription "Future Progress" on the flags?[69]

Such an orientation, argued Herzen, was tantamount to the subjection of individual human beings to an idea, to some social conception and collective name, to some Moloch or another. Basically, it was nothing but a "continuation of man's offering, the slaughter of the lamb to conciliate Jehovah."[70] What is love of mankind? asked Herzen. Love that embraces the whole of humanity, "everything that has ceased to be a monkey,"[71] was something that Herzen was unable to appreciate. True enough, Herzen tended at times to celebrate "virgin" Russia and even divine for her people a veritable mission in the future to come. For this reason, indeed, he was warned by Turgenev against transforming the "Russian sheepskin coat"[72] into another idol, not unlike "Humanity," "Progress," and other absolutes he was so determined to dethrone. But even when inspired by this populist afflatus, Herzen recognized only well that such selfless abandonment to enthroned abstractions is often accompanied by the lack of respect, if not contempt, for the concrete individual.

Underlying Herzen's social philosophy was his devotion to the "true monad of society," the individual, his affirmation of the value of human personality. For this unabated concern with the individual and his self-determination, Herzen was indebted to the *Sturm und Drang* as well as the early German romantics. Throughout his life, Herzen grappled with that "rare chimera" of Don Carlos—the respect for man—even though he rationalized this chimera by seizing on a variety of ideas. In pointed contrast to the Slavophiles, who viewed the world through the groove of the commune resuscitated from the past, Herzen judged the past, the present, and the future in the light of the *principium individui.*

On this salient principle—the autonomy of man and of personality— Herzen found himself in complete agreement with other Westerners. "The foremost task of mankind," wrote Ogarev, "is to secure for the individual full freedom along with the highest development of social life."[73] In a letter to the Aksakov family, Turgenev not only refused to concede that the commune was the "universal panacea, the alpha and omega of Russian life,"[74] but also asserted that the same commune deprived its member of freedom. It is for this freedom, he concluded, that "I am fighting and will fight to the end."[75] Nor was Turgenev assuaged by Bakunin's word *congrégationiste*; on the contrary, bent on remaining an "individualist till the end," Turgenev detected in this new concoction still another threat to "individual freedom."[76]

With the *Sturm und Drang*, Herzen tended to regard the opposition between the individual and society, liberty and authority, and inner values and social forms as inevitable and irreconcilable. This sense of unease about man in society, combined with the insistence that the individual must remain true to his own self, made Herzen prone at times to reject in an anarchist vein all forms of authority, law, and tradition as needless restraints imposed by society. For the sake of ensuring the absolute autonomy of the individual, of making him a law and measure unto himself, Herzen came close to espousing a conception of freedom divested of all historical and institutional contingencies, leaving the individual without any props save his own self-will.

Yet, with all recognition of these, Herzen's anarchist quest for the world of unfettered freedom led him to seize on that sphere of life in which mutual confidence, spontaneity, personal bonds of intimacy or, as he called them, "profound ties unaffected by any events,"[77] prevail, and to which individuals belong by reason of their very *Eigentuemlichkeit.* Beyond the significance of sinews of individual freedom, this circumscribed sphere of interpersonal life possessed a further significance to Herzen—one in keeping with the humanistic motif of his thought. The burden of this motif may be seen from the following *locus classicus:* "Were people to desire to save themselves instead of the world, to deliver themselves instead of humanity, how much they could do for the salvation of the world and the emancipation of humanity."[78] Implicit in this passage is a call to "salvation" that seems closely akin to that of Goethe and the early romantics: of Wilhelm Meister, when he addressed Werner, "What good is it for me to manufacture perfect iron, when my own breast is full of dross?"[79] or even of Schlegel, when he proclaimed that the highest calling of man is the *Bildung* and *Entwicklung* of his individuality.[80] Herzen echoed a similar view when he wrote *From the Other Shore*, "To renounce one's development means to renounce oneself."[81]

Belinsky and the Intelligenty: The Sphere of Ideological Commitment

An extreme hostility toward established order—the existing political as well as religious, familial, and other institutions—underlies the ideological outlook of the intelligentsia. This feeling of resentment among them is so diffuse and the corresponding indictment of society so generalized that one can hardly find a single conventional value or traditional pattern of life of which they would approve. If they favored, for example, the village commune and argued that it ought to be preserved, this was not because it harbored traditional values, because it represented an indigenous institution, as the Slavophiles believed, or because the Russian peasant continued to evince his attachment to it, but rather because, as Chernyshevsky stated, "The higher stage of development coincides by virtue of its form with the original stage."[82] To Chernyshevsky and his populist disciples, therefore, the institution of commune, far from being a relic of bygone times, was the cornerstone of the future society, heralding the advent of a collectivistic order. Anything but tradition-minded or history-oriented, the *intelligenty* turned their ire against the traditional order that to them seemed evil and corrupt beyond redemption, condemning it in the name of "progress," "reason," and "truth." "To the devil with all traditions!" exclaimed Belinsky in 1841. "Anathema and death to all those who think differently. Down with those dreadful ties."[83] "Protest," wrote Pisarev, "was a prime necessity for Russian society in the person of its most progressive representatives."[84] Men of letters were thus urged to direct all their efforts toward "one single target"—the emancipation from all the trammels imposed by "caste prejudices, the authority of tradition," in short, from all "antiquated rubbish."[85] By writing literary reviews, critical essays, and even novels, the intelligentsia repeatedly returned to this self-assigned task of categorical repudiation. Under the guise of an historical essay entitled "Russian Satire under Catherine's Reign," for example, Dobroliubov time and again assailed eighteenth-century writers for their moderate demands and their failure to go to the root of evil. What Russia needed, asserted Dobroliubov more than fifteen times in the same article, was a "basic," "total," "principal," "root and branch" transformation of her social order. The Russian reader, emphasized Dobroliubov, must be constantly tormented, pursued, taunted with all the abominations that go on, given no respite until he is made to cry in rage: "Why, this is as bad as penal servitude! Better let my miserable soul perish; I have no wish to live in this slough any longer."[86]

Noteworthy here is the fact that the prime target of attack was not so much the oppressive polity, which provided little if any protection for legal rights and individual freedom, as the social order based on inequality of rank and wealth, and the very institution that served the Slavophiles as the model of human association—the family and kinship.

> Relations between husband and wife, father and son, mother and daughter, tutor and pupil—these are matters that should be weighed and examined from the most varied angles.... Ideas and convictions regarding the conditions of domestic life should be expressed not with the purpose of imposing such ideas upon contemporary society, but to encourage the latter to realize the necessity of boldly and thoroughly revising existing forms hallowed by the passage of centuries and therefore motheaten.[87]

Chernyshevsky's diary dramatically records the expansion of this attack from the social to the political sphere of life and unveils, among other things, the subterranean hue to his condemnation of society.

> Gentlemen, you think that matter depends on the word of republic, but there is no power in that word. What matters is to relieve the lower class from slavery, not to law, but to the inevitability of things, as Louis Blanc says.... I do not care a bit for those people who shout freedom, freedom—and there it ends. Freedom for what? It is not a question of whether there should be a Tsar or not, but a question of social relations, of whether one class should suck the blood of another.[88]

Chernyshevsky's adjuration that an emphasis on "legal rights" of individuals would hinder the establishment of "superior social order," his insistence on the equalization of status and "hatred in principle of any kind of aristocracy,"[89] led him to prescribe this strange political remedy:

> Therefore I think that the only, and probably the best, form of rule is an autocracy, or better still, a hereditary unlimited monarchy, but one which understands its function; that it must stand above all classes, and is especially created for the protection of oppressed people, whose interests it defends. It must act with energy and conviction, and it must know of course that its role is temporary and dual; first, it must champion the lower class ... secondly, because it is obliged to prepare for the realization of future equality—not formal but real—of that class with the higher one—equality in means of living, in order to raise it up to the level of the higher. Peter the Great acted thus, in my opinion.[90]

It was only two years later that Chernyshevsky abandoned the idea of the autocracy for the oppressed, significantly enough, on the ground that the "absolute monarch" was nothing but the "pinnacle of an aristocratic hierarchy to which he belongs body and soul."[91] He concluded, therefore: "Perish— the sooner the better; let the people enter into their rights unprepared, or prepared only by a time of struggle."[92]

It is apparent that neither the Slavophiles nor Herzen would have agreed with that point of view. They recognized only too well that the use of another autocratic protector of equalitarianism would culminate in the annihilation of all traditional immunities and would leave the individual at the mercy of the despotic state. Yet it was precisely this "generalized equality" of social and economic condition, this freedom from all "antiquated rubbish," that the Russian intelligentsia craved. They loathed the past no less than the present and assailed customs, conventions, and traditional institutions in the name of a vaguely conceived millenial future. Pisarev expressed this deep distrust of the past while reviewing Chernyshevsky's ideas propounded in *What Is to Be Done*:

> All the author's sympathies are without reserve on the side of the future: they are undividedly on the side of the embryos of the future that are already noticeable in the present. These embryos are at present hidden under a heap of social fragments of the past, and the author's attitude toward the past is naturally quite negative. As a thinker he understands and excuses all its digressions from rationality but as a man of action, as a champion of an idea striving to be realized, he fights all that is ugly and pursues with his irony and sarcasm all that weighs on the earth and darkens the sky.[93]

Unlike Herzen and the Slavophiles, the *intelligenty* were determined to install the tyranny of doctrine over life and, indeed, argued that it was a mark of moral superiority to possess convictions and to measure everything against the yardstick of "rationality," to judge "everything from the standpoint of those convictions."[94] It is far from paradoxical to assert that this repudiation of everything that savored of the past for "reason," renunciation of traditions and conventional values for convictions made in the name of an eventual utopia, actually blurred their reason and rendered them incapable of understanding both themselves and the social world they so much despised.

If one inquires into their millenial expectations of a "golden age" in which all would be "reasonable" and "equitable," they all share a remarkable weakness in detailed reconstruction. Despite this deficiency, it is possible to present in a bare outline the future society as envisioned by the first Russian *intelligenty*. Belinsky's paradisiacal theme may serve as a starting point of this analysis:

> And there will come a time—I fervently believe it—when no one will be burnt, no one will be decapitated, when the criminal will plead for death as a mercy and salvation and death will be denied him, but life will serve as his punishment as death does now; when there will be no senseless forms and rites, no contracts and stipulations of feeling, no duty and obligation, and we shall not yield to will but to love alone; when there will be no husbands and wives, but lovers and mistresses, and when

the mistress comes to the lover saying: "I love another," the lover will answer: "I cannot be happy without you, I shall suffer all my life; but go to him whom you love," and he will not accept her sacrifice, should she through her generosity wish to remain with him; but like God, will say to her: "I want blessings, not sacrifices ...!" Woman will not be the slave of society and man, but, like man, will fully follow her inclinations without losing her good name, that monstrosity of conventional ideas. There will be neither rich nor poor, neither kings nor subjects, there will be brethren, there will be men, and, at the word of the apostle Paul Christ will pass his power to the Father, and Father-Reason will hold sway once more, but this time in a new heaven and above a new world.[95]

Although one is more than adequately informed by Belinsky of what will be eliminated in a new heaven—and this includes the institution of the family, the state, institutional restraints, that "monstrosity of conventional ideas," laws and customs, those "senseless forms and rites," civil bonds (contracts and obligations), and inequality of status and rank—one is left much less enlightened as to how this new society will be held together. It is clear that neither familial nor contractual and civil ties will bind the brethren in a new heaven. It is explicitly stated that the individuals will not enter the relationship of husband and wife, superior and subordinate, subject and ruler. Nevertheless, Belinsky's three concepts provide a clue into how his brethren, divested as they are of all particular identities, will form a solidary collectivity. They are *sociality, humanity*, and *rationality* and surely not the "police and the laws."

The word sociality was used by Belinsky to refer to the paramount principle of ideal social order, one that no longer depended on the authority of custom and law, social differentiation, and individual self-interest, but was based instead on commitment to "ideals" and commonly held "convictions." In contrast to civil society, the social order informed by sociality was endowed with a comprehensive unity and to that extent allowed neither for distinctions of rank or status, nor for conflicting group or individual interests. Belinsky was convinced, indeed, that a society formed of "heterogeneous elements" and "held together by material interests alone" would be "pitiable and inhuman."[96]

Implicit in this notion of sociality is the image of a "new man," ever ready to renounce his personal identity in order to be consumed in the ideal *moi commun*—in humanity or *narod*. Unlike a member of the civil society, an independent and egoistic individual, this new man is imbued with the spirit of sacrifice for and "love of mankind, but a love cultivated by the consciousness and education."[97] Although Belinsky might have thought that his idea of mankind was akin to the *Humanitaet* of Goethe and the German romantics, it must be noted that neither Goethe, nor Schlegel and Schleiermacher, nor, for that matter, Herzen, were concerned with the development of mankind as a whole. To Herzen, as has been pointed out, love of a hypostatized abstraction was the harbinger of fanaticism, and the very claim that the whole world could become one's brother was tantamount to having no brothers. More important, however, is the fact that Herder, Goethe, and the early romantics did not regard *Humanitaet* as a self-subsisting whole endowed with symbolic significance, but as the quality observed in man or the quality that should be his ideal, as a "Kennzeichen der Menschennatur, als Menschentum."[98] That is why Schleiermacher declared, "Thus, there dawned upon me what is now my highest intuition. I saw clearly that each man is meant to represent humanity in his own way,"[99] and that is why he was "not satisifed to view humanity in rough, unshapen masses, inwardly altogether alike."[100] Such a conception of humanity, and the personalistic orientation it entailed, led Goethe and the early romantics to urge individuals to deliver themselves rather than the world, to focus on their own *Gesinnung*, their inner intentions, rather than on external forms of life, on the development of their own personalities rather than on the salvation of mankind.

To Belinsky and his disciples, however, humanity became a symbolic focus of identification with the new dispensation in which the millenial expectations of the meek and the disinherited would be fully realized. It conjured up the vision of "collective salvation" born out of bloodshed and mass extermination. What was necessary, therefore, was to save "brothers in mankind" rather than engage in the pursuit of knowledge or seek liberty for individual development. Regarded in this light, "love of humanity" betrayed the incorrigible disposition of the *intelligenty* to convert abstract concepts, like mankind, *narod*, or class, into expressive symbols in order to find identity in something beyond themselves—in the new heaven on earth presided over by men freed of all conventional restraints and attachments and inspired solely by the spirit of devotion to these symbols.

The ideal "new men," as envisioned by Chernyshevsky, Dobroliubov, Pisarev, Lavrov, and others, may be considered as an elaboration on Belinsky's theme. Love of mankind *(narod)* and total commitment to whatever creed they embraced remained the two basic ingredients of their personality structure. "Where are the men of integrity," asked Dobroliubov, "who have been from childhood imbued with a single idea, who have merged themselves with that idea so thoroughly that they must either achieve its triumph or perish in the attempt."[101] A man who fails to merge "his soul with any great cause," claimed Dobroliubov, "cannot fight for it as if he were fighting for his own joy, his own life, his own happiness."[102] The whole charm of these "new men" supposedly "lies in the grandeur and sacredness of the ideas" that permeate their whole beings.[103] They may be fanatics, Pisarev readily conceded, "but they are fanaticized by a sober thought."[104] The important point is that they become enthusiastic over the ideas they worship, the ideas with which the "names of Owen, Fourier and a few other true friends of humanity are connected."[105]

Even before the traditional order and its ramshackle institutions have become undermined, the "new men" proceed to establish new social bonds—based, however, on "definite convictions" and service to humanity. We are informed by Chernyshevsky's hero that whenever these men act, they act not to satisfy their "personal passions, but for mankind in general," that what they say, they say "from principle and not from passion, from conviction and not from personal desire."[106] They are even drawn into most intimate relations by professing to each other their convictions.

> I fell in love with you (declared Vera Pavlovna) when, speaking to me for the first time on my birthday, you expressed pity for woman's lot and pictured for her a better future.

> And I—when did I fall in love with you? On the same day, as I have already told you, but exactly at what moment?

> At what moment? When I asked you if it were true that we could so act as to make all men happy.[107]

Chernyshevsky's "pure people" avoid familiarity as they would fire and readily give up "relatives and friends, all personal attachments and all individual joys of human life"[108] in exchange for service to the cause.

For the sake of liberating mankind, the intelligentsia advanced a conception of man deprived of the most enduring human qualities. Such a man "was throughout his life, in all the spheres of his life and activity, in all his acts decisively consistent and devoid of conflicting qualities."[109] He was expected to renounce "all good things of life," including "personal attachments," and be ready to sacrifice "everything and everyone in the world"[110] for the sake of realizing his convictions in life. The singleness of purpose and the total commitment to fleeting idols rendered this "new man" incapable of appreciating the diversity of social life, of recognizing the significance of personal relations and required that he be both deficient in understanding the reality he so much abhorred and devoid of human sensibility. Under the guise of alleged rationality there lurks a zealot unable to question or judge critically the very convictions that permeate his whole personality. What does this Don Quixote express? asked Turgenev.

> Don Quixote is imbued with devotion to the ideal, for which he is prepared to subject himself to every possible deprivation, to sacrifice his life; he values his life only to the extent that it will serve as a means for the realization of the ideal, for the establishment of truth and justice on earth.... To live for himself, to care about himself Don Quixote would consider to be shameful. He lives only (if it is possible to express it this way) outside of himself, for others, for his brethren, for the sake of destroying evil.... A constant striving toward one and the same goal lends a certain monotony to his ideas, a one-sidedness to his mind; he knows little, but he need not know much.... At one moment Don Quixote can seem a complete maniac, because the most indubitable materiality

disappears before his eyes, melts like wax in the flame of his enthusiasm (he really sees live Moors in wooden dolls, knights in sheep)—at another moment, limited because he does not know how to sympathize easily, or to enjoy himself, but, like an ancient tree, he has struck his roots deep in the soil and cannot change his convictions, nor can be shifted from one subject to another....[111]

Did the Russian *intelligenty* seriously expect the Russian society to conform one day to this telocratic model of the world in which one system of belief, one goal, one "true consciousness," and one type of man would prevail? Judged on the basis of their statements, there can be no doubt that a good many of them did. Dobroliubov, relying on the information supplied by Turgenev's fictional hero, Insarov, quoted him with approval: "In Bulgaria every peasant, every beggar, and I—we all want the same thing, we all have the same goal."[112] In Russian society, Dobroliubov remarked regretfully, "every class, even every circle, lives its own separate life, has its own separate goal and strivings, has its own appointed place."[113] Chernyshevsky assured his readers that the time would come when this "new man" will no longer be "any special type, and it will be difficult for anyone to understand that there ever was a time when it was regarded as special and not as the common nature of all mankind."[114] Significantly enough, they found these men, as did Belinsky and Chernyshevsky, among friendship circles of the generation of the "remarkable decade." So much so that Belinsky tried to persuade Botkin that their relationship exemplified the principles of rationality and sociality. Chernyshevsky praised the Slavophiles for the "passionate commitment to their convictions."[115] Needless to add, such people as Kireevsky, Samarin, Herzen, Granovsky, Botkin, Stankevich, Turgenev, Annenkov, and others would have certainly disclaimed Chernyshevsky's contention that they were bound by an absolute identity of convictions and strivings and that they allowed their individualities to become absorbed in the unity of the ideological outlook. Obviously, Belinsky, like Chernyshevsky and Dobroliubov, failed to appreciate the cult of friendship among the members of the generation of the "remarkable decade" and branded their self-assured sociability, their leisurely style of life, that "active idleness," to cite Herzen, "which is conducive to the thinker's meditation, to the poet's reveries and to the epicurean enjoyments, the exuberant, capricious poetic development of our aristocratic personalities,"[116] as nothing more than a manifestation of superfluity and idleness.

There can be little doubt, however, that the members of the friendship circles of the generation of the "remarkable decade" were neither idle people nor conviction-ridden zealots, but primarily a community of friends maintained, to use Goethe's phrase, by inner intentions (*Gesinnung*) over and above the identity or the divergence of opinions. Kireevsky, for example, conceived of friendship as an ethical imperative, and, while urging the historian Pogodin to improve his character in the company of close friends, pointed out that one can never be sufficiently convinced that "man is cultivated by another man."[117]

Such is the main thrust of social ideas found in the *Weltanschauung* of the Slavophiles, Herzen, Belinsky, and the intelligentsia of the post-1850 generation. If compared, these ideas can be seen to disclose distinct conceptions of social order as well as varied images of man and his relation to society. The only significant point of convergence among them seems to derive from their insensitivity to the civil order, even though underlying this particular attitude were diverse value orientations. The communal society of the Slavophiles was too undifferentiated to allow for the separation of various spheres of life; its touchstone, as has been noted, was *Sittlichkeit* rather than the rule of law. For what the Slavophiles opposed was not so much social change (economic and technological innovation) as the spectre of advancing secularization—the erosion of the sacred from society and culture—which threatened their vision of social order integrated on the basis of an overarching religious creed and capable of forging various spheres of life into a single whole. On the other hand, the Westerners, unlike their Slavophile opponents, lacked the concept of a fixed social order and made instead the individual the focal referent of their orientation. To some Westerners, like Ogarev for example, "there existed only one thing: the individual with his humane disposition and historical contingency."[118] The idea of community consonant with this orientation was constituted on personal bonds and was thus too esoteric to allow for the "particularization" (in the Hegelian sense) of its members. It served primarily to accommodate unique individuals who preferred the sphere of spontaneity and interpersonal relations to the system of governance by rules. Without doubt, this sphere of "personal life" was highly valued by the Westerners; in fact, Ogarev tended to subsume under it everything else, including *"das Allgemeine."*[119] Although it is true that Herzen spoke on behalf of "civil liberties" and that both—Herzen and the Slavophiles—appreciated the "calm freedom" of England, there is little evidence to attest to their abiding interest in her legal institutions—the protection of individual rights, due process provisions, the tradition of autonomous judiciary, or other English liberties. Finally, the vision of future society projected by Belinsky and the *intelligenty* following him was not only incompatible with the civil order but also subversive of familial attachments and personal ties. Its hallmark was unity between the individual and collectivity, between the real and the ideal, the insistence that "reality itself" should be raised "to the level of the rational demand,"[120] and unity of purpose, which defined both the program of collective action and the ends of individual lives. Affective attachments and personal sympathy were considered a threat to "societal solidarity," admittedly because they "divided the people into many groupings."[121] This assumption of the oneness of society, combined with the emphasis on the ideological *Gleichschaltung* of diverse spheres of social life, and on the subjection of individuals to a collective ideal, not only precluded the establishment of a differentiated civil order, but rendered the rule of law virtually superfluous in the new heaven.

Chernyshevsky's praise of the Slavophiles for their antiindividualism and for their sound view of the relationship between the individual and society, his livid hatred of liberal ideas and their proponents—from Chicherin in Russia to de Tocqueville in France—and his apprehension lest "legal rights" of individuals, once firmly instituted, might stand in the way of "superior social order," testify to the ease with which the Russian intelligentsia exchanged "legal fictions" and "legal idols" for a future utopia.

The Problem of the Social Determination of Ideas

The foregoing account has pointed out the radicalization of Russian thought and the ideologization of its carriers within the short span of two generations. The leading ideas of the members of the "remarkable decade" clustered around *conservatism* (the Slavophiles)—akin on many points to that of the French conservatives and German romantics, *genteel liberal* (Turgenev, Granovsky) and *radical individualism* (Herzen, Ogarev); those of Belinsky and the intelligentsia of the post-1850 generation tended toward ideologically inspired *collectivism* and *doctrinaire radicalism*, with its heavy reliance on utopian socialism. Compared to the West, Russian social thought may be said to have developed in a reverse fashion. Whereas romantic conservatism in the West formed an intellectual counter-movement to the ideas of the *Aufklaerung*, the Russian version of the *Aufklaerung* (ideological nihilism) represented a reaction against the romantic conservatism and radical individualism of the generation of the "remarkable decade." If it is true that conservative ideas in Germany were worked out to their "logical conclusions," it was doctrinaire radicalism in Russia that was carried to its extremes and has also remained a dominant style of thought for over a century.

Was this failure of the intelligentsia to overcome the dominant perspective a result of the dearth of people among them whose sensibility marked the quality of their thought? As is well known, Mannheim located such people in a "relatively classless stratum" of the "socially unattached intelligentsia" (*freischwebende Intelligenz*).[122] This stratum of the intelligentsia is ostensibly best equipped to transcend the limitations of any single perspective by virtue of its unanchored location in the social order and diverse class composition of its members. To delve further into this epistemologically privileged position of the intelligentsia would not suit our present purpose. Here it is sufficient to note that such *déraciné* synthetizers, like other men of ideas, must be bent on overcoming interest-bound orientation, must adhere to a set of standards conducive to the pursuit of truth rather than be fanatically convinced of possessing "truth in its final form." The social conditions under which Russian intellectual life developed in the course of the nineteenth century militated against the establishment of an open intellectual forum, with its free exchange of ideas and its body of traditions and values favorable to that flexibility of mind and detachment that are the basis of the critical attitude.

The history of the Russian intelligentsia lends little support to Mannheim's thesis. It suggests instead that the rise to dominance of a socially unattached intelligentsia was closely bound with the ideologization of cultural life and an abundant supply of zealots bent on measuring all social reality with the yardstick of doctrine. Moreover, as will become clear below, the major ideas of the *intelligenty* as well as their mode of attachment to these ideas tend to accord with this unanchored position in the social order.

It has been noted that little more than change of family names is required to present the life histories of the leading Slavophiles (at least with regard to their early years). "On the rich soil of serfdom, regularly like oaks, developed those families, with their roots deep in the life of a people and nourished by its fruits, they reached European enlightenment by their tops."[123] All the leading Slavophiles came from the landowning gentry and were members of a few old families still engaged in the management of their estates. "These large families," according to Riasanovsky, "were linked by marriage and by blood and formed a closely knit group of relatives and friends."[124] The Slavophiles thus grew in an atmosphere of kinship complaisance, in quiet gentry nests permeated by ancient customs and traditions. If one looks at the internal relations prevailing in the Slavophile families, they were characterized by deep personal attachments of their members to each other. "A feeling of mutual concern," observed Kireevsky, "has been refined in our family to the impossible."[125] It is said that Peter Kireevsky died out of grief shortly after the death of his brother and that Konstantin Aksakov "died from longing for his father, in fact, the entire illness consisted only in that."[126]

Compared with the Slavophiles who belonged to the landed nobility, the Westerners were recruited from a less exclusive matrix of social life. Nevertheless, most of them, as Bogucharsky pointed out, hailed from similar gentry nests: "Khomiakov and Turgenev, Samarin and Kavelin, Aksakov and Panaev," and one may add, Stankevich, Annenkov, Herzen, and Ogarev, "equally belonged to the generation of the forties, all possessed many common and dear memories, behind all of them stood a manorial orchard ... with its shadowy parks and poetical conversations, with its abundance of beautiful womanly faces."[127] Despite this rootedness in the privileged ambience and similarity of social background, members of the generation of the "remarkable decade" evolved intellectual perspectives sufficiently variegated to extend over the whole spectrum of political ideas—from conservatism of the Slavophiles and liberal individualism of Granovsky and Turgenev to the radicalism of Herzen.

But the key individual standing apart from his own generation of the "remarkable decade" is Belinsky, the foremost paragon of the *déraciné* intelligentsia in Russia. Unlike his contemporaries—both the Slavophiles and the Westerners—who harbored many of the virtues and vices of the "old world," Belinsky, as Herzen noted, "was one of the freest people," he was bound by neither traditional beliefs nor conventions of his milieu.[128] Coming from the family of a poor provincial official, "Belinsky left it without retaining a single pleasant memory. His parents were harsh and uncultured. When he was ten his father struck him so strongly that he fell to the floor."[129] The idea of revenge pursued him for long, Herzen continued, but the awareness of personal helplessness "changed it into a hatred of any familial authority which he retained to the end of his life."[130] Belinsky himself readily admitted that he had received no affection from his mother. "Furthermore, my father could not stand me ... he beat me unsparingly and squarely. I was a stranger in the family."[131]

What kind of life did such transplanted young men face in Petersburg or Moscow? Belinsky found himself in a milieu in which there was no place as yet for an uprooted commoner—an expelled student without established status in society. "Behind his friends," wrote Miliukov, "there stood their families who looked askance upon association of their sons with Belinsky."[132] It was here that he viewed every moment as an anticipation of a new insult and injury, and was made exaggeratedly conscious of a deep chasm that divided him from his friends and made him resentful of his station in life. This "Chandala feeling" that one is disadvantaged and not considered equal prompted Chernyshevsky to approach individuals of higher standing by an act of self-effacement. Expressing his gratitude to a young lady who danced with him, Chernyshevsky let her know readily: "I'll never forget this distance that separates me from you."[133] Dobroliubov's resentment of the world from which he suffered the stings of rejection led him ultimately to look for a formula that would eliminate the "inequality of status" and, if need be, "turn everything upside down."[134]

A dislodgment from primordial environment and from an enduring network of personal and intimate relations marks one of the most striking characteristics of Belinsky and the first *intelligenty*. Even Chernyshevsky, who had scarcely any reason to be driven by family chagrin, spoke the language of an outsider when he recorded in his diary that: "I don't enter into any family affairs, I have no knowledge of what is taking place in our home."[135] It is this fact of disinheritance and the accompanying feeling of being outside of all social ramifications that renders meaningful their mode of attachment to ideas. Jolted loose from the bonds of kinship, "attracted by life" and yet unable to relate to people, outsiders to the social world to which they aspired and from which they had come, these first *intelligenty* fell on ideas as poor rustics would on "white loaves" of bread in a large city:

> Imagine a peasant who did not eat anything all his life besides bread mixed with sand ... and who, after an arrival to a large city, found mountains of white loaves, confection and fruits. Is it just to say that he lacks self-control and human restraint if he looks on those things with the eye of a tiger ... and, after having got hold of them, devours them in an animal-like fashion, ready to break his head in case someone tried to take them away.[136]

In this last sense, ideas to the Russian *intelligenty* were not merely an effective instrument for channeling their animus against the existing social order—for expressing their obsession with the idea of annihilating all social arrangements—but also a means of relating themselves to people and uncovering meaning in the world around them. Belinsky's ideological wanderings, his revolt against romantic individualism, may well be interpreted as a compulsive search for a rigid system of beliefs helpful in overcoming a haunting sense of dispossession. Indeed, he blamed the circle of Stankevich for its exclusiveness and Fichte's individualism for the fact that it estranged him from Russian society by turning him into an abstract man.

> Woe to a man who intends to be only a man and does not add to that abstract and sonorous calling that of a merchant, a landowner, an officer, an official, an artist, or a teacher. Society will punish him. I experience this punishment myself. Were it possible to attach myself to any official journal I would do it at once. This move would secure me a position, without which a man is nothing but a phantom, and could also offer security in case of illness and other misfortunes.[137]

While he turned away from Fichte to Hegel, and, by equating reality with God, embarked on adjustment to society, he also continued to complain in the same old vein: "Friends, friends, you are in Moscow and I—the devil knows where. If I left for Moscow, I should escape only from Petersburg but not from myself. Homeless in the world and without a kindred soul—dreadful!"[138] On another occasion he again complained to Botkin: "Oh, my Botkin, I am alone, alone—no one is close to me."[139] Even worse, it was precisely during these frantic attempts to merge with reality that Belinsky lost interest in "prosaic life" and felt "more and more as a citizen of the universe"[140]—so much so that he became indifferent to human company and women: "the ability of love was lost, the ties of marriage seem to be nothing more than ties."[141] "What is to be done?" asked Belinsky in this state of personal despair and aloneness. The answer he provided was of epochal significance, for it contained the core element of the intelligentsia's orientation: "the death of the particular for the sake of the general—this is the law of the universe."[142]

The more Belinsky felt himself to be estranged from life and people, the more his soul was filled with "flame and energy," the more he was ready "to die and suffer for convictions" and to dedicate himself to the service of collective good. His heart was now filled with rage at the sight of a crowd wallowing in the dirt. "And after all this," exclaimed Belinsky indignantly, "has *a man* the right to forget himself in art, in knowledge!"[143]

What we witness here is a phenomenon of the utmost interest. The same Belinsky who lacked the capacity to experience the warmth of personal relations or to establish affective ties and love, who lost the sense of his own identity and belonging, who, indeed, branded all human attachments as nothing but constraint, displayed at the same time a distant affectivity toward the *narod* and mankind in general—a manifest predisposition for attachment to collective entities and symbols. The same Dobroliubov, who at the age of six-teen felt that without love and personal attachments his heart would become "hard and cold as a stone," declared a few years later: "I found the strength within me to resign myself to my personal lot: the pleasure of work served to compensate me for the former pleasure of indolence, acquisition of the mind for the infatuation of the heart, love of mankind for love of kin."[144] The lead-ing Fourierist, Butashevich-Petrashevsky, spoke of similar experience while reflecting on his personal past. "Finding no one worthy of my attachment—whether among women or among men—I have devoted myself to the service of mankind ... striving for the common good has supplanted in me egoism and the instinct for self-preservation, and respect for truth has freed me from every trace of self-regard."[145] In a very real sense, then, the first Russian *intel-ligenty* identified with abstract collectivities to compensate for their failure and/or inability to relate to individual human beings; they suffered over the plight of the *narod* because they were insensitive to themselves and to people close to them; they were ladies bountiful and served causes that were not their own because they seemed to be lacking in human compassion and not because their love was too abundant to be confined to individual persons.

It is important to note that the intelligentsia's conception of the ideal society was, on crucial points, congruent with their social position. For what they proposed, in brief, was a society in which its members and, foremost, they themselves, would relate to one another in terms of ideals and beliefs rather than in terms of status, specific interests, or personal qualities. It would be a social order in which Belinsky and Dobroliubov would not be viewed as unre-fined provincials, in which Chernyshevsky's wife-to-be would not be embar-rassed by his social background, in which Chernyshevsky himself would not be kept in a porter's lodge, as he was on one occasion, because of his outward appearance and the mode of transportation used (he came on foot), but would find identity and recognition as men of convictions. Moreover, the basic per-sonality components of the "pure people" remind us in many ways of the *intelligenty* themselves. It is as if the *intelligenty* projected onto these "pure people" some of the qualities and orientations they themselves exhibited and, in the process of doing so, created ideal men in their own image.

Notes

1. Quoted in A. A. Kornilov. "Obshchestvennoe Dvizhenie pri Aleksandre II," *Minuvshie Gody (February 1908), p. 96.*
2. *N. G. Chernyshevsky, Selected Philosophical Essays* (Moscow: Foreign Languages Publishing House, 1953), p. 468.
3. Ibid., p. 473.
4. *See* V. Zaitsev, "Belinskii i Dobroliubov," *Russkoe Slovo*, 6 (January 1864): 1–68; N. A. Dobroliubov. *Selected Philosophical Essays* (Moscow: Foreign Languages Publishing House, 1948), p. 395.
5. V. G. Belinsky, *Polnoe Sobranie Sochinenii*, ed. V. S. Vengerov (St. Petersburg, 1900), II, p. 488.

6. Chernyshevsky, *Selected*, p. 457.
7. V. G. Belinsky, *Izbrannye Pisma* (Moscow, 1955), I, p. 128.
8. F. F. Nelidov, ed., *Zapadniki 40kh Godov* (Moscow, 1910), p. 125.
9. Chernyshevsky, *Selected*, p. 411.
10. D. Pisarev, *Selected Philosophical, Social and Political Essays* (Moscow: Foreign Languages Publishing House, 1958), p. 108.
11. Quoted in N. Kosy, "Literaturnye Zakonodateli," *Vremia* 6 (1861): 109; *see also* N. Strakhov, *Iz Istorii Literaturnogo Nigilizma: 1861–1865* (St. Petersburg, 1890, p. 88.
12. K. S. Aksakov, *Polnoe Sobranie Sochinenii*, ed. I. Aksakov (Moscow, 1875–1889), I, pp. 279–80.
13. I. V. Kireevsky, *Polnoe Sobranie Sochineii*, ed. M. Gershenzon (Moscow, 1911), I, p. 207.
14. Ibid., p. 113.
15. Ibid., p. 187.
16. Ibid.
17. Ibid., p. 192.
18. Ibid., p. 206.
19. Ibid., p. 202.
20. Ibid., p. 115.
21. Ibid.
22. Ibid.
23. Ibid.
24. Ibid., p. 205.
25. Ibid.
26. Ibid., p. 209.
27. Ibid., II, p. 242.
28. Ibid., p. 253.
29. Ibid., p. 252.
30. Ibid., I, p. 109.
31. Aleksei S. Khomiakov, *Polnoe Sobranie Sochinenii*, 4th ed. (Moscow, 1911), I, p. 127.
32. Ibid., p. 108.
33. Ibid., p. 129.
34. A. S. Khomiakov, "On Humboldt," in *Russian Intellectual History: An Anthology*, ed. Marc Raeff (New York: Harcourt, Brace and World, Inc., 1966), p. 217.
35. Khomiakov, *Polnoe*, I, 130.
36. I. Aksakov, *Sochineniia*, (Moscow, 1886), II, p. 449; quoted in Nicholas V. Riasanovsky, *Russia and the West in the Teachings of the Slavophiles*, "Harvard Historical Studies," Vol. 61 (Cambridge: Harvard University Press, 1952), p. 105.
37. L. Brodsky, *Rannie Slavianofily* (Moscow, 1910), p. 121.
38. K. S. Aksakov, "O Sovremennom Cheloveke," *Bratskaia Pomoch: Postradavshim Semeistvam Bosnii i Gertsegoviny* (St. Petersburg, 1876), p. 251.
39. Khomiakov, *Polnoe*, I, p. 137.
40. I. Aksakov, *Sochineniia*, II, p. 267.
41. Ibid., V, p. 557.
42. Paul Kluckhohn, *Das Ideengut der Deutschen Romantik*, 3d ed. (Tuebingen: Max Niemeyer Verlag, 1953), p. 61.
43. K. Aksakov, *Bratskaia Pomoch*, p. 259.
44. K. Aksakov, "On the Internal State of Russia," in *Russian Intellectual History: An Anthology*, ed. Marc Raeff (New York: Harcourt, Brace and World, Inc., 1966), p. 235.

45. Ibid., p. 231.
46. Ibid., p. 234.
47. I. V. Kireevsky, "On the Nature of European Culture and Its Relation to the Culture of Russia," *Russian Intellectual History: An Anthology*, ed. Marc Raeff (New York: Harcourt, Brace and World, Inc., 1966), p. 202.
48. A. I. Herzen, *Selected Philosophical Works* (Moscow: Foreign Languages Publishing House, 1956), p. 343.
49. Ibid, p. 344.
50. Ibid.
51. Ibid., p. 343.
52. Ibid.
53. Ibid., p. 342.
54. Ibid., pp. 455–56.
55. Ibid., p. 457.
56. Quoted in Edward H. Carr, *Romantic Exiles* (London: Gollancz, 1933), p. 135.
57. Ibid., pp. 135–36.
58. *See* Martin Malia, *Alexander Herzen and the Birth of Russian Socialism* (New York: Grosset and Dunlap, 1965), p. 221.
59. Herzen, *Selected*, p. 591.
60. Ibid., pp. 385–86.
61. Ibid., p. 430.
62. Ibid., p. 585.
63. Ibid.
64. Ibid., p. 586.
65. Ibid., p. 582.
66. Ibid., p. 594.
67. Ibid., p. 595.
68. Ibid., p. 586.
69. Ibid., pp. 362–63.
70. Ibid., p. 452.
71. Ibid., p. 412.
72. Edgar H. Lehrman, ed., *Turgenev's Letters: A Selection* (New York: Alfred A. Knopf, 1961), p. 143.
73. N. P. Ogarev, *Sotsialno-Politicheskie i Filos of skie Proizvedeniia*, eds. M. Jovchuk and N. Tarakanova (Moscow, 1956), II, p. 288.
74. "Iz Perepiski I.S. Turgeneva z Semeiu Aksakovykh," *Vestnik Evropy* 165 (February 1894): 495.
75. Ibid.
76. Michail Dragomanov, ed., *Konstantin Kawelins und Iwan Turgenjews social-politischer Briefwechsel mit Alexander Iw. Herzen*, Vol. 4 of *Bibliothek Russischer Denkwuerdigkeiten*, ed. Theodor Schiemann (Stuttgart, 1894), p. 61.
77. Herzen, *Selected*, p. 434.
78. Ibid., p. 446.
79. Goethe, *Wilhelm Meister's Apprenticeship*, Carlyle translation (Boston, 1883), p. 261.
80. F. Schlegel, *Ideen 60 in Kritische Schriften*, ed. W. Rasch (Munich: Hanser Verlag, 1956), p. 93; *see also* Lilian R. Furst, *Romanticism in Perspective* (New York: St. Martin's Press, 1969), p. 65.
81. Herzen, *Selected*, p. 445; *see also* Paul Kluckhohn, *Persoenlichkeit und Gemeinschaft: Studien zur Staatsauffassung der Deutschen Romantik* (Halle: Max Niemeyer, 1925), p. 2.
82. N. G. Chernyshevsky, *Izbrannye Filosofskie Sochineniia* (Moscow, 1950), II, p. 490; for an analysis of Chernyshevsky's view of the commune, *see* William

F. Woehrlin, *Chernyshevskii: The Man and the Journalist* (Cambridge: Harvard University Press, 1971), pp. 209–15.
83. Belinsky, *Izbrannye*, II, p. 145.
84. Pisarev, *Selected*, p. 94.
85. Ibid., p. 79.
86. N. A. Dobroliubov, *Izbrannye Sochineniia* (Moscow, 1947), pp. 169–217; *see also* Dobroliubov, *Sochineniia*, IX, p. 408.
87. Pisarev, *Selected*, p. 89.
88. N. G. Chernyshevsky, *Polnoe Sobranie Sochinenii* (Moscow, 1939), I. p. 75.
89. M. Antonov (Bulgakov), *N.G. Chernyshevskii: Sotsialno-Filosofskii Etiud* (Moscow, 1910), p. 93; Chernyshevsky, *Polnoe*, I, p. 121.
90. Ibid.
91. Ibid., p. 356.
92. Ibid.
93. Pisarev, *Selected*, p. 627.
94. Chernyshevsky, *Selected*, p. 51.
95. V. G. Belinsky, *Selected Philosophical Works* (Moscow; Foreign Languages Publishing House, 1948), pp. 164–65.
96. P. N. Sakulin, ed., *Sotsializm Belinskogo: Stati i Pisma* (Moscow, 1925), pp. 81–83.
97. V. G. Belinsky, *Izbrannoe: Estetika i Literaturnaia Kritika v Dvukh Tomakh* (Moscow, 1959), II, p. 686.
98. Kluckhohn, *Das Ideengut*, p. 54.
99. *Schleiermacher's Soliloquies*, trans. Horace Leland Friess (Chicago: The Open Court Publishing Co., 1926), p. 54.
100. Ibid.
101. Dobroliubov, *Selected*, p. 417.
102. Ibid., p. 408.
103. Ibid., p. 417.
104. Pisarev, *Selected*, p. 649.
105. Ibid.
106. N. G. Tchernychevsky, *What's to Be Done*, 4th ed., trans. Benjamin R. Tucker (New York: International Book Store, 1909), p. 212.
107. Ibid.
108. Pisarev, *Selected*, p. 673.
109. Chernyshevsky, *Polnoe*, I, p. 153.
110. P. Lavrov, *Komu Prinadlezhit Budushchee?* (Tipografiia Gruppy Starykh Narodovoltsev, 1902), p. 8.
111. I. S. Turgenev, *Sobranie Sochinenii* (Moscow, 1956), XI, pp. 170–71; quoted in Rufus W. Mathewson, *The Positive Hero in Russian Literature* (New York: Columbia University Press, 1958), pp. 137–38.
112. Dobroliubov, *Selected*, p. 420
113. Ibid.
114. Tchernychevsky, *What's to Be Done*, p. 156.
115. N. G. Chernyshevsky, *Izbrannye Ekonomicheskie Proizvedeniia* (Moscow, 1948), I, p. 93.
116. Herzen, *Selected*, pp. 383–84.
117. Kireevsky, *Polnoe*, II, p. 216.
118. Ogarev, *Sotsialno*, II, p. 398.
119. Ibid., p. 338.
120. Dobroliubov, *Selected*, p. 396.
121. P. Lavrov, "Sotsialnaia Revoliutsiia i Zadachi Nravstvennosti," *Vestnik Narodnoi Voli*, no. 3 (1884), pp. 26–28.

122. Karl Mannheim, *Ideology and Utopia*, trans. Louis Wirth and Edward Shils (New York: Harcourt, Brace and Co., 1936), p. 155.
123. M. Gershenzon, *Istoricheskie Zapiski* 2d ed. (Berlin, 1923), p. 44.
124. Riasanovsky, *Russia and the West*, p. 29.
125. Quoted in Gershenzon, *Istoricheskie*, p. 24.
126. V. Smirnov, *Aksakovy, Ikh Zhizn i Literaturnaia Deiatelnost'* (St. Petersburg, 1905), p. 47.
127. V. I. Iakovlev (Bogucharsky), *Iz Proshlago Russkogo Obshchestva* (St. Petersburg, 1904), p. 229.
128. A. I. Herzen, *O Razvitii Revoliutsionnykh Idei v Rossii* (St. Petersburg, 1907), p. 128.
129. Ibid.
130. Ibid.
131. A. N. Pypin, *Belinskii: Ego Zhizn' i Perepiska* (St. Petersburg, 1876), II, p. 39.
132. P. Miliukov, *Iz Istorii Russkoi Intelligentsii* (St. Petersburg, 1903), p. 117.
133. Chernyshevsky, *Polnoe*, I, p. 408.
134. N. A. Dobroliubov, *Sobranie Sochinenii v Deviati Tomakh*, ed. B. E. Bursova et al. (Moscow-Leningrad, 1961–65), VIII, p. 522.
135. Chernyshevsky, *Polnoe*, I, p. 418.
136. Belinsky, *Izbrannye*, II, p. 26.
137. Ibid., pp. 16–17.
138. Ibid., p. 13.
139. Ibid., p. 123.
140. Ibid., p. 158.
141. Ibid., p. 134.
142. Ibid., p. 81.
143. Ibid., p. 172.
144. N. A. Dobroliubov, *Dnevniki*, ed. V. Polansky (Moscow, 1932), p. 70.
145. V. Semevsky, "M. V. Butashevich-Petrashevskii," *Golos Minuvshago* (January 1913), p. 32.

7 Men of Action: Intelligentsia and the Legacy of Domination

Our understanding of the intelligentsia's "love affair" with the people remains disconcertingly deficient, even though so much Russian and Western ink has been spilled over it. There prevails in the West a hackneyed image of the intelligentsia as a group of enlightened individuals living off the ideas prefabricated abroad, and estranged from the tsarist autocracy above, and the mass of humanity below. It has been suggested, accordingly, that:

> The whole notion of "going to the people" was central and specific to Russia—because the intelligentsia, having been artificially created, was particularly aware of its artificial position and this provided it with an extra incentive to worship, idolize and feel the pangs of conscience towards the people.[1]

The members of the intelligentsia need not have been lucid on the nature of their social predicament; like their literary protagonists, however, they seemed to have been painfully aware of occupying the pariah status in their own "blessed land."

Many ingenious explanations have been proffered in the past to account for this trying plight of the intelligentsia. More recently, an American author has endeavored to shed light on this plight of the intelligentsia by resurrecting two of its favorite ideas: "spontaneity" and "consciousness." The individual members of the intelligentsia ostensibly related to the world by oscillating between two modes of orientation: they either attempted to dissolve in and/ or fuse with such "spontaneous forces" as the peasant folk or the laboring masses, or sought to cast the world in the image of their own consciousness, thereby reasserting their own identity.[2]

Whatever the merit of this view (originally formulated by Potresov),[3] the intelligentsia's quest for unity with the *narod* should not be taken for a collective urge to dissolve into the world of the toiling masses—be they peasants or workers. Only two major groups of the populist intelligentsia—Bakunin's *buntari* and Lavrov's propagandists (including their individual followers from Chaikovsky's circle)—went to the countryside to merge with the peasant masses (even though they differed with regard to their respective conceptions of this merger). All other populist groups expressed little desire to let themselves be absorbed by the peasant masses. More significant, perhaps, is the fact that both the *buntari* and the propagandists hoped to merge with the people on their own terms, as there can be no loophole for doubt that the "renowned fusion" with the people was inseparably bound up with the "question of ideals."[4] The very image of *narod* conjured up those very values and beliefs that various groups of the intelligentsia themselves professed. To the populist intelligentsia, *narod* represented a collective Stenka Razin endowed with the revolutionary élan and ready to burst off imminently. *Narod* embodied the "universal idea" of collective solidarity and equality or, finally, stood for that "glorious achievement" of Russia—the village commune, with its harmony and unanimity based on commonly shared values. Lavrov cast *narod* in the image of God, albeit unaware of being omnipotent.

> *Narod* is truly a suffering God, but God unaware of his omnipotence. He was neither crucified nor put on the crown of thorns by his own free will. He bleeds profusely, but he is endowed with the God-like prowess, and the mighty heroes who rush to the Calvary to rescue him are but microscopic midges before him. *Narod* alone is strong enough to smash the cross to which he remains nailed down. The only thing that the weak creatures, standing in the feet of his huge cross, can do is to murmur to him: "you are God, you are omnipotent! Smash your cross and crush your enemies!"[5]

Narod thus acquired in the consciousness of the populist intelligentsia a symbolic significance capable of evoking a whole gamut of bizarre images ranging from the "tsardom of truth" to the "heavenly music."[6] In response to this *narod*, many populist *intelligenty* were moved to extreme acts of heroism and sacrifice; some literally went to the gallows with the word *narod* on their lips at the same time that the living members of this *narod* looked numbly at the sorry spectacle of execution.[7] Moreover, the common people of the hinterland knew little and cared less about the martyrdom of their devotees.

In the populist hierophany the *narod* partook of both the actual and the ideal elements: on one hand, *narod* designated the toiling masses of the countryside, a social category definable in terms of objective characteristics; on the other hand, *narod* expressed the subjective dispositions—the sentiments and aspirations—of the populist intelligentsia and to that extent served as the chief symbol of the populist ideology. Even the unsuccessful exodus to the countryside failed to erode completely the populist conviction that the "people possess, as men of action claim, and ought to possess, as theorists believe, all the requisites for the attainment of our goal."[8] As late as 1877, Lavrov reiterated his often-professed belief that:

> in the Russian people there is a mighty socialist future. Several conditions beneficial to socialism are contained in the agricultural commune

(obshchina) and in the artisan commune (artel) ... but this is only the point of departure—much more important is precisely that absence of tradition and idols."[9]

In the final analysis, *narod* became the object of devotion to whom the populist intelligentsia addressed prayers, made recurrent pledges of exclusive loyalty, and professed a "sacred hatred" of its foes—both real and imaginary. For this reason alone they could not but view with suspicion any dispassionate study of *narod*, that "narrow-bureaucratic" activity worthy only of "old-fashioned pedants." As one of them indignantly asked:

What is this celebrated study of *narod*'s way of life in the social sense, in the sense of solving the "cursed questions," in the sense of acquiescing the tormented conscience of the intelligentsia, in the sense of relieving the suffering of those who thirst for *truth*, in the sense of saving them from the sultry and gloomy prison of apathy and despair? Oh yes, from the vantage point of abstract scholarship this kind of study may not be without interest, but from the social point of view it represents nothing but a compromise, a detraction and a self-satisfying deception. This deception is the more so dangerous because it is liable to substitute means for ends.[10]

The impatience of the populist *intelligenty* with "abstract scholarship" was not solely due to their apprehension that a scholarly approach to the object of their attachment might uncover evidence unfavorable to it. The populist attitude toward the *muzhik* was supple enough to accommodate ultimately the most derisive opinions about him. Suffice it to note here that the *muzhik* was not only praised for being the most magnificent creature on earth, but was also compared to a "beast of burden"[11] and likened to a creature dangerous by his savagery and stupidity ("*Rusticus* ist zu dumm");[12] he was not only extolled as a "communist" or "socialist by instinct" and "revolutionary by nature,"[13] but also branded as a swine.[14] But while this magnificent creature was being slowly unhallowed and, in the end, debased to the abject position of a swine, the populist *intelligenty* showed little inclination to turn into swineherds, let alone get down on all fours in order to submerge in the swinish multitude. Instead, they continued to channel their effusions onto *narod* that excited "human heart" and provided "new vistas, new ideas and images"[15] rather than onto the *bête noire* residing in the countryside. By this time, of course, this *narod* became dissociated from the peasant masses and existed solely in the consciousness of the intelligentsia as the focus of symbolic identification.

To argue that the populist *intelligenty* endowed with symbolic significance their own creation is not to suggest that they were cognizant of this folly. They seemed to have been unaware for some time that what they worshipped so passionately and even died for was an abstraction devoid of objective reference. Indicative of this was the tendency of the populist *intelligenty* to confound their own concocted image of *narod* with the *muzhik* whom they encountered on the pilgrimage to the countryside. On the one hand, they tended to see the people awry, since they looked at them through the veil of ideas they held onto so zealously; on the other, they turned to the people seen awry in order to uncover evidence in support of these ideas. What evolved from this muddle was an ingenuous technique of "poetization" or "idealization," whereby the populist *intelligenty* transformed the people into the "guiding ideal" and then proceeded to relate themselves to the people in response to this "guiding ideal." Aside from being convinced that the people deserved to be "idealized," they also justified "idealization" on the grounds that:

> as everywhere else, the facts of narod's life are confounded and even sad; as a result of it, we idealize these facts, transform facts into ideals by purifying them of the extraneous admixture that complex conditions of life entail.[16]

What the populists failed to come to grips with was the fact that different groups of the intelligentsia claimed to have uncovered in the people different values and ideals. Even if it is conceded that the Russian people harbored a "uniquely beautiful notion of truth"—one that combined "thought" and "action," "social ideals," and the "facts of life"[17]—and were equally blessed with a unique talent for infusing their collective life with disparate values, it was still incumbent on the populist intelligentsia to decide what specific aspect of that life was worthy of being poeticized. There is no evidence to suggest that the populists extolled the people, as the Slavophiles did, for their submission to authority so tellingly evinced by the "adoration of the Tsar" or "intense loyalty to Christ's Church,"[18] or that they ever contemplated transforming this loyalty to autocracy into their own "pearl of consciousness." Nor is there evidence for assuming that the populist intelligentsia betrayed the romantic *Sehnsucht* of the Slavophiles for the idyllic life that the family and the "unadulterated organism"—the commune—admittedly provided and in which respect for the patriarchal *ordo*, with its filial piety, "neighborly love," and "choral singing," reigned supreme.[19] The populist intelligentsia found instead in the village commune a prefabricated *phalanstère* whose members—the people—led a "full and balanced" life devoid of monotony and contradictions. Membership in this *phalanstère* ostensibly provided the people with an ample opportunity to perform diverse tasks and thus acquire mastery of varied occupational skills. Some populist wits thus proclaimed the *muzhik* the most versatile individual on earth.[20] This same village commune was also compared to a *communauté,* since it was cast in the image of social organization based on economic equality, common ownership of land, and collective liability. So thoroughly committed were the people to this collectivistic order and, at the same time, so uncompromisingly did they recoil from the Roman dominium, if not from the "bourgeois order" in general, that any attempt at undermining this order would have required the use of force—the bayonet and the whip, according to Tkachev.[21]

By fashioning the people in the image of the ideas they professed, the populist *intelligenty* rendered indistinct their own vision of the people as "socialists" or "revolutionaries" by nature from the people themselves. Once the duality of the ideal and the real had been obliterated, the cloud-cuckoo land of socialism and/or anarchy acquired a phenomenal presentment at the same time that the people of the hinterland became hallowed into a collective idol. At the height of this adulation, the populist *intelligenty* may be said to have yearned after unity with their own ideal reflection, as they sought to fuse with *narod* patterned after their own sentiments and values. Had they desired instead to assimilate into the rustic world, the cruel predicament of their isolation from the people would have been resolved with relative ease. A propitious step toward "personal union" could have been taken had the populist *intelligenty* poured their love onto individual members of the people. Such individualized response to the object of their attachment would have enabled them to establish contacts based on more enduring personal or familial ties. However, the populists found close association with the people little to their liking; indeed, they preferred the company of their own "enlightened" female consorts dressed like "unenlightened" peasant matrons. The only noticeable advance made by the populist *intelligenty* toward rapprochement with the people was in outward appearance: on their sojourns in the country they took to wearing simple peasant attire. But all such rustic paraphernalia—from sarafans to bast-shoes—served merely as a disguise designed to mislead not only the Tsarist police but also the people whose ranks they sought to join.

No less revealing was the reluctance of the populist intelligentsia to establish "functional ties" with the people. It is true, of course, that some of them tried to master a trade before venturing on the pilgrimage to the people; still others came close to acquiring a profession through formal training. But whatever their skill or training might have been, there could be hardly any doubt that they evinced little desire to serve the people as expert agronomists, physicians, teachers, or other trained specialists, let alone to establish enduring ties with the people on the basis of such professional services. Rather, they heaped scorn on all those men of "microscopic interest" whose prime aim in life was to dispense such "narrow" and "shallow" benefits.[22] Some of them bluntly dismissed academic training as an immoral and criminal diversion unworthy of their attention. Neither is there reason for suggesting that the populists yearned after an "occupational union" with the people and, as a result, rushed into the country to become calloused like other tillers of the soil. For those few who had settled among the people under the guise of itinerant laborers (*batraki*) or artisans ultimately followed the suit of their literary protagonists and vanished from the countryside like a "pack of wolves,"[23] unable to endure any longer the proximity of a "deaf" *muzhik*. So overpowering was their sense of aloneness in the midst of *narod* that one of them justified his *congé* as follows:

> I wanted to speak with the people of my own kind; I wanted to read books since I was becoming completely uncouth ... I longed so much to speak "our language" that on one occasion I addressed an oven and imagined to be talking to my own friends.[24]

It seemed as if the separation from the people was destined to last *in aeternum*: for the closer the populist *intelligenty* came to establishing contacts with the people the more apprehensive they were of being estranged from the people. The exposure to the peasant world all but crushed the fondest dream of unity with the people, making them eventually realize that, despite their peasant attire and calloused hands, they would sooner get drunk than fuse with the people.[25]

What impelled the populist intelligentsia by the hundreds to go to the people was neither dedication to a life of toil nor compassion for the tillers of the soil; so too the vision of unity with the people that they held onto transcended both the external empeasantment and occupational assimilation to the rustic mode of life. Rather, true to their self-image, the populists went to *narod* out of commitment to their own cause—anarchy, socialism, or revolution. Although most of them might have been armed with little more than the "Don-Quixotic sword and the pasteboard cuirass,"[26] there was always inscribed on their fragile armour some kind of a "guiding theory." If they believed, as did the populist *buntari*, that the "people's force" would explode imminently and flood all of Russia, there remained little else to do but to rush to the countryside to organize the people into a revolutionary army. Since very few of the peasant folk volunteered to join the ranks of this army, the populist *buntari* turned to organizing themselves. Some established a foothold on the outskirts of a few villages and, while waiting impatiently for a *Walpurgisnacht*, busied themselves polishing pistols and saddles.[27] If they believed instead, as did Lavrov's "pure" propagandists, that the "tsardom of light" would triumph only after the people had become enlightened and were made conscious of their collective strength, they went to the countryside armed with "little books" rather than pistols. For as Lavrov argued:

> The people alone possess enough strength, enough energy, and enough vigor to make the revolution. But the people are unaware of their own strength, they fail to see any *possibility* of overwhelming their economic and political enemies. It is necessary to enlighten them. And the foremost task ... of the Russian intelligentsia is to awaken them.[28]

Convinced, as they were, that the people must be ideologically mobilized through protracted propaganda, they turned to a "verbal uncorking" of themselves, dispensing "truth" to all who would listen—from sectarian peasants to roving *batraki*. So determined were some of them to enlighten the people that in at least one instance they literally pursued a fleeing *muzhik* shouting to him all kinds of slogans.[29]

But whatever the approach used, it became patently clear that the descent from heaven to earth was far from pleasant. The very attempt to take on the semblance of a poor *muzhik* apeared to be "harmful doctrine," since regardless of how impoverished the peasants themselves might have been, they looked with distrust at destitute individuals. It was also discovered that long beards and bast-shoes did not adorn the whole of rural Russia, indeed, the Ukrainian peasants only became frightened by the sight of bearded *katsapy* (derogatory for Russians).[30] Above all, it became increasingly apparent to the populist *intelligenty* that the contretemps of their exodus to the countryside was ominously similar to that which befell Voltaire's irresistible Pangloss: the peasant closed the door in his face. Neither the tsardom of anarchy nor that of socialism, but the pressing issues of daily life—from the shortage of land and taxation to family welfare and poor harvest—tended to preoccupy the attention of the people. Although this thundering finding was accepted only reluctantly, there is little doubt that by the middle of the 1870s the populist *intelligenty* came to recognize that the *narod* they prayed to and worshipped seemed never to have existed in the natural habitat. Some, looking forward to a brighter future, found their sole consolation in composing verses "From Behind the Bars."

> *Perhaps—what man may tell—my blood shall be*
> *As drops of molten lead, that falling, wake*
> *The people's conscience from its long, deep sleep;*
> *There face to face with me, their own pale ghost*
> *At least that people's conscience understand*
> *What horrors they allow, and yet are dumb.*[31]

Others alleged that the *intelligenty* were themselves to blame, since they loved the people like "dogs and horses" and, in fact, conceived of the object of their affection as an "ignorant" and "immoral beast."[32] Most of the populists, however, found fault with the people: the "civilized" (Tkachev) or "enlightened" (Lavrov, Mikhailovsky) minority—the intelligentsia—faced the peasant masses steeped in torpor, superstition, and savagery. "As long as the people remain unenlightened in the broad sense of the word," wrote one such disenchanted populist, "we can expect from them the most barbarous and despicable acts."[33] The former "revolutionaries by instinct" were now degraded to "revolutionaries *in posse*"[34] and compared to "little savages" who should be treated without "malice or pity."

The populist is one of the most realistic positivists rooted firmly in the positive science and proceeding in his actions from positive facts of knowledge. The phrase "everything for and through the people" is not at all the phrase of former demologists who approached *narod* as a king of some religion. Quite the contrary, our view is similar to that of any dedicated teacher versed in the latest science and, consequently, aware that a child's nature should not be ignored but developed in terms of its capabilities. Considered in this light, we preach neither the hatred of the intelligentsia nor the adulation of *narod's* ignorance, superstition and savagery.[35]

It was not so much the *muzhik's* lack of knowledge or valid information that worried the intelligentsia as the peculiar character of his outlook. The peasant might have continued to believe, of course, that St. George protects the cattle or that the whales support the earth. Although the story about the whales perturbed some populists (Mikhailovsky), they were duly reminded by others that from Moses and Solon onward many a wise man have been equally lacking in valid knowledge. But what tormented the intelligentsia was the fact that the *muzhik's* range of vision was somehow confined to the *hic et nunc*. In his daily round of activities, he tended to fall back on the traditional ways of his ancestors or on some circumscribed and pragmatic considerations. As a result of this failure to respond to whatever went beyond his narrow groove, the *muzhik* was proclaimed a victim of double idiocy: the "primordial," because he was attached, and uncritically so, to the *mores majores* of his forefathers, which hedged him in on every side; and the "functional," because he let himself be absorbed by the pursuit of narrow interests. His actions were governed by such maxims as, "it is the way of former times," "like our fathers and forefathers," "other people act this way," and "this is not our business."[36]

Despite this growing disenchantment with the object of their adoration, the populist *intelligenty* were reluctant to give up hope in the people. None other than the leading populist writer, Uspensky, argued boldly that the initiative displayed by the uprooted Russian peasants in the pogroms of Tartars in Baku and Jews in the Ukraine testified to their emancipation from the "swinish" mode of existence. At home, in Russian villages, the peasants tended to be acquiescent and submissive, whereas in the Ukraine, "among strange people," they were given a unique opportunity to think and act "according to principles."[37] Here they did violence to others not as a "beggarly crew of robbers," but as human beings aware of their individual worth and dignity. Continuing along this curious line of reasoning, Uspensky arrived at a startling conclusion that the pogroms of Jews and Tartars have an "enlightening effect upon the Russians."[38] The illegal populist press used the pogroms of Jews to measure the growth of revolutionary consciousness among the people. In one such article, the readers were reminded that the Jews somehow reproduce all the evils inherent in the social order and that the French Revolution began also with the massacre of Jews.[39] But what incensed the populists, Uspensky's argument notwithstanding, was the fact that the "beastly excitement" of the people was "unprincipled," in that their "crusade" against the "Semites" lacked a "comprehensive outlook" admittedly necessary for a truly enlightened action.[40] Too immersed in the "little world" of the family and the commune, the people were utterly "unconscious" of their "collective existence," let alone of belonging to the "unnoticed guardians" of "brighter future." All "social forms" of their life stemmed from "spontaneous historical development" rather than from carefully thought out convictions and principles.[41] So much was this the case, claimed the populists, that in "Ivan's head" all principles and ideas (including socialism) tended to be translated into his own language of "immediate needs and notions."[42] This particular proclivity of the *muzhik* posed a hovering difficulty of how to relate to the people without betraying cherished principles. The Land and Freedom populists thought they had found a solution: on one hand, they sought through agitation to establish a permanent link with the people and, in so doing, mobilize the people on the basis of their immediate needs and interests; on the other, they hoped through a separate organization—formally structured, disciplined, and centralized—to provide the revolutionary struggle of the people with organizational unity as well as to preserve intact their own "guiding ideals" lest in the *muzhik*'s head they become "adulterated" and "confounded" beyond recognition.[43] This Janus-faced solution premised the establishment of the "vanguard party" bent on maintaining its organizational identity and on keeping alive the "spark of truth and ideal" amidst the peasant masses mired in the traditional mode of life.

One final attempt was made by the Land and Freedom populists to institute a foothold in the countryside in order to organize the "revolutionary forces" among the people "by word and above all by deed."[44] The Chigirin conspiracy, which resulted from this attempt to reach the people, was taken by some Land and Freedom members for a qualified success, as it seemed to have convinced them that it was possible to create a "purely peasant and revolutionary organization" based on "local demands and interests."[45] At the same time, the Chigirin venture, perpetrated, as it was, by means of fake Tsarist manifestoes and other "unacceptable principles," led a growing number of the populists to terminate their activity in the countryside, thereby accelerating the shift from the "agitation by word" to the political struggle (assassination and terror) as the sole weapon of agitation.

The uneasy union of agitation and organization was not destined to last for long, as the factional conflict accompanying this drift away from the people split the Land and Freedom party into two opposing groups—the "agitators" (Black Repartition) and the "organizers" (Will of the People).[46] Clinging desperately to their faith in the people, the Black Repartition populists, in particular their chief spokesman, Plekhanov, continued to reassure themselves that the people would ultimately rise in defense of their interests, narrow and immediate though these interests might be, thereby transforming the whole of rural Russia into a jacquerie. For this reason, Plekhanov considered agitational activity among the people the paramount task of the populist intelligentsia. He argued accordingly that:

> it would be highly regrettable if, by becoming exclusively engrossed in the political struggle, we would permit the peasant revolts to take place without our participation, our guidance and influence. By acting in this way, we would only confirm our isolation from the people—a view so dear to our enemies. The socialist "party" without a basis in, and influence upon, the people is sheer nonsense, a general staff without an army, an illusory value.[47]

On the other hand, the Will of the People populists displayed little patience for "idle talk"—whether that of Lavrov's propagandists or Plekhanov's agitators—and dismissed their activities among the people as "inactivity" and "bourgeois sitting" in the countryside.[48] Unconvinced that the people were fit to articulate their interests by evolving the rustic version of trade union consciousness, let alone to carry on an organized struggle on behalf of these interests, they concluded instead that:

> at present, our peasant represents less than nothing. He is a beast of burden, a kind of ram that exists only in order that a shepherd may eat his meat or make clothing out of his wool and hide. He is a zero.[49]

Rather than follow the futile path of "revolutionary onanism,"[50] as the propagandists and agitators admittedly did, the populist organizers turned to setting up a "revolutionary vanguard" powerful enough to carry on a concerted struggle on behalf of the people. In unison with other populists, they believed themselves to be acting in the name of the people, but they also thought that very little, if anything, could be accomplished by, and/or through, the people. They seemed to have concluded instead that the liberation of the people was to be carried out without ever consulting with the people, that any service to the people (including the seizure of power) ought to be rendered without expressed consent of the people.

> The organization of the peasant forces does not come into our purview, even though the popularization of our party through acts of terror has cleared the way for a direct influence upon the people. We consider it necessary to channel our activity in that direction only to the extent to which it may clarify to the people the true nature of our demands as well as insulate the masses from the reactionary overtures of their enemies in time of insurrection.[51]

The very possibility of establishing a mass organization among the peasants was now dismissed as a harmful dream.[52] True enough, individual peasants, if enlightened, would be able to join the ranks of the vanguard organization, but, in so doing, they would become merely the "agents" of this organization, cooperating "consciously and systematically" with its plan of action.[53] Since this vanguard organization was to constitute an exclusive formation of professional revolutionaries, it was to engage on its own in the struggle for power, without any attempt at organizing a broad social movement based on the peasant masses. Only such a "superior" organization of revolutionaries—strictly centralized, conspiratorial, and elitist—was best prepared to carry on the revolutionary struggle with a "merciless consistency."[54]

Enough has been said to show that among the populist intelligentsia, the *buntari* advanced the most exalted image of the people, so exalted, in fact, that they virtually equated the *narod* of their own caprice with the inhabitants of rural Russia. Not only were the people ready to revolt, they seemed, even more so, innately endowed with the spirit of revolt.[55] Unlike the "educated" socialists from the intelligentsia, the people were also "socialists" by virtue of their "social position," even though they hardly ever heard of the word socialism.[56] In still another sense, the *buntari* came close to obliterating the distinction between themselves and the people of their own caprice and, having done so, they quite logically envisioned the process of fusion as direct and imminent. There remained thus one decisive move to be made by the populist *buntari*—to descend on the countryside and there to merge with the peasant masses molded in the image of collective Stenka Razin. On the opposite end of this populist spectrum were the organizers who had given up all hope of ever seeing themselves and the people joined by one "triumphant idea" and marching arm in arm into the "tsardom of socialism." Rather, they came to share Tkachev's view that the propaganda would bear fruit only after the "revolutionary party had seized political power."[57] They were also unconvinced that the people could be pulled into the revolutionary struggle if continually exposed to the populist agitation. What obsessed the populist organizers was the establishment of the vanguard organization capable of capturing political power on behalf of the people. For it was via power wielded by the vanguard that the populist organizers hoped to gain access to the people and, by mobilizing their latent forces, establish the "despotism of the people"—a form of domination that was to serve as the "direct precursor of socialism."[58]

Finally, standing in the middle between these two populist positions were the propagandists and the agitators. Both of these groups maintained that some contact with the people was imperative and feasible. But whereas the former hoped to achieve a terminal merger with the people by mobilizing them through the propaganda of socialist ideas, the latter sought only to institute a lasting bond with the people by leading them in the struggle on behalf of immediate needs and interests.

The populist encounter with the people dealt a serious blow to the integrity of Russian *pravda*; it became torn apart as never before. The alleged "temple of truth" was found to resemble the "orgy of noisy peddlers" and "unthinking slaves."[59] All attempts at idealizing the people were now denounced by Tkachev as the "most dangerous and widespread illusion,"[60] seemingly unperturbed that only a few years before he had proclaimed the same people "always ready for the revolution."[61] The peasants were relegated collectively to the petty bourgeois class and, like other members of this class, they were found to represent "cannibalistic individualism" emptied of every "social and political principle."[62] The peasant commune (*obshchina*)—the very solidarity of which was to serve Lavrov and his followers for a starting point of social- ist propaganda—came now to represent little more than a "fiscal affair."[63] The peasant himself, this "apostle of toil and endurance," was figuratively proclaimed "dead" and duly dispatched to a final resting place. What had begun on the hopeful note of merger with the people terminated in the frantic confession of isolation from them.

> At present, the people and society have parted company to such an extent that they lead their own separate lives, have their own ideals, aspi- rations, interests, etc., which not only sharply contrast but oftentimes contradict.... The point has been reached at which the people and society fail utterly to understand each other.[64]

From the adventurous *buntari* who dreamt of imminent fusion with the "tsar- dom of anarchy" to the assertive organizers bent on establishing the "despot- ism of the people" prior to the triumph of the "tsardom of socialism," the populist intelligentsia traversed the road to complete estrangement from the object of its attachment.

Once the populist idol—the silent *narod*—was all but forsaken, there remained the desolate altar and the isolated *intelligent*, whom the poet, Nadson, likened to a "crying voice in the desert."[65] What followed was a period of growing confusion and ideological groping among the populist intelligentsia, causing its wavering members to hurl themselves "from one doctrine to another, from one ideal to another ideal."[66] No less disturb- ing than this ideological impasse was the rising tide of "deviant" ideas and perspectives often parading under the guise of populist orthodoxy. One such group of self-styled populists—the so-called genuine populists—dared to attack all other populists, dismissing them en bloc as "demophiles" and "bureaucratic intelligentsia."[67] The leading exponent of this "antipopulist" populism, Kablits, was one of the most perceptive critics of the populist intelligentsia, despite his insistence on orthodoxy. He assumed for the start- ing point of his critique that the prevailing populist movement in Russia, far from being genuine, represented some kind of deviant demophily. The central identifying feature of the followers of demophily was "love of the people" coupled with "complete disrespect" for the individual peasant and his rights.[68] Apart from confounding "love" with "contempt," these demo- philes were determined to dominate the people by forcibly imposing on them their own ideals disguised under such pompous words as "science" and "pro- gress." From Lavrov to Mikhailovsky and Tkachev, the demophiles looked

down on, if not completely ignored, the opinions of the people, thereby fail-
ing to recognize the fact that:

> The worth of any societal form is not so much to be judged on the basis
> of how closely it approximates one or another scientific ideal as in terms
> of its adaptation to the desires of individual human beings who consti-
> tute a given collectivity. The most perfect form will be detrimental to a
> society if it fails to be consonant with the desires of its members, since in
> such a case it can only be maintained by sheer force.[69]

In contrast to the demophiles, Kablits' "genuine" populists argued that
it made little sense to defend the interests of the people without taking into
account their values and opinions. Above all, they warned against undue
meddling in the life of the people as well as any forcible attempt to impose
on the people some set of uniform ideas. Russian society, like every complex society, did not form "one unitary whole devoid of subdivisions"[70]—be
they subdivisions of class, regional, or national character. Unfortunately, the
demophiles seemed to have taken for granted the "all-Russian uniformity"
and, what is worse, concocted for the future a far more thorough uniformity.
The "enlightened Manilov" of the future—the demophile—argued Kablits:

> aspired to subordinate human life to one template; he was bent on
> destroying all kinds of differences.... He could not tolerate between
> himself and another individual any impediment capable of restraining
> his unreasonable impulses, consequently, he undertook, so to speak, to
> pulverize society into isolated individuals.[71]

Much more perilous than the ideological breakdown of populism was the
psychological demobilization of the populist *intelligent* that threatened his
very personality and led to the rise of the so-called balanced and demagnetized type of individuals.[72] These new individuals among the intelligentsia displayed a curious proclivity "to spit at principles" rather than at the
"unprincipled" humanity around them. More so, they seemed to be insolent
enough to transform the very act of spitting into a principle of their own
and ended up embracing "unprincipled" principles. In the populist language,
these demagnetized *intelligenty* were the paragons of *meshchanstvo*, since
they guided their life by such maxims as "gradually, silently and slowly."[73]
Far from being perturbed by the "cursed questions," they only reinforced
the "silent tide" of "small deeds" among the intelligentsia. Once freed of all
ideals, these "triumphant swines" among the intelligentsia raised the "fact of
their swinish outlook to the principle of the universe."[74] They even dared to
join the *zemstvo* institutions as statisticians, doctors, or teachers, satiating the
ranks of *meshchane* whom Lavrov and other populists so much despised.[75]

The spectre of ideological putrefaction compelled the populist intelligentsia to search for a new cause—for some "basic guiding ideas acceptable to

all"[76]—that would replace the fallen *narod* and thereby mend the crumbling
populist edifice. Not unexpectedly, this cause was found in the Marxian
ideology, as a growing number of disconcerted populists gravitated "instinc-
tively" toward the service of the proletariat before turning into "conscious
social democrats."[77] It was now the proletariat rather than the *narod* that
for many of them had come to embody "the ideas of modern life by virtue of
the very conditions of its existence."[78] So smooth was this shift of allegiance
from the *muzhik* to the worker that according to the testimony of at least one
such populist: "we became social democrats in one minute."[79] Among the
many converts from the populist intelligentsia were Akselrod, Aptekman,
Deich, Plekhanov, Potresov, Zasulich, and even Lenin himself—all of whom
found life-long employment in the service to the proletarian cause. These
and other populist converts to Marxism could with good reason claim to be
symbolically "reborn," since they worshipped a new idol (even if this idol was
installed on the emptied populist altar) and went to the people under a new
banner. Psychologically, however, they represented little more than "rejuve-
nated" populists who turned to the "substitute *narod*"—the proletariat—to
reinforce their ideological frame of mind.[80]

The Marxian Phase: From *Narod* to the Proletariat

The spread of Marxism among the intelligentsia proceeded not only at the
expense of, but also in opposition to, the populist ideology. The many doc-
trinal differences between the populist and Marxian intelligentsia have been
extensively explored by both Russian and Western historians. At times, these
differences have been taken too literally and without due regard to the deeply
ingrained propensity of the intelligentsia to fight with the fullest of venom the
nearest neighbor.

The Marxian intelligentsia spared no effort to resolve the old populist
problem of the relationship between the "enlightened few" and the "unenlightened many." True enough, this populist problem became at least
lexically updated: the "conscious fighters" supplanted the "enlightened individuals" and the Marxian proletariat the populist *narod*. Lenin believed,
of course, that the populists, uninitiated as they were in the new science of
society, failed to grasp "the connection between the intelligentsia ... and the
material interests of definite social classes."[81] But it remains to be shown
how much Marxism helped him to understand what was admittedly mis-
understood by the populists. It is sufficient to state here that the Marxian
analysis of the class position of the intelligentsia was on the whole immate-
rial to his view of the relationship between the "conscious fighters" and
the proletarian class. Rather, the populist legacy, which Lenin only too
often disowned, had a decisive influence on the way he posed this problem and even on the character of the solution he provided. So well versed
was Lenin in the populist heritage that in at least one instance he rightly
reminded the Marxian "revisionists"—the economists—that they confused

the "magnificent organization" of the Land and Freedom revolutionists with that of the Will of the People.[82]

The Marxian intelligentsia sought initially to mobilize the working class ideologically via propaganda of socialist ideas. This attempt succeeded only in recruiting individual workers into small circles (*kruzhki*), which remained largely isolated from the masses of workers. Except for the "conscious few" who joined the circles, the workers showed little ideological zeal or desire to serve the cause of "scientific socialism." Like the peasants, they tended to be more concerned with the conditions of daily life than with the abstruse issues of ideology. As Martov confessed:

> In my circle I twice delivered talks on the aims and methods of social-ism, but real life kept on interfering. ... Either the members of the circle would themselves raise the question of some event that had occurred in the factory, ... or someone from another workshop would appear, and we would have to spend the time discussing the conditions there.[83]

To obviate this threat of isolation, the Russian Marxists turned to agita-tion in the hope of forging a lasting bond with the workers on the basis of economic interests ("petty needs and demands") rather than socialist ideas.[84] But the involvement in the "spontaneous struggle" of the workers seemed to pose another danger to the Marxian intelligentsia: it threatened its ideologi-cal identity as well as organizational independence, and led ultimately to the spread of a heresy known as "Economism." In the face of this dilemma, Lenin devised a scheme that claimed to secure for the tribunes the exclusive character of their organization and, at the same time, bind them inseparably to the working class movement.

What, then, was the principal function of the tribunes whom Lenin dis-patched in "all directions" and to "all classes of the population?" To follow him, the tribunes were expected to perform the interrelated roles of expert agitators, propagandists, and organizers. In contrast to the populist agita-tors, the tribunes were not primarily concerned with the "palpable" demands and economic needs of the masses. Agitation (economic exposure) was not allowed to become the "predominant part of their activities" in society.[85] Neither were the tribunes, in the fashion of the Lavrovite propagandists, mainly engaged in indoctrinating the working masses with socialist ideas. Nor were they, like Tkachev's organizers, exclusively preoccupied with the establishment of the "fighting" organization of revolutionists. Rather, the tribunes combined all three populist archetypes. Nowhere else is this more apparent than in the analysis of the relationship between the tribunes and the proletarian masses. Lenin ignored, for example, the cherished belief of the Lavrovites that the *narod* as a whole might be so thoroughly enlightened as to become indistinguishable from the "critically thinking individuals." Even more it was true of the naive expectations of the populist *buntari* that they would be able to assimilate themselves with the peasant masses. He simply ridiculed those who extolled the "mighty fists of hundred fools" and dismissed with contempt the very idea that "any fool can help the spontaneous birth of a new social order."[86] Quite the contrary, Lenin assumed without hesitation, what some populists had discovered to their surprise, the lasting distinction between "consciousness" and "spontaneity," "ideological elements" and "material elements" or, finally, between the "organization of professional revolutionists" and the "pure and simple labor movement."[87] What would henceforth preoccupy the attention of Lenin was not fusion—imminent or terminal—or, as he called it, "organic unity," but the establishment of manifold links between the "conscious few" and the "unconscious many." Three major bonds were to link them together: the economic (via economic interests), the ideological (via socialist ideas), and the political (via organizational power). The economic bond was to provide the basis for the initial rapprochement between the tribunes and the proletarian masses. The establishment of this bond was necessary because, like Plekhanov and the populist agitators, Lenin considered the masses to be most susceptible to "propaganda by facts" closely related to their "daily and palpable interests."[88] The concerted response to such specific demands, evolved in the "drab daily struggle," would lay the ground for the formation of proletarian mass organizations. Such "workers' organizations," claimed Lenin, "must in the first place be trade organizations; second, they must be as wide as possible; and third, they must be as public as conditions will allow."[89] The inclusive membership in these organizations was to make the mass of workers more readily accessible to the control and leadership of the exclusive organization of tribunes. "The wider these organizations are," argued Lenin, "the wider our influence over them will be."[90] From the very outset, however, the scope of tribunes' activity among the masses of organized workers would not be confined to the "economic struggle" alone or reduced to that of trade union leaders representing the workers in relation "to a given group of employers." For the economic mobilization of the masses, while necessary, was to serve only as a "starting point for the awakening of class consciousness" and "for the beginning of class struggle."[91] By its very nature, it imposed a "restricted outlook" on the initiative and energy of tribunes and, as a result, made them prone to succumb to the spontaneous labor movement of the "pure and simple" *Nur-Gewerkschaftlerei.*[92] Such a submission to "elemental forces," that is, bowing to what exists at the present time, stemmed from the "fundamental fallacy" of the economists to keep "at the tail end of the movement."[93] Above all, it was dangerously symptomatic of the "disease" called "subservience to spontaneity," which Lenin assailed in the name of tribunes:

> But the working class Social-Democrat, the working class revolutionist (and their number is growing) will indignantly reject all this talk about fighting for demands "promising palpable results" etc., because he will understand that this is only a variation of the old song about adding a *kopeck* to a *ruble.*[94]

Lenin detected with little difficulty that the solution offered by the economists, aside from representing the acme of opportunist perfection, belittled the role of tribunes as well as impaired the unity of the movement on the "principal question" of tactics. Not only was he opposed to any scheme designed to downgrade the tribunes to mere trade union officials, he also refused to allow the masses to acquiesce in spontaneity and be carried away by the belief that a "*kopeck* added to a *ruble* is worth more than Socialism."[95] Even the compromise solution, akin to that of the populist agitators—whereby the organization of the "enlightened few" would uphold consciousness but would be willing to accommodate to the spontaneity of the "unenlightened many"— seemed to have dissatisifed Lenin. What was necessary, contended Lenin, was to link up the "conscious activity" of the tribunes with the "spontaneous movement" of the masses. Such a link was obviously impossible to institute via the economic struggle alone, which would only culminate in complete subservience (namely, the economists) or, at best, adaptation (namely, the populist agitators) to the spontaneity of the masses.

Such considerations led Lenin to expand the function of tribunes rather than limit it to the economic mobilization of the masses. He called accordingly on the tribunes to imbue the masses with the ideas of socialism and class consciousness and not simply pull them, by slavishly cringing before the "palpableness of concrete results," along the line of least resistance; to subvert the "spontaneity of the masses" by a "mass consciousness" of their own rather than gaze with awe, as the economists admittedly did, on the "posteriors of the Russian proletariat";[96] to mobilize the masses ideologically and thereby make them advance, apart from concrete demands, an increasing number of individuals into the ranks of "conscious fighters." Only when the economic struggle for "palpable results" has been subverted and the narrow outlook characteristic of the labor movement undermined, and only when the workers have become responsive to the socialist cause and not solely to the plight of their children, only then would still another, the ideological bond, "inseparably connect" the tribunes with the masses.

Considered in this light, two discordant roles seemed to have been assigned to the tribunes as well as two incompatible ties that bound them to the masses. On the one hand, the tribunes engaged in the "economic exposure" of factory conditions, mobilized the masses on the basis of their economic interests, and guided them in the "economic war" against the exploiters. Inasmuch as they called the masses to "concrete actions" and fought with them against the exploiters, the tribunes ostensibly catered to "concrete demands" advanced by the masses and to that extent maintained the economic link with the organized labor movement. On the other hand, the tribunes represented the working class not only in "its relation to a given group of employers" but also in "its relation to all classes in modern society" by engaging in the "universal exposure" of the existing social order.[97] To the extent, then, that the tribunes mobilized the proletarian masses ideologically, they sought to subvert their spontaneous struggle on behalf of palpable demands and, by smuggling in the Marxian doctrine, transform it into the ideological struggle of classes. Although logically they might appear incompatible, these two types of relations with the working class were actually complementary. It will be recalled that the "economic exposure" and "economic struggle" served as a *point d'appui* for the spread of socialism and, if properly utilized, as a "beginning and a constituent part of Social Democratic activity."[98] If the tribunes actively participated in the trade union movement, it was because by so doing, they endeavored to secure direct access to the "mighty force of millions and millions of workers 'spontaneously' rising for the struggle."[99] If they supported the "economic war" against the employers and fomented unrest among the workers, it was for the sake of transmuting such "spontaneous conflicts" into a "conscious struggle" of classes.

The ideological mobilization of the workers through the propaganda of socialist ideas—the second major function of the tribunes—was presumably necessary due to the inherent inability of the masses to overcome spontaneity and develop socialist consciousness from within. The lengthy statement of Kautsky to the effect that the "vehicles of science are not the proletariat, but the bourgeois intelligentsia" and that, consequently, modern socialism originated "out of the heads" of the members of this stratum,[100] seemed to have convinced Lenin that the socialist consciousness must be imposed on the proletarian masses from outside. Yet, Kautsky belabored only the evident by his claim that ideas—both socialist and nonsocialist—originate out of the heads of the men of ideas, i.e., the intellectuals. Similarly evident was another assertion of Kautsky that the members of this stratum, being the "vehicles of science" and not magic, openly communicate socialist ideas to other people, counting among them, as he noted, the "more intellectually developed proletarians."[101]

Lenin posed an altogether different problem by his demand that members of the exclusive group monopolize one particular system of ideas (Marxism), elevate their organization to a position of the "vanguard party," and then proceed, first, to pull the masses along the line of least resistance in order to indoctrinate them with the ideas of socialism, and then to pull and mobilize ideologically the masses for the sake of pushing and, in fact, pushing the masses a "hundred times more forcefully."[102] Such professional *pullers*, *indoctrinators*, and *pushers* of the mass of humanity have but little in common with the stratum of the intelligentsia as conceived by Kautsky. The members of the intelligentsia are the "vehicles of science" precisely because as a stratum they occupy an unanchored position in the class structure of society. By virtue of this position they can more readily comprehend collective life from the perspective of a broader intellectual horizon. As he formulated it:

> ... it is that stratum of the population which can most readily transcend classes and the limited perspectives of status groups, which may feel itself idealistically superior to passing and partial interests, and which is

capable of perceiving and representing the long-range needs of the entire society (my translation).[103]

On the other hand, Lenin showed little patience with such men of ideas. He tolerated them no more than he did those "supermen of literature" whom he dismissed with a well-known injunction, "Down with the supermen of literature" and, indeed, promised to reduce them to a "small cog and a small screw in the social-democratic mechanism, one and indivisible—a mechanism set in motion by the entire conscious vanguard of the whole working class."[104] His vision of the social world was too watertight to allow for the existence of the intelligentsia or the intellectual perspective unbound to either the "bourgeois" or the "proletarian" class. With an impudence worthy of the Russian *intelligent*, Lenin announced that

> the only choice is: Either bourgeois or socialist ideology. There is no middle course (for humanity has not created a "third ideology"), and, moreover, in a society torn by class antagonisms there can never be a non-class or above-class ideology.[105]

History might have destined the proletarian masses to regenerate Russia, if not the world at large; nevertheless, the vanguard organization of tribunes treated them as but "material elements" to be pulled from within and pushed on from outside. As a collectivity, the working class constituted little more than the crowd of "mighty fists" forever destined to remain at the disposal of the vanguard party. If this crowd took an "active part in the movement" it was largely in the sense that it advanced "from its ranks" an increasing number of "consistent proletarians." However, in this instance, too, the working masses served as a reservoir of recruits for the organization of tribunes whose distinct identity was to remain unimpaired even after an extensive exposure of the masses to the propaganda of socialism. The organization of tribunes represented the vanguard of the "vast masses of the working class, the whole (or nearly the whole) of which works 'under the control and guidance' of the Party organizations, but which does not and should not, as a whole, join the Party."[106] So determined was Lenin to preserve the exclusive character of this vanguard and so categorically opposed to confusing the organization of tribunes with that of the workers that he not only dismissed any attempt to eradicate the "line of demarcation" between them as "absurd and dangerous," but also branded it as *khvostism* (following in the tail of events) on "questions of organization."[107] Toward this resurgent *khvostism*, Lenin's attitude was equally adamant; in fact, the conflict over it caused a schism in the party, giving rise to organizational opportunists—more commonly known as the Mensheviks.

It will be recalled that the economists had been also implicated in *khvostism*; unlike the Mensheviks, however, they dragged "at the tail" on "principal questions of programme and tactics" by compromising with the "pure and simple" labor movement.[108] As a result of this lapse into the struggle for a *kopeck*, the economists tended to confound the tribunes with trade union leaders and, *pari passu*, conceived of the organization of tribunes as being identical with the trade union organization of workers. So much was this the case, claimed Lenin, that, on questions of organization, they talked "in different tongues" and, indeed, referred to "different things," since what concerned them were "strike funds, mutual aid societies, etc." and hardly a centralized and militant organization of tribunes.[109] To speak of the latter and, at the same time, to put forward "concrete demands," as the economists did, made but little sense, according to Lenin:

> The "economic struggle against the employers and the government" does not in the least require—and therefore such a struggle can never give rise to—an all-Russian centralized organization that will combine, in a general attack, all the numerous manifestations of political opposition, protest and indignation, an organization that will consist of professional revolutionists and be led by the real political leaders of the whole people.[110]

Although the demise of Economism helped to restore "sufficient unity and definiteness" in the party program and tactics, Lenin found this unity to be only a "necessary but far from adequate condition for Party unity and for centralized Party work."[111] To achieve the latter, it was imperative to effect the "unity of organization," sadly wanting in a party "which has grown to be more than a mere family circle."[112]

> The issue is whether our ideological struggle will have forms of a higher type to clothe them, forms of a Party organization obligatory for all, or the forms of the former dispersion and the former circles. We have been dragged back from the higher to the more primitive forms. And this is being justified by the argument that the ideological struggle is a process and forms are merely forms.[113]

This "higher form" of organization was designed to unite under the guidance of a central authority hitherto disconnected circles into a hierarchical and formally structured "party machine." The relations inside and between circles, thus far dependent on "personal friendships and a confidence which had not to be accounted for and for which no reasons had to be given," were to be founded instead on "formal, 'bureaucratically' (from the point of view of the undisciplined intellectual) worded rules."[114] If effectively enforced, these rules would endow the party organization with a "rigid form," making it free of the "willfulness and the caprices" endemic to informally structured circles and "circle scramble methods," known as the free process of "ideological struggle."[115]

To the Menshevik proponents of organizational *khvostism*, argued Lenin, formal rules seemed "irksome," "burdensome," and "degrading," the "higher form" of organization a "monstrous factory," and the "division of labor" a means for "converting men into wheels and screws."[116] In the fashion of all "gentlemanly anarchists," they failed to recognize that the factory, far from being a bogey, represented that "highest form of capitalist cooperation," which brought together and organizationally disciplined the workers, placing them at the head of the "exploited population."[117] Castigating the Menshevik detractors for their "anarchist phrase-mongering," Lenin wrote:

> Let me tell you gentlemen, who are so solicitous about the younger brother, that the proletariat is not afraid of organization and discipline!
>
> The proletariat will not worry about professors and high-school students, who do not want to join an organization....The proletariat is trained for organization by its whole life much more radically than are many puny intellectuals.[118]

With this assertion that the working classes would acquiesce in the discipline imposed by a "higher form" of party organization for the sake of their ultimate liberation, Lenin seemed to have provided a final answer to the "accursed question" of the intelligentsia. What began with the commitment to the idea of "superior" social order, which was to be installed for the benefit of all laboring people, was consummated in the passion for a "superior" form of party organization—one designed to pull the same people from within, mobilize them ideologically, and push them from the outside. This dreadful paradox—that men who claimed to serve the cause of total liberation should have devised a scheme of total domination—is one of the most striking ironies of modern times. Viewed historically, Lenin's vanguard organization represented the most elaborate form of domination—of seizing and maintaining power in society—even though, with respect to its formal structure, it differed but little from the "fighting" or "superior" type of organization as advanced by Tkachev and the Land and Freedom populists, respectively.

Notes

1. *See* the statement of Hugh Seton-Watson in "To Define Populism," *Government and Opposition* 3 (Spring 1968): 140–141.
2. Leopold H. Haimson, *The Russian Marxists and the Origin of Bolshevism* (Cambridge: Harvard University Press, 1955), p. 11; For a literal view of the intelligentsia's attempt to integrate itself with the people, *see* Philip Pomper, *The Russian Revolutionary Intelligentsia* (New York: Thomas Y. Crowell Co., 1970), pp. 101–102.
3. A. N. Potresov, *Etiudy o Russkoi Intelligentsii* (St. Petersburg, 1906), pp. 266–71.
4. N. Oransky, "Narodnyi Vopros: V Nashem Obshchestve i Literature," *Russkoe Bogatstvo* (May 1880), p. 3.
5. P. Lavrov, *Russkoi Sotsialno-Revoliutsionnoi Molodezhi. Po Powodu Broshury: "Zadachi Revoliutsionnoi Propagandy v Rossii"* (London, 1874), p. 20.
6. "Posledniaia Ispoved': Otryvok iz Dramy, "*Narodnaia Volia*, no. 1 (October 1879) in *Literatura Partii "Narodnaia Volia,"* ed. A. V. Iakimova-Dikovskaia et al. (Moscow, 1930), p. 11, henceforth referred to as *Narodnaia Volia.*

7. "Khronika Presledovanii," *Narodnaia Volia*, no. 1 (October 1879), p. 17; *see also* "Posle Kazni 4 Noiabria," *Narodnaia Volia*, no. 4 (December 1880), p. 93.
8. N. Morozov, "Literaturnaia ZlobaDnia," *Otechestvennye Zapiski* (January 1877), p. 47.
9. Quoted in Philip Pomper, *Peter Lavrov and the Russian Revolutionary Movement* (Chicago: Chicago University Press, 1972), p. 178.
10. Oransky, *Russkoe Bogatstvo* (June 1880), p. 2.
11. "Zadachi Partii," *Narodnaia Volia*, no. 2 (November 1879), p. 23.
12. L. Tikhomirov, "Zaprosy Vremia," *Vestnik Narodnoi Voli*, no. 4 (1885), p. 263.
13. P. N. Tkachev, *Izbrannye Sochineniia na Sotsialno-Politicheskie Temy*, ed. B. P. Kozmin (Moscow, 1933), III, p. 91; P. Lavrov, *Narodniki-Propagandisty 1873–1878 Godov* (St. Petersburg, 1907), p. 144.
14. G. Uspensky, *Polnoe Sobranie Sochinenii*, 6th ed. (St. Petersburg, 1908), II, p. 73; *see also* L. Obolensky, "Do Chego Dogovorilsia Gleb Uspensky," *Russkoe Bogatstvo* (July 1883), p. 168.
15. "Nashi Molodye Belletristy," *Mysl* (March 1880), p. 92.
16. "Narodnik v Apartamentakh *Vestnika Evropy*," *Russkoe Bogatstvo* (August 1883), pp. 202–203; L. Obolensky, "O Nashei Filosofii i Narodnichestve," *Russkoe Bogatstvo* (March 1883), pp. 706–23; P. Lavrov, *Istoricheskie Pisma*, 2d ed. (St. Petersburg, 1905), pp. 171–95.
17. N. K. Mikhailovsky, *Sochineniia*, (St. Petersburg, 1896), IV, p. 405.
18. A. I. Koshelev, "Pismo k Redaktoru," *Russkaia Mysl'* (February 1880), p. 66; *see also* K. Leontiev, *Sobranie Sochinenii* (St. Petersburg, 1913), VII, p. 227.
19. "Golos K Zemstvu," *Russkaia Mysl'* (February 1880), pp. 76–78.
20. Uspensky, *Polnoe*, IV, p. 302.
21. Tkachev, *Izbrannye*, III, p. 91; *see also* "Selskaia Obshchina v Olenetskoi Gubernii," *Otechestvennye Zapiski* (February 1874), p. 219.
22. *See* A. Mikhailov, "Obyknovennaia Istoriia," *Russkoe Bogatstvo* (November 1883), pp. 225–43; "Prevrashchenie Moshek i Bukashek v Geroev," *Delo*, no. 2 (1871), p. 2.
23. I. N. Potapenko, "Ne Geroi," *Sochineniia* (St. Petersburg, 1904), V, p. 351.
24. V. Aptekman, *Obshchestvo 'Zemlia i Volia' 70-kh Godov*, 2d ed. (Moscow, 1924), p. 382.
25. Uspensky, *Polnoe*, IV, p. 293.
26. Oransky, *Russkoe Bogatstvo* (June 1880), p. 18.
27. V. Debogorii-Mokrievich, *Vospominaniia* (St. Petersburg, 1906), p. 270.
28. Lavrov, *Narodniki-Propagandisty*, p. 101.
29. V. Kallash, ed., *Protsess 193-kh* (Moscow, 1906), p. 5.
30. Debogorii-Mokrievich, *Vospominaniia*, p. 227.
31. "Po Povodu Kaznei," *Narodnaia Volia*, no. 3 (January 1880), p. 48.
32. Ia. I. Kablits (Iuzov), *Intelligentsiia i Narod v Obshchestvennoi Zhizni Rossii* (St. Petersburg, 1886), p. 40.
33. "Vnutrennoe Obozrenie: Uzhasnye Produkty Krestianskogo Nevezhestva," *Russkoe Bogatstvo* (November 1887), p. 175.
34. Tkachev, *Izbrannye*, III, p. 242.
35. "Narodnik v Apartamentakh," *Russkoe Bogatstvo* (August 1883), p. 197.
36. G. Uspensky, "Iz Putevykh Zametok," *Otechestvennye Zapiski* (May 1883), pp. 258–60; *see also* "Soznatelnaia i Traditsionnaia Obshchestvennost'," *Russkoe Bogatstvo* (March 1883), pp. 731–41; P. Semeniuta, "Iz Vospominanii ob N. I. Zhelabove," *Byloe* (April 1906), p. 210.
37. Uspensky, *Otechestvennye Zapiski* (November 1883), p. 222.
38. Ibid., p. 223.

39. "Po Povodu Evreiskikh Besporiadkov," Prilozhenie k *"Listku Narodnoi Voli,"* no. 1 (1883), p. 200.
40. "Vnutrennoe Obozrenie," *Narodnaia Volia*, no. 6 (October 1881), pp. 136–38.
41. "Programma Ispolnitelnogo Komiteta," *Narodnaia Volia*, no. 3 (January 1880), pp. 49–50.
42. Aptekman, *Obshchestvo*, p. 155.
43. Ibid., pp. 181–98.
44. Quoted in Franco Venturi, *Roots of Revolution*, trans. Francis Haskell (New York: Alfred A. Knopf, 1960), p. 574.
45. Ibid., p. 622; *see also* G. Plekhanov, *Chernyi Peredel*, no. 1 (October 1878), in *Pamiatniki Agitatsionnoi Literatury* (Moscow, 1923), p. 191, henceforth referred to as *Chernyi Peredel.*
46. Vera Figner, *Memoirs of a Revolutionist* (New York: International Publishers, 1927), p. 51.
47. G. Plekhanov, *Chernyi Peredel*, no. 2 (September 1880), p. 189.
48. "Peterburg 8 Dekabria," *Narodnaia Volia*, no. 7 (December 1881), p. 149.
49. "Zadachi Partii," *Narodnaia Volia*, no. 2 (November 1879), p. 23.
50. Tkachev, *Izbrannye*, III, p. 56.
51. "Polozhenie Partii v Dannyi Moment," *Narodnaia Volia*, nos. 8–9 (February 1882), p. 159.
52. "O Zadachakh Deiatelnosti Partii v Narode," *Narodnaia Volia*, no. 10 (September 1884), p. 218.
53. Ibid.
54. *Narodnaia Volia*, nos. 8–9 (February 1882), p. 165.
55. M. A. Bakunin, *Polnoe Sobranie Sochinenii*, ed. A. I. Bakunin (St. Petersburg, 1907), II, p. 260.
56. Lavrov, *Narodniki-Propagandisty*, p. 144.
57. Tkachev, *Izbrannye*, III, p. 226.
58. "Zhelatelnaia Rolia Narodnykh Mas v Revoliutsii," *Narodnaia Volia*, no. 4 (1880), pp. 92–94; *see also Narodnaia Volia*, no. 10 (September 1884), p. 215.
59. L. Obolensky, "Obo Vsem," *Russkoe Bogatstvo* (April 1885), p. 197.
60. Tkachev, *Izbrannye*, I, p. 326.
61. Ibid., Ill, p. 66.
62. P. Akselrod, "Sotsializm i Melkaia Burzhuaziia," *Vestnik Narodnoi Voli*, no. 2 (1883), pp. 204–205.
63. P. Lavrov, "Sotsialnaia Revoliutsiia i Zadachi Nravstvennosti," *Vestnik Narodnoi Voli*, no. 4 (1885), p. 159.
64. "Ocherki Narodnoi Literatury: Narodnaia Deiatelnost' Intelligentsii," *Russkoe Bogatstvo* (July 1892), p. 147.
65. Obolensky, *Russkoe Bogatstvo* (April 1885), p. 199; S. Nadson, *Stikhotvoreniia*, 17th ed. (St. Petersburg, 1899), p. 119.
66. *Narodnaia Volia*, nos. 11–12 (October 1885), p. 239.
67. Kablits (Iuzov), *Intelligentsiia*, p. 39.
68. Ibid., p. 43.
69. Ibid., p. 49.
70. Ibid., p. 107.
71. Ibid., p. 112.
72. *See* N. Nikitin, "Uravnoveshennyia Dushi," *Delo* (March 1877), pp. 100–101; "Geroi Zabyvshii Umeret'," *Vestnik Narodnoi Voli*, no. 4 (1885), pp. 109–20; N. Rubakin, "Razmagnichennyi Intelligent," *Na Slavnom Postu (1860–1900): Literaturnyi Sbornik*, posviashchennyi N. K. Mikhailovskomu (St. Petersburg, 1906), Part 2, pp. 327–40.
73. Nikitin, *Delo* (March 1877), p. 111.

74. "Geroi," *Vestnik Narodnoi Voli*, no. 4 (1885), p. 110.
75. Lavrov, *Istoricheskie*, p. 128; *see also* Ivanov-Razumnik, *Chto Takoe Intelligentsiia?* (Berlin, 1920), p. 13.
76. "Obo Vsem," *Russkoe Bogatstvo* (April 1887), p. 119.
77. Iu. Steklov, "Iz Vospominanii o Sotsial-Demokraticheskom Dvizhenii Sredi Odeskikh Rabochikh v 1893–1894 Godakh," *Minuvshie Gody*, no. 9 (1908), p. 225.
78. P. Akselrod, "Sotsializm i Melkaia Burzhuaziia," *Vestnik Narodnoi Voli*, no. 3 (1884), p. 209.
79. Steklov, "Iz Vospominanii ...," *Minuvshie Gody*, no. 9 (1908), p. 223; for a perceptive analysis of the relationship between populism and Marxism, *see* Richard Pipes, "Russian Marxism and Its Populist Background: The Late Nineteenth Century," *Russian Review*, no. 4 (October 1960), pp. 316–37.
80. More recently, the Marxian *intelligenty* have discovered the "substitute proletariat" among students, blacks and "sections of intellectuals." *See* Alvin W. Gouldner, "Prologue to a Theory of Revolutionary Intellectuals," *Telos*, no. 26 (Winter 1975–76), p. 5.
81. V. I. Lenin, *Sochineniia*, 4th ed. (Leningrad, 1952), II, p. 481.
82. "But the magnificent organization that the revolutionists had in the seventies and which should serve us all as a model, was not formed by the *Narodovolists*, but by the adherents of *Zemlya i Volya*.... And only a gross failure to understand Marxism ... could give rise to the opinion that the rise of a mass movement relieves us of the duty of creating as good an organization of revolutionists as *Zemlya i Volya* had in its time, and even a better one." (V. I. Lenin, *Collected Works*, trans. J. Fineberg (New York: International Publishers, 1929), IV, pp. 208–9.
83. Quoted in J. L. H. Keep, *The Rise of Social Democracy in Russia* (Oxford: Clarendon Press, 1963), p. 46.
84. Anonymous, *Ob Agitatsii, S Poslesloviem P. Akselroda* (Geneva, 1896), p. 17.
85. Lenin, *Collected*, IV, p. 139.
86. Ibid., p. 133.
87. Ibid., p. 185.
88. Ibid., p. 138.
89. Ibid., p. 187.
90. Ibid., p. 189.
91. Ibid., p. 138.
92. Ibid., p. 180; *see also* V. I. Lenin, *Selected Works*, ed. J. Fineberg (New York: International Publishers, 1943), III, p. 121.
93. Lenin, *Collected*, IV, p. 133.
94. Ibid., p. 152.
95. Ibid., p. 120.
96. Ibid., p. 183.
97. Ibid., p. 138.
98. Ibid.
99. Ibid., p. 130.
100. Ibid., p. 122.
101. Ibid.
102. Ibid., p. 197.
103. Karl Kautsky, "Die Intelligenz und die Sozialdemokratie," *Die Neue Zeit* 13, no. 29 (1894–1895): 76.
104. Lenin, *Sochineniia*, X, p. 27.
105. Lenin, *Collected*, IV, p. 123.
106. Lenin, *Selected*, II, p. 360.

107. Lenin, *Collected*, IV, p. 200.
108. Lenin, *Selected*, II, p. 438.
109. Lenin, *Collected*, IV, p. 187.
110. Ibid., p. 176.
111. Lenin, *Selected*, II, p. 437.
112. Ibid.
113. Ibid., pp. 438–39.
114. Ibid., p. 444.
115. Ibid.
116. Ibid., p. 442.
117. Ibid.
118. Ibid., p. 439.

8 Ideologization: The Problem and Its Background

The ideologization of Russian thought and its carriers has been explained by reference to varied sources. It has been traced to Western intellectual influences ("spiritual enslavement" to the West), to political conditions prevalent in Russia, to class composition (plebeian origin) of the intelligentsia, and even to the national character and the "Russian soul."

One of the oldest explanations may be conveniently dubbed the intellectual-ideological one. The proponents of this explanation, many of them people of conservative orientation, blame Western intellectual influences, imported ideas to which the Russian intelligentsia uncritically cleaved at the expense of indigenous values. As a result of this "spiritual enslavement" by the West, the Russian *intelligenty* estranged themselves from the "Russian soil" and thus turned, as one official conservative argued at the beginning of this century, into "outcasts in their own fatherland."[1] As can be readily seen this interpretation contains the concealed assumption that ideas somehow win their way by their own power and that, consequently, they can be grafted on men as sprigs on trees.

The crux of the problem here is why various groups of the Russian men of letters not only embraced different ideas, but also responded differently to the same ideas and their proponents. It is known, for example, that Voltaire and the French *philosophes* were no less read by Catherine's contemporaries than by Belinsky and Pisarev; that Goethe, Schiller, and Byron evoked an eager response not only in Belinsky, but also in Zhukovsky, Pushkin, Lermontov, and the generation of the "remarkable decade"; that Hegel and Feuerbach, Proudhon and Fourier, had among their avid readers not only Chernyshevsky and Dobroliubov, but also Herzen, Granovsky, and Khomiakov. Yet Catherine's contemporaries found in Voltaire and other *philosophes* good arguments for ridiculing on occasions the Russian clergy or office scribes, whereas Belinsky and Pisarev looked at Voltaire as the harbinger of "new dispensation"[2] and the apostle of total negation. Karamzin, Zhukovsky, Turgenev, and other members of the generation of the "remarkable decade" saw in Schiller and Goethe distinguished artists and humanists, or censored the former, as did Karamzin, for turning into heroes those deserving least praise, whereas Belinsky proclaimed Schiller the "emancipator of society from bloody prejudices and traditions," the modern "Tiberius Gracchus"[3] imbued with *Weltverbesserungswahn*.

What is in need of careful consideration here are these divergent modes of response to the same Western intellectuals and their ideas. For it would be highly unrealistic to assume that the Russian men of letters accepted mechanically all the ideas swarming from Paris and Berlin. The ideological development of some of them illustrates clearly that this was far from true. Thus, on reading Hegel, young Chernyshevsky reproached him for the fact that his "thoughts are for the most part ... moderate and devoid of innovations."[4] He, therefore, dismissed Hegel's discussion of *Moralitaet* on the grounds that its author was a "slave of the existing state of affairs, of the existing structure of society."[5] Indeed, all of Hegel's works, according to Chernyshevsky, were marked by "die zarte Schonung des Bestehenden" and Hegel himself was completely unresponsive to the "stormy changes" taking place around him.[6] It may be added that Belinsky's and Pisarev's criticism of Hegel and of philosophy in general was based on similar considerations.

What we witness here is no doubt a response to imported ideas based not so much on their formal and material validity as on the individual predispositions and the amorphous convictions of their recipients. In the absence of an intellectual tradition of critical inquiry, the factor of "personal equation" becomes only too evident. This very fact prompts the student of Russian cultural history to look carefully not only at doctrines but also at their upholders. One may state with certainty that the Russian *intelligenty* possessed incipient convictions and passed through "decisive experience" in the formative period of their lives, which made them prone to accept and/or discard Western ideas and doctrines. Pisarev himself made this point clear, when reflecting on his own personal experience, that these imperceptibly formed values were not derived from a "conscious, reasonable, and fruitful reading of good books," but "collected bit by bit, abstracted from a multitude of varying impressions" and sown in the mind "by all sorts of events in your private life and the life of society."[7] It was only then, Pisarev continued, that a conscious and critical evaluation of authors and books takes place and ideological opponents are classed "in the crowd of writers who are idiots and rascals."[8] So much was this the case, that in their search for evidence that would reinforce their underlying attitudes "developed under the impact of life and not at all through literary study," some enterprising members of the intelligentsia "found it everywhere even where there was none...."

> In defending our populist convictions we borrowed arguments from Lassalle regardless of the fact that Lassalle, as is well known, referred to the workers and not at all to the peasants, whom, in his works and speeches, he plainly considered a reactionary element. But we ignored this essential distinction and transferred everything that Lassalle said about the workers to our peasants ... we substituted workers for peasants,

the Western European bourgeoisie for our privileged stratum and, as "repentant nobles," turned to self-accusation.[9]

This differential response to and selectivity of ideas casts doubts on the view of those who blame Western intellectual influences ("systematic Germanization" of Russia) for the ideologization of Russian thought and its carriers—the intelligentsia. Furthermore, such a view of ideologization ignores the problem of why the Russian *intelligenty* embraced these Western ideas "po russki" (in the Russian manner), that is, with their whole beings. It is this zealous and combative commitment to ideas—the "fanaticized consciousness" of the intelligentsia—rather than the substantive content of these ideas that is of crucial significance here. There seems to be no necessary connection between a specific set of social theories and ideas and definite behavior patterns and psychological attitudes. The fact is that similar theories may lead to different consequences—actions and attitudes—and, conversely, similar actions and attitudes may follow from different theories. Patterns of ideological domination over human beings, of coercion and terror on behalf of ideas, may be evolved not only by apostles of "reactionary" or "evil" ideas, but also by apostles of "progressive" or "noble" ideas and even by the "children of God." A belated recognition of this fact among the Soviet intelligentsia may be glimpsed from these reflections of Eugenia Ginzburg:

> As I lay awake in my plank bed, the most unorthodox thoughts passed through my mind—about how thin the line is between high principles and blinkered intolerance, and also how relative are all human systems and ideologies and how absolute the tortures which human beings inflict on one another.[10]

The second interpretation, widely held among Russian and Western authors alike, relates the ideologization of intellectual life to political conditions. The extreme proponents of this view, many of them people of radical persuasion, blame the autocratic regime—with its censorship and the Third Section, with its opposition to every autonomous social and cultural activity, and with its suppression of freedom of speech—for everything that happened in nineteenth-century Russia. At its best, it amounts to the general observation that the radical movement in Russia was an "indigenous, authoritarian response to the environment of the Tsarist absolutism which nurtured it."[11] In other words, as the same author added, "Autocracy generates its own authoritarian antibodies and endows them with its own peculiar contours."[12] Herzen most likely had the same thing in mind when he wrote over one hundred years ago that

> in every opposition which openly fights the government there is always something from the latter's character, but in a reverse sense. And I think that there is some grain of justice in this fear that the Russian government

begins to display toward communism: *communism is the Russian autocracy turned upside down.*[13]

We should be on very slippery ground, however, if we accused the Tsarist regime entirely for all the moral and intellectual aberrations among the intelligentsia. It is not our purpose to rectify the injustice brought on the Russian autocracy or, worse, to serve as belated apologists for it. But to blame the Tsarist absolutism for the fact that the Russian *intelligenty* came to live in an atmosphere of negation, that they transformed various *isms* into dogmas seeking realization in collective life, that they evolved an unprecedented disdain of disinterested intellectual pursuits, thus preparing the ground for their own subjection, that they were determined to purify themselves of "all personal affection" and to sacrifice "not only their lives, their future, their position, but their very souls"[14] to one grand idea or cause and that they expounded a conception of man bent on sacrificing "ten thousand heads" for the "good of humanity"—such a view would seem oversimplified and, in the final analysis, unjust.

It is, of course, possible, by selecting appropriate historical evidence, to depict exaggeratedly the ruthlessness of the Tsarist autocracy and the arbitrariness of its censorship and thought control. Yet a careful scrutiny of government repression and of the vicissitudes of censorship, even during the so-called pre-historic period, reveals a series of mitigating facts. First, the Tsarist censorship, unlike the Soviet one, was on the whole negative. Its principal task was to prevent authors from expressing and discussing openly certain ideas rather than to force them to say things they did not believe.[15] Significantly enough, the Russian men of letters said almost everything they were bent on saying. Second, Russian censorship was neither administratively nor ideologically comprehensive in scope and, as a result, allowed for a considerable measure of intellectual expression. Finally, the policy of the government with regard to literature and intellectual life in general was basically defensive. The annals of Russian censorship present in many ways a grotesque mixture of tragedy and comedy. The very arbitrariness of the censorship does not suggest efficacity so much as capriciousness of individual censors. When one censor decided to change the statement, "I am going to Russia; people say the climate there is colder than here" to "I am going to Russia; all the people there are honest"; when another one could not tolerate the phrase "naked truth," for, as he reasoned, "truth is feminine (in Russian) and it does not behoove her to appear naked in public";[16] when Krassovsky, another of the censors whose verdicts are classic, deleted the passage in which the writer referred to the heavenly smile of his lady, adding that "a woman is unworthy of having her smile called heavenly";[17] or when he could not put up with the line, "One of thy tender glances is dearer to me than the attention of the whole universe" on the ground that "there are in the universe tsars and legitimate authorities whose attention we must rightly prize"[18]—this pointed not so much to a uniform and comprehensive policy of thought control as to the capriciousness and naiveté of individual censors. When the Soviet censor, almost one hundred years later, opposed the expression "weak (waterish) Soviet tea" because tea is either "weak" or "Soviet" and that it is impermissible that it be both "weak" and "Soviet,"[19] this decision can be assumed to result from the idiosyncracies of the individual censor rather than from the watertight system of Soviet thought control, at that time (1921) hardly existent.

Without denying that the Tsarist censorship was annoying and frustrating, it certainly did not succeed, as the late Professor Karpovich pointed out, "in stifling independent creative activity or in preventing the growth of the critical spirit."[20] This observation is even more applicable to the second half of the last century, during which censorship held little danger for the artistic and scientific literature. Yet—and this is the salient point—it was not the generation of the "remarkable decade" that so generously provided the "new men," but the generation of the 1860s, whose members had scarcely experienced the oppressive policy of Nicholas I and had begun their careers with the accession to the throne of the Tsar-Liberator, Alexander II.

The authors who hold the Russian autocracy responsible for the ideologization of the intelligentsia brush aside the fact that it was postreform, liberalized Russia that furnished such a fertile soil for the "new men." Moreover, they also leave unexplained a serious rift that divided the members of the generation of the "remarkable decade" from the "spiteful sons" of the 1860s. To blame the autocratic regime for this breakdown in the continuity of generations is hardly enlightening, let alone convincing. As we see it, the Tsarist regime and its cultural policy may be considered as at best a precipitating cause of the ideologization of the intelligentsia. By its use of administrative decrees and force in fighting "dangerous" ideas, by its attempt to ban such terms as "progress" and "republic" from the public usage, it helped only to reinforce the fanaticism of its detractors, and to endow their convictions with the halo of "truth" and "justice." That is why, among other things, some of them welcomed the Tsarist persecution, calling on the authorities for more of the same:

> More exiles, more arrests!—irritate and strengthen the dissatisfaction of the public opinion, make the members of the revolutionary party be constantly on the alert, but do not forget that all these measures will only bring nearer the day of revolution and that the greater the oppression the more ruthless will be the vengeance.[21]

A third popular view accounts for the ideologization of the intelligentsia by reference to a shifting class base of its members. Mikhailovsky was one of the first to expound this view when he replied to a self-addressed query: "What happened?—The *raznochinets* arrived. That is all that happened."[22] Lenin assimilated the populist concept of *raznochintsy* to his class periodization of the ideological movement in Russia. It amounted, in effect, to the threefold division: (a) the period of the gentry, from 1825 to 1861, during which the movement was dominated by individuals of gentry origin; (b) the period of *raznochintsy*, characterized by the advent to dominance of individuals drawn from the nongentry strata; and (c) the proletarian period preempted by the workers and their "conscious" representatives. Convinced, as Lenin was, that the formation of ideological trends and political parties in Russia "offers the most brilliant support of the Marxist theory," he saw clearly "three genera-tions, three classes acting in the Russian Revolution."[23]

A look at both Western and Russian literature reveals that this "class" approach to the intelligentsia, with some minor modifications, is rather widely accepted. Its measure of validity will be assessed in the analysis that follows. To begin with, we present again the data on the social background of the members of the military and religious elites, the professional, schol-arly, and literary groups, born between 1800 and 1849. By comparing them with those of the second half of the eighteenth century, we should be able to estimate the overall changes wrought in the social character of the Russian cultural elite during the last century.

Several observations having an important bearing on our problem can be advanced on the basis of the data offered in Table 8.1. In the first place, the social composition of the military and religious elites hardly changed at all. The military and religious hierarchies continued to be appropriated by the gentry and the clergy, respectively. Of significance, however, are the changes in the cultural sphere, in the social composition of literary and scholarly groups. They disclose, among other things, that the individuals of gentry origin turned increasingly to scholarly and professional occupations. Indeed, there can be little doubt that by the 1880s the gentry's share in these occupa-tions was nearly equal to that of the clergy. This very readiness to embark on scholarly and professional careers points clearly to the underlying shift in the value orientation of the gentry. It is sufficient to recall that throughout the eighteenth century and the early decades of the nineteenth, scholarly and professional pursuits were regarded as demeaning to the gentry.

Two main trends are manifest here: the "aristocratization" of the scholars and professionals and the "democratization" (albeit less pronounced) of the men of letters. Despite the fact that the individuals of gentry origin remained numerically dominant among the literati (67.6 percent), there is no denying that the influx of commoners affected considerably the social character of the literary community. There are, therefore, some reasons to argue that this change in the social composition of the men of letters was in part reflected in the conflict of generations. But to concede so much is not to suggest that the infusion of plebeian blood in the literary community taken per se is sufficient for explaining the rise of "new men" among its members. To be consistent, any advocate of this view would have to conclude that the Russian scholars should have provided such "new men" as early as the end of the eighteenth century. On the contrary, as is well known, the Russian scholars—recruited as they were from the clergy and other non-gentry estates—furnished the

Table 8.1 Social Origin of Cultural, Military, and Religious Elites, Born 1800–1849*

Social and occupational status of father	Literati		Artists		Scholars		Doctors		Religious Elite		Military Elite	
	No.	%	No.	%	No.	%	No.	%	No.	%	No.	%
Nobility	117	67.6	14	12.8	46	22.5	51	22.5	4	5.8	291	92.1
Minor officials & Military	2	1.2	8	7.3	17	8.6	14	6.2	1	1.5	6	1.9
Clergy	22	12.7	5	4.6	59	29.8	95	41.9	64	92.8	1	.3
Burghers & Merchants	12	6.9	27	24.8	19	9.6	31	13.7	–	–	2	.6
Professionals	10	5.8	20	18.4	22	11.1	16	7.1	–	–	10	3.2
Peasants	10	5.8	22	20.2	3	1.5	5	2.2	–	–	–	–
Foreigners	–	–	13	11.9	32	16.2	15	6.6	–	–	6	1.9
Total	173		109		198		227		69		316	

* Source: See Table 2.2.

Table 8.2 Social Origin of Members of Four Revolutionary Groups: Nechaevtsy, Trial of 193, Trial of 50, Trial of 21*

Social and occupational status of father	Nechaevtsy		Trial of 193		Trial of 50 Trial of 21	
	No.	%	No.	%	No.	%
Nobility	39	37.1	80	44.4	24	35.8
Officials & Military	21	20.0	17	9.4	11	16.4
Clergy	17	16.2	32	17.8	9	13.4
Merchants	11	10.5	7	3.9	–	–
Burghers (Meshchane)	12	11.4	27	15.0	14	20.9
Peasants	5	4.8	17	9.4	9	13.4
Total	105		180		67	

*Source: B. P. Kuzmin (ed.), *Nechaev i Nechaevtsy: Sbornik Materialov—Tsentrarkhiv—Politicheskie Protessy 60–80 Godov* (Moscow, 1931); V. Kallash (ed.), *Protsess 193-kh* (Moscow, 1931); B. B. Glinsky, *Revoliutsionnyi Period Russkoi Istorii (1861–1881 g.g.)* (St. Petersburg, 1913), II, 88–92; *Golos Minuvshago*, No. 7 (1914).

autocracy with obedient servants and official conservatives, whereas the gentry-recruited men of letters became its first critics. Underlying this view is the unwarranted assumption that the so-called *raznochintsy* had a monopoly on radicalism. Yet a look at the social make-up of the several ideological groups whose members—modeling themselves in the image of fictional heroes (all those Lopukhovs, Rakhmetovs, Bazarovs, and Insarovs)—formed the first revolutionary coteries (Nechaevtsy, 1869) and went to *narod* in the 1870s, discloses the shallowness of this explanation.

If anything, the data presented in Table 8.2 clearly show that the gentry, numerically one of the smallest groups in Russian society, contributed the largest contingent to the ideological movement during the reign of

Alexander II. That is why one prerevolutionary author, himself a participant in the populist exodus to *narod*, claimed that the initiative of the populist movement belonged to the gentry and that the commoners were but joiners.[24]

These and other considerations cast a serious doubt on the putative connection between the ideologization and the class character—plebeian background—of the intelligentsia. An alternative view advanced here relates instead the rise of "new men" among the intelligentsia to social dislocation, with the accompanying loss of a durable network of social ties and attachments, and regards their alienation as a consequence of ideological response to this condition of existence. Stated thus, it goes beyond class origin, which is liable to divergent interpretations and, indeed, allows one to attribute an equal weight to the gentry and the *raznochintsy* alike. What remains to be considered are the factors conducive to the supply of individuals set outside the established order and its circumscribed network of relations.

Social Structure and Cultural Life

Any serious analysis of this complex problem must give due weight to the social and economic transformation that attended the reforms of Alexander II. The import of these reforms on the social and economic spheres of life has been duly recognized by many authors. They have often been compared to the reforms of Peter the Great. "The emancipation of serfs and other reforms of the sixties marked the watershed between the old and the nineteenth-century Russia, much as the reign of Peter the Great marked that between the old Muscovy and the New Russia."[25] Interestingly enough, the effect of this transformation on cultural life, on the literary community, has been traditionally played down.

As a preliminary to such an evaluation, it is necessary to spell out in general terms some of the salient features of the pre-reform Russia. Of immediate interest here is the urban segment—the center of artistic and intellectual life. Thus, by the early 1840s, Russia had 4,727,619 urban inhabitants—50.15 percent of them were burghers (*meshchane*), 4.5 merchants, 5.5 gentry and officials, 0.15 so-called honorary citizens, and 1.4 clergy; the remaining 38.5 belonged to the category of people of "various ranks" (*raznochintsy*).[26] As might have been expected, the bulk of the urban population was made up of burghers. Yet this percentage (50.15) is utterly misleading. For what one encounters here is the inverse relationship between the proportion of burghers and the size of a city. No more than 9 percent of the Petersburg district were burghers; in Moscow they made up 21 percent, whereas in other towns and cities their percentage ranged from 66 to 91.[27] The overwhelming majority of those cities in which burghers formed a dominant group were small towns—some 568 of them out of the total number of 700 had a population of 10,000 or less.[28] This concentration of burghers on the periphery of urban life sheds light on the social character of the Russian cities as well as on the occupational composition of their inhabitants. One

English observer found as late as 1870 that most of the Russian towns "were but little villages in disguise."[29] As regards burghers, his impression was that the majority of them "have come from the country and have brought their country homes with them."[30] That is why there was no room for such burghers in Petersburg, at that time the largest city in Russia.

The category of the Russian bourgeoisie in turn—all the merchants and tradesmen—comprised only 4.5 percent of the urban population. An overriding characteristic of the Russian merchant class, like that of the peasantry, was its traditionalism. By its outlook and way of life it was "more tradition-minded than the bureaucracy or the aristocracy."[31] Even on the eve of the great reforms, the Russian merchants still betrayed such qualities of their Muscovite forebears as "immobility, lack of initiative, unwillingness to go beyond traditional practices, fear of innovation," and a peculiar penchant for secrecy.[32] Socially and culturally they were largely isolated from other urban groups.

> The merchant family lived in complete retirement and isolation. Social calls were frowned upon, and the entertaining of friends was considered a sign of flighty, lazy wastefulness. The merchants shunned public entertainments as well. He disliked the opera because, as one of them explained, the music prevented him from understanding the words. He avoided ballet performances because he considered the "gyrations" of ballerinas an unsuitable spectacle for the female members of his family. He got up at dawn when the residents of the aristocratic western section of Moscow on the other side of the river were still soundly sleeping, and went to bed when the evening in the western sector had hardly begun.[33]

Cut off from the nobility by the barriers of legal status and style of life, the Russian merchants at the same time were loath to associate on an informal footing with other urban residents, and formed a world apart in an urban environment.

To return again to the social composition of the two largest cities and two cultural centers—Petersburg and Moscow—the dominant category of their residents consisted of "men of various ranks." Who were these *raznochintsy* that belonged neither to the gentry nor to burghers and merchants? According to Ditiatin, they were artisans, laborers, carriers, coachmen, and other servants.[34] Despite this seeming differentiation, the bulk of them may be safely relegated to the status group of household servants attached to high officials and the nobility in the two capitals. The nonserving nobility, however, formed an "extraterritorial" group, moving in the spring with their own enserfed musicians, actors, artisans, maids, and porters to the country estates and returning back in the late fall.

Russian urban structure reflected in a miniature form the structure of the society as a whole. At its bottom there was a mass of submerged humanity of village and town peasants—bound legally and economically to their masters—the serving and nonserving nobility at the top. During the 1830s and 1840s, almost half of the population of Moscow and Petersburg was made up of "household servants and peasants" and close to 75 percent of them were enserfed.[35] There was an empty space, to speak metaphorically, in this social order founded on service and bondage, a social vacuum that the tiny, socially marginal stratum of the Russian bourgeoisie never filled. Culturally, it never passed through a process of Westernization analogous to that of the Russian nobility. It was never captivated by Western culture in the form of literature and science and never questioned its submerged position in society, but followed the road of an easy adjustment to prevailing social and political conditions.

What, then, was the place of the intellectual community, more specifically, of its literary segment in the two capitals of Russia? As has been repeatedly emphasized, it was the manor house, the aristocratic salon, that formed the principal ambit within which the intellectual life unfolded, the latest European ideas were voiced, and critical thought asserted itself. Obviously, the very survival of this institution depended on the existence of the privileged group of nobility. It cannot be said, therefore, that Russian letters and art found their most favorable channel in urban intercourse of "towered cities ... and the busy hum of men."[36] Whereas urban centers in the West provided the middle class milieu in which literature and science developed and from which many men of letters came, a fact that prompted Goethe to argue that the middle classes are more favorable to talent, the cities in Russia were preeminently administrative centers. Although urbanization in the West laid a ground for the rapprochement of different social strata and the formation of a *tiers état*, the Westernization of Muscovy by Peter the Great, the administrative urbanization of Catherine II led ultimately, as Bendix rightly noted, to the "intensification of class differences."[37] Instead of a "busy hum of men" related by multiple ties, corporate and civic interests, the Russian cities presented a spectacle of semi-closed social strata, insulated from each other and held together internally by kindred and other particularistic bonds. "All the Muscovites," observed Chicherin of pre-reform Moscow, "lived within familial circles ... enjoyed life and worried little about the future."[38] The Russian cities lacked an impersonal civil milieu, a social "melting pot," to which refined gentlemen (Zhukovsky, Pushkin, Lermontov) would descend, and enlightened commoners ascend. The conflict between the members of the generation of the "remarkable decade" and the first *intelligenty* partially expressed on psychological and ideological levels this polarized structure of the Russian society—the conflict between the gentlemen recruited from the privileged estate of nobility on the one extreme, and enlightened commoners from the mass of humanity on the other.

What was the impact of reforms on this social edifice? Briefly stated, the reforms led to the transformation of a relatively stationary and semi-closed estate order into an open and increasingly differentiated class system. The very change in the legal status of some fifty million inhabitants of European

Russian introduced a dynamic element into the social structure. It let loose forces hitherto dormant and lent new impetus to social change and mobility. It undermined the economic security of the gentry estate and brought about the *Verlumpung* of many of its members by depriving them of the exclusive privilege to own serfs. Finally, as a corollary, it was this crumbling estate order that came increasingly to provide individuals for the déclassé intelligentsia—a social formation pertaining to all estates and to no class. The magnitude of social transformation ushered in by the reform may well be illustrated by the accelerated growth of urban populations. As has been noted by many authors, the urban population relative to the population as a whole remained stable in Russia throughout the eighteenth century (3 percent in 1724 and 3.1 percent in 1784).[39] As late as the middle of the nineteenth century, it did not exceed 6 percent of the total population. From the 1860s onward, the urban population began to increase constantly and disproportionately. Between 1863 and 1897, the total population of Russia increased by 53.3 percent, whereas the population living in cities and towns grew by 97 percent.[40]

Of particular importance in this context was the adverse effect of reforms on the estate of the nobility, which undermined the foundation of its traditional style of life. The break-up of a household economy based largely on villein service called for an economic readjustment that many a Russian landlord was incapable of doing. After having spent the cash compensations in a manner of former traditions, which entailed a costly and extravagant style of life, the landlords were left with some land, but with no labor force to cultivate it. "As they did not know how to work," to cite Tikhomirov, "they sold their estates in all directions."[41] Added to this was the fact that the bulk of the Russian landowners were poor and that the liberation of the serfs only aggravated their economic plight. About 41,000 landowners out of a total number of 100,247 possessed less than twenty-one male serfs in 1861—that is to say, found themselves in strained economic circumstances.[42] Within a short span of time, the deserted gentry houses and estates became a familiar sight of the Russian countryside. Some of their owners lived off the rent, others entered service, swelling the ranks of officialdom, or turned to other occupational pursuits. On the other hand, the aristocratic section of the city of Moscow, with its salons and night life, fell into oblivion within one decade. That is how Kropotkin described it on his visit to Moscow in 1871.

> The rich serf-owners, who once were so prominent here, had gone. After having spent in a reckless way the redemption money which they had received at the emancipation of the serfs, and after having mortgaged and remortgaged their estates in the new land banks which preyed upon their helplessness, they had withdrawn at last to the country or to provincial towns, there to sink into oblivion. Their houses have been taken by "the intruders"—rich merchants, railway builders, and the like—while in nearly every one of the old families which remained in the Old Equerries'

Quarter a young life struggled to assert its rights upon the ruins of the old one.[43]

Youth and Ideological Groups

The reforms of Alexander II and the accompanying change generated by them called for a readjustment to the emergent order marked by a growing differentiation of its institutional and occupational structure. It can be safely asserted that one of the symptoms of this readjustment was the "parent-children" conflict, which testified to the increased differentiation between the generations. Judged by its scope, the conflict was comprehensive enough to extend over the broad range of attitudes and behavior patterns—from symbolic acts of rebellion (external appearance, dress) and a clamor for independence from all parental authority, often coupled with an intense hatred of one or both parents (Nozhin, Perovskaia, Volkenstein), to a generalized rejection of the parental generation (as reflected in the proposal to eliminate each and every person over thirty) and of the personal life associated with it. This latter kind of response, with its accompanying sense of estrangement, may be seen from Uspensky's biographical reflections, in which he renounced his own past till the age of twenty:

> All my personal life, the circumstances of my life till the age of twenty, condemned my mind to a total blackout, complete ruin, profound savagery of values.... For this reason, when 1861 came, there was nothing in my personal past worthy of being taken with me on the "long journey of life"; on the contrary, in order to live somehow it was incumbent upon me to forget that past to the last drop and to destroy all its qualities instilled in me.... It was necessary to spend years attending many a funeral of all those people among whom I had grown up and who faded from this world without a murmur.... The very atmosphere of acquiescence that prevailed among those dying people, a deep awareness on my part that everything they stood and lived for represented a falsehood and a lie, and, finally, their helplessness—all this convinced the people of my age and conditions of life that it is neither possible nor desirable to retain from that past even the slightest reminiscence.[44]

The very magnitude of this conflict presents a spectacle hitherto unprecedented on the Russian social scene and prompts one to look carefully at some of its manifestations. First, it poses the problem as to why the revolting sons were so much impressed by the first "Petersburg Daniels"—Belinsky, Chernyshevsky, Dobroliubov—that they transformed them ultimately into consciously recognized models. It is as if they passed through similar experience, perceived the world in a similar manner and, consequently, found a psychological and ideological affinity between themselves and their teachers. Second, a careful scrutiny of evidence bearing on the age of Russian

Table 8.3   Median Age of Nechaevtsy

Social Origin	Number	Median Age
Nobility	39	23
Officials & Military	21	21
Clergy	17	23
Merchants	11	23
Burghers (Meshchane)	12	23
Peasants	5	22

Source: See Table 8.2

historical Lopukhovs and Insarovs leaves no room for doubt that they were recruited almost exclusively from the school-going youth and formed age-homogeneous groupings (see Table 8.3). So transparent, indeed, was this "spiritual paedocracy" to many Russian contemporaries that it led them to use the word *intelligenty* as a synonym for students. Sociologically, however, they were something more than mere age-peer groups, friendship circles similar to those of the generation of the "remarkable decade." They were pre-eminently the formations of "holy unions"—ideological groups—whose internal solidarity and mutual relations were based neither on personal, diffuse ties characteristic of particularistic groupings, nor on the impersonal, specific ones of the functional collectivities. One of the most striking features of those groups was their vehement opposition to any display of personal affective attachments among their members. Ideally, they were expected to forsake willingly all familial and personal ties on behalf of such central symbols as socialism, revolution, *narod*, or proletariat. The few individuals who tended to form personal attachments within and without them were suspected and, indeed, found themselves standing apart from the rest of the members. They belonged to the category of those to whom ideological groups could not become "country, family, everything."[45] One such member in the Land and Freedom organization was characterized as follows:

> Many features of his character were the cause of it, his sarcastic and sometimes haughty bearing.... But the main reason, it seems to me, was the fact that Alexander Ivanovich underestimated the moral qualities of those he was in contact with and this was felt instinctively by others. He loved some, but *not all*; valued some, but not all. In the meantime, if I am correct, all of us in our friendly relations did not *individualize*—for us the knowledge that one is a man totally committed to the revolutionary cause and is ever ready to offer for it his liberty and life—evoked love to him, created a certain emotional nimbus around him.[46]

Continuing this theme, the same writer deemed it necessary to add that "between him and other distinguished revolutionists there did not exist close relations...he could not fuse with them and did not admit of *full revolutionary intimacy*."[47]

A mere glance at such expressions as "individualize" and "full revolutionary intimacy" points to the unique type of relationship that was supposed to exist among the members of those groups. Basically, they all related to that particular individual's failure to make his attachment to other members transferable and universalistic. Yet love and close friendly relationships entail individualization; they presuppose that an attachment be particularized. In the Land and Freedom organization, however, this same differential response and the accompanying tendency to individualize undermined "full revolutionary intimacy" and also precluded the establishment of close friendly relations. May it not be that the so-called revolutionary intimacy has nothing in common with the intimate interpersonal relationship between friends or between husband and wife? That this is the case can be gauged by the attitude toward those few individuals who, like one of them, "loved women and was loved in turn,"[48] or like another who "loved all the passions and charms of life" and followed the dictum: "life was given to us in order to live it."[49] Significantly enough, these few individuals of "unusual spiritual physiognomy" were singled out because their relationship to "women-revolutionists was completely different from other friends."[50] Whereas most of the members displayed "simple friendship," these exceptional ones "dispersed sparkles, followed and pursued, attempted to satisfy whims, evoked caprices and laughter."[51] To put it succinctly, their uniqueness lay in the fact that they responded to individual women, that they introduced spontaneity and permitted personal feelings to enter into the relationship. Because of this, they were scarcely desirable individuals in those circles. "One such man can be in our party, two is still possible to retain, but three of them is impossible."[52] Even the Chaikovsky circle, which was admittedly based on "friendly relationships full of mutual trust and respect,"[53] deemed it proper to expel one member for falling in love with a young lady of no radical bent and another one for associating with "unprincipled" youths.[54] It is far from paradoxical, therefore, that the exemplary type of individual who best fitted those "close" and "friendly" relations was a young man who was cold and indifferent to the people surrounding him and burned only with "social passion," who "had no family and whom love did not disturb,"[55] or a young woman who did not have the "slightest trace of the desire which almost every woman had of displaying her beauty" and was "incapable of the spontaneous friendship of young and inexperienced minds."[56] Such a young woman had no "special friends" because she "distributed her attachments more equitably and, consequently, more uniformly."[57] Indeed, they were expected to forget "all ties of kinship and all personal sympathies, love and friendship,"[58] to be emptied of all affective dispositions toward other human beings and of all personal needs and inclinations. It is for this reason that some obervers were struck by the very slight account they took of "personal interests connected with their profession, their future, and even of the pleasures which are said to grace the morning of life."[59]

One encounters here an extremely significant phenomenon: the terms *intimacy* and *close* and *friendly* relations connote complete lack of personal intimacy, or personal and affective attachments. More than that, the same intimate and friendly relationships demand that their subjects be deprived of all "romanticisms, all sensitivity and enthusiasms," that they be inimical to all private considerations, "personal hatred," that they refuse to allow themselves to be guided by personal impulses, that they obliterate "all the soft and tender affections arising from kinship, friendship, and love,"[60] so much so that the members of the same "fraternal groups" should have "no personal inclinations, no business affairs, no emotions, no attachments, no property, and no name."[61]

Formulated in general terms, ideological groups require, first of all, that their members divest themselves of all personal ties and attachments. More specifically, they demand that their members obliterate completely the sphere of privacy and lay bare all their innermost feelings and desires. This is achieved through the revolutionary intimacy that makes it possible to control "every little weakness, every lack of devotion to the cause."[62] One of the leading members of the Will of the People organization left this injunction in his testament:

> I enjoin you, brothers, to keep guard over each other in every practical activity, in all the small concerns of everyday life. It is necessary that this guarding should enter into the conscience and thus turn itself into a principle, that it should cease to seem offensive, that personal considerations should be silenced before the demands of reason. It is necessary for all the closest friends to know how a man lives, what he wears, how he takes notes and what kind of notes he takes, how careful, observant, and resourceful he is—in this is our power, in this is the perfection of the activities of our organization.[63]

It is not surprising, then, that ideological groups preclude any manifestation of personal sentiment, any display of genuine intimacy and affectivity. These are most likely to thrive in the sphere of privacy. Indeed, the more intense the "revolutionary intimacy" between the members of ideological groups, the less likelihood there is that personal sentiments of liking or disliking will appear. The personal intimacy is thus inversely related to the ideological one, that is, the reassertion of the former is indicative of the weakening of the latter. It is precisely those individuals to whom the ideological group cannot become "country, family, everything," who cannot merge themselves completely with other members of the ideological group, who do not admit of "full revolutionary intimacy," who form personal affective attachments with outsiders, are prone to individualize, to stand aloof, to like some and dislike others, and, indeed, to display personal sentiments of affection toward other members of the same ideological group. Those individuals, in contrast, who intensely interact with other members of an ideological group, who, in fact, confine their whole relationship to the small circle of zealots and are completely insulated from the surrounding world, are least prone to individualize and thus evolve sentiments of personal affection for one another. They are, in effect, those who develop "full revolutionary intimacy."

Considered in this light, the basic components of ideological orientation may now be identified as follows: First, ideological orientation is *total*—involving a response to the whole person as nothing but a belief-possessed being. Phrased differently, members of ideological groups respond to ideas and beliefs as if these were qualities of persons rather than objects of cognitive or appreciative orientation and, conversely, conceive of themselves as solely the carriers of ideas, not the possessors of various personal qualities. The end result of this orientation is of far-reaching consequences: ideas and beliefs become "personalized" and human beings "ideologized."

Ideological orientation is thus total in a twofold sense. It is total because it is all-inclusive and requires that the individuals empty themselves of all personal interests and identifying attributes, forgetting even their names, and act and respond to one another solely in terms of their symbolic significance. It is also total because it is exclusive of multiple-group loyalty and, as such, demands that the individuals sever all personal ties and primordial attachments and, indeed, stand outside all conventional relations.

Second, ideological orientation is *dichotomous.* This dichotomy is deeply imbedded in ideological orientation and is expressed on several levels. It is expressed, first, in the so-called authoritarian syndrome characterized by the intolerance of ambiguity and rigid all-or-nothing formulas. More basically, it is a dichotomous orientation because it conceives of the social universe in terms of black and white, hopelessly divided into two irreconcilable parts—"two principles"[64] of social life (collectivism-individualism), "two forces"[65] (state-people), "two ideologies" (bourgeois-socialist), "two classes," "two parties," and so on. Consequently, it gives rise, as one member of the Will of the People noted, to a kind of primitive morality, to two sets of directly opposed rules for approaching and judging people.

> In a moral sense I discover plainly that the ideas of Lavrov lead merely in some degree to a revival of a quite primitive, imperfect kind of morality. Instead of a universal brotherhood and a higher justice which governs all private interests (including those of the circles), Lavrov revives the Old Testament circlelike solidarity. According to this, within the circle (or party) the closest relations develop, but all the rest, the external world so to speak, represents some *goys* and *giaours*; it comes about that they are looked upon as enemies, as *nemtsy, nemy* (the dumb) with whom the Lavrovites cannot communicate (there is no common language). No doubt, this external world they have in mind to save, but in the first place, as a collectivity, as mankind, while individuals who come under the heading of "enemies of socialism" have no right to expect justice. In their attitude towards the latter, as is evident from the above, the revolutionists permit themselves to drop all ideas of honor. In the matter of "saving," neither honesty nor regard is shown to the external world.[66]

The persistent attempts made by ideological groups to draw clear-cut bounds between themselves and the hostile world reflect this dualistic orientation. The clearer such a line of demarcation, the more intense are the hatred and suspicion of the outside world and, consequently, the more cohesive the ideological group. This external world to be hated in toto is identified, as a rule, in terms of social entities (*narod*, proletariat) destined to be collectively saved. It is as if the ideological groups could thrive only as long as there were objects to be hated—be they real or imaginary.

Third, ideological orientation precludes seeing a human being as a composite of personal ascribed qualities and performances. These aspects of individual human beings have no meaning in ideological relationships. In other words, ideologists neither value each other for what they are nor for what they achieve as individual persons. Ideally, they are completely deindividualized, and by renouncing all personal qualities, conceive of themselves as nothing but the carriers of beliefs. To the extent that they do this, the most important criterion is *commitment.* Once it is known that an individual is totally committed to a set of beliefs and is ever ready to sacrifice everything for them, he is showered, as has been pointed out, with "love" and also endowed with an "emotional nimbus." "I, *and all of us,*" wrote Bakunin in his letter to Nechaev, "love you sincerely and have a great respect for you because we have never met a man more unselfish and devoted to the cause than you are."[67]

Finally, ideological orientation precludes a direct affective disposition toward individual human beings. Tyrannical to themselves and to others, the individuals in an ideological relationship attempt to subdue, if not entirely to eliminate, any direct expression of personal affection. At the same time, it is not an affectively neutral orientation. In fact, ideologists channel all personal passions and emotions on to the collective cause they cherish. Human beings share in this *displaced* and *collective affectivity* to the extent to which they are its vessels. It is, thus, a profoundly antipersonalist orientation, characterized by an all-pervasive insensitivity to the needs and sufferings of concrete human beings—whether they be peasants or workers. "Not the concrete and real peasant," observed one populist writer, "attracted all our attention, was liked by us, made us ready to sacrifice everything decisively for the sake of improving his life—we wished well to and loved the abstract peasant. More than that, we feared the peasant closest to us, and so to speak perceptible."[68] Far from being the Christian caritas, this kind of love for symbolic collectivities—*narod* or proletariat—may go hand in hand with utter callousness toward individual peasants and workers. It is safe to assert, indeed, that in terms of the displaced affectivity described above, ideologists are not inconsistent when they suffer and die for people, and also exclaim in the same breath that concrete human beings are nothing to them, that the cause of the people is everything. It is even doubtful whether they are inconsistent when, on the one hand, they deceive individual peasants by forging manifestoes, and terrorize human beings en masse, and on the other hand, convince themselves and others that they are servants of the same people, striving disinterestedly for their liberation.

The four components of ideological orientation can be most likely expressed through diverse organizational structures. This is readily recognized when one compares, for example, the internal structure of a small populist circle with that of a centralized ideological movement of the Leninist type. Wherein does this difference lie?

One way of approaching this structural differentiation is to specify the basic difficulty that constantly besets small ideological groups. Evidence exists that such groups are impelled from within to degenerate with time into friendship cliques in which the spontaneous flow of emotion and personal likes and dislikes reassert themselves. It is known, for example, that the members of populist circles indulged recurrently in so-called little banquets at which they poured out their hearts to each other. "This need of giving unrestrained expression to feeling, so natural among the people allied more by community of effort, ideas and dangers, than by ties of blood, communicated to these rare gatherings something poetical and tender, which rendered them beyond measure attractive."[69] It is also known that behind the facade of ideological asceticism there tended also to evolve personal ties between men and women who were members of the same circles. As one of them readily admitted a few decades later: "When I look back at that period of my life, I recall that among the people surrounding me there were quite a few couples in love and that many of those couples culminated their intimate relations in marriage."[70] Finally, this same personal factor is manifest in the mode of recruitment of new members into small ideological circles. Available evidence suggests that they cannot but rely exclusively on mutual confidence and individual acquaintance and contacts.

To obviate the danger of relapse into the sphere of privacy and thus secure ideological identity and organizational continuity, small ideological circles resort to what might be called "bureaucratization." It will be recalled here that this very move split the Land and Freedom organization into two opposing factions. One of them contended that new members ought to be recruited on the basis of personal acquaintance and confidence; the other insisted that impersonal considerations of the individual's integrity and usefulness should suffice for acceptance into the organization. Underlying this particular disagreement, however, was the central problem of the development of the "superior form" of organization on which "revolutionary continuity" and the successful accumulation of "revolutionary experience" depend.[71] This superior form of organization was to recruit new members on the basis of formally prescribed rules rather than on personal confidence; it was to regulate, in an explicitly stated manner, the duties of its members; it was to be centralized and thus capable of coordinating the activities of dispersed circles; and finally, it was also to be hierarchically structured and disciplined.

Such "bureaucratization" of the organizational structure notwithstanding, the ideological character of these groups remained intact. True enough, they were built on the principle of hierarchy and a consistent system of formalized rules, but they were most certainly different from any functional associations. It matters little, of course, what names one gives to these two types of ideological groups. They may be conveniently called here, respectively, ideological informal and ideological formal groups. The important point is that they not be confused with personal groups or functional associations. Ideological formal groups do not admit in the fashion of the latter either the separation of public and private spheres of life, or the clear-cut segregation of the individual's roles. Their members do not participate in them merely in the capacity of one narrowly defined and functionally specific role of "official." They continue to demand, like informal ideological groups, a total commitment to the cause, which is now authoritatively defined and institutionalized. It is here that they differ strikingly from ideological informal groups. Members of ideological informal groups are recruited on the basis of individual contacts and mutual confidence, members of ideological formal groups on the basis of formal requirements and regulations. The former groups are held together by "inner convictions" of their members, the latter by the organizational structure which has come to embody them. By establishing, as it were, an "immediate rapport" with their ideas, members of ideological informal groups are inwardly compelled to adhere to them. Members of ideological formal groups, in the fashion of Lenin's "tribunes," adhere primarily to organizational principles. What we witness here is both "formalization" of the organizational structure and "institutionalization" of ideas. The former leads to the rise of professional ideologists; the latter results in the establishment of a doctrine.

From what has been said, it can be seen why the category of individuals best fitted to join ideological formations would have to be looked for among those who have no personal responsibility, who have severed for one reason or another all personal attachments and primordial ties, and who are not bound, as adults are, by specific obligations to corporate groups and associations. Ideally, they would be individuals who have left the family of orientation but have not yet established the family of procreation; who have ceased to be dependent children but have not yet become responsible adults. In short, the category of people most closely approximating this condition of liminality is youth. On this point there can be hardly any doubt that ideological groups in Russia were almost completely monopolized by young people. Yet it is evident also that not every Russian youth in any conceivable social circumstance was psychologically prepared to transform mankind, *narod*, or some other symbolic collectivity into an exclusive "object of cathexis," that not every youth was ready to accept devotion to the cause and give up, in exchange, attachment to individual persons. The recruits for ideological groups should not only be young but should also belong, as Bakunin recognized, to that "classless class" of young vagrants without a niche in the social order. In this sense, then, the condition of deracination—of being torn loose from the fabric of society—may be considered as logically necessary for membership in ideological groups.

Why did the postreform Russia wrench so many young men and women from the circumscribed network of particularistic relations and other anchors in the social order? We shall place this problem into better perspective by way of a contrast between the generations of the 1840s and the 1860s. What characterized all those fictional Oblomovs, Beltovs, and their historical counterparts—Stankevich, Herzen, Samarin, Kireevsky, Aksakov—was a certain smoothness and continuity in their life careers. The childhood experience of those young squires was on the whole quite similar. They had private tutors who treated them with the utmost leniency; as a result they were allowed to learn as little as they chose. At eighteen, if they were of average intelligence, they entered service, as did Mackenzie Wallace's typical landowner of the old school—Ivan Ivanovich. This particular squire had no inclination for any activity. The old friend or his father, the army colonel, would have accepted him to the cavalry regiment, but Ivan was not enthused by military service. In deference to his father, he wished to gain an official rank; at the same time, in deference to his mother, he wanted to remain at home and continue his indolent mode of life. The dilemma was happily resolved by the Marshal of the Nobility who inscribed him as a secretary in bureau. Since all the duties of his office could be easily discharged by a paid secretary, Ivan, the nominal occupant, would be periodically promoted as if he were an active official. He readily accepted the offer and in the course of seven years achieved the rank of collegiate secretary. Immediately after the termination of his service by proxy, Ivan found himself on the high road of matrimony. The whole affair was arranged with the assistance of his parents and he again entered the role of husband with little effort on his part. Since then "the daily life of this worthy couple is singularly regular and monotonous, varying only with the changing seasons."[72] Variations there were, of course. Some of them entered military service, others served actually and not nominally, some refused to serve and turned instead to intellectual pursuits, some stayed in Moscow and Petersburg, others returned to their country estates. But beyond these minor differences there is one basic similarity. Wallace identified it when he observed of Ivan Ivanovich that "of struggle, disappointment, hope, and all the other feelings which give to life a dramatic interest, he knows little by hearsay and nothing by experience. He has, in fact, always lived outside of that struggle for existence which modern philosophers declare to be the law of Nature."[73]

What impressed the English observer here was the smooth transition from the indolent youth to an adult member of the society—an official, a husband, a man of leisure—a transition that required in many instances a minimum of individual effort. Furthermore, this very smoothness was effected by the helpful hand of his family. Had he decided on a military career, his family would have arranged it. But since the help of his family made it possible to achieve the rank by proxy, Ivan followed the road of least resistance. So much so that the same parental contacts facilitated his marriage. It was not so much individual effort and performance, as family contacts and other personal ties, that is, particularistic considerations, which helped people like Ivan Ivanovich to achieve the status of adults. It is as if such individuals never faced all the difficulties and disappointments by themselves, as if they never entered the stage of the world on their own, but freed only one foot from the shelter of kinship particularism. Even those of them who intellectually outgrew their parents (as did most of the members of the generation of the "remarkable decade") and turned from service to intellectual pursuits, remained, in a way, grown-up children. Viewed from the economic standpoint, most of them were not professional men of letters but rather *rentier* intellectuals financially secure by virtue of their family income. They also relied socially on the family in making contacts with high officials and similarly found support and refuge in the family on their exile from Moscow and Petersburg. In many instances, indeed—to mention only the exile of Kireevsky, Ogarev, and Turgenev—it was nothing more than a forced return to the family fold—the country estates. None other than Belinsky recognized this fact when he remarked on one occasion that his friends, notably Aksakov, remained children throughout their lives and that they never tasted (as he did) reality, that "great school of life."[74]

A look at the Russian young men who embarked on an independent way of life following the reforms of Alexander II shows how strikingly their status differed from that of the members of the generation of the "remarkable decade." Since many of them received neither economic nor social support from their parents, the familial base that the generation of their "fathers" possessed, and in time of trouble relied on, was knocked out from under their feet. Almost half of the students enrolled at the University of Moscow in 1863 endured penury, some of them living on the edge of starvation.[75] One of the first post-reform studies bearing on the economic status of Russian students, made in 1872—at the time when close to 70 percent of them were of gentry origin—reveals their deplorable poverty. At that time, the Russian student needed about 375 rubles annually to exist tolerably. Yet only 10 percent of the students at the University of Kiev had an income higher than 300 rubles; 4 percent stayed with their parents; and 86 percent lived virtually in poverty. Some 40 percent of them received no aid whatsoever from their parents.[76]

Obviously, the sons of former Oblomovs faced for the first time Belinsky's accursed reality. Gone were the manorial orchards and shadowy parks, gone was the leisurely if not indolent style of life of grown-up children in a cozy family nest. Hard work, personal initiative, and self-reliance, more than familial contacts and other particularistic considerations, were required now for becoming a full-fledged member of society, for making successful careers in nonfamilial spheres of life. The significance of this development lay thus in the introduction of the "breaking point" in the former relatively smooth growth from youth to adulthood, from kinship to larger society. For the individual it required a basic reorientation with respect to attitudes and behavior patterns that were hitherto uppermost in the value system of Russian society.

The main social condition underlying the rise of the ideological movement in Russia, if placed within the framework of the foregoing analysis, may be identified as follows: ideological groups of Russia emerged in the wake of transition from the semi-closed estate order founded on bondage and service to an increasingly open, individualized, and occupation-integrated system—that is, one marked by a growing differentiation between the state and society, office rank and personal status, kinship and occupational achievement. The argument advanced here suggests that not the obduracy of the autocratic regime and its oppressive policy, but the modernization and liberalization of Russia (the social changes operating beneath the outworn crust of this regime) laid the ground for an abundant supply of young men and women for "holy unions."

Concluding Remarks

The preceding analysis of factors operative in the emergence of ideological groups in Russia does not and cannot account for individual variations among those who joined them. We know that among the Russian *intelligenty* and their youthful myrmidones there were not only the uprooted and dispossessed, but also misfits and failures (e.g., Obruchev, Pryzhov), romantic adventurers (e.g., Ossinsky and Yurkovsky from among the Ukrainians), some escapees from authoritarian family control (e.g., Karpova-Rogacheva), some "repentant nobles" (e.g., Kropotkin, Lysogub, Lebedintsev), some who by their "personal constitution" were responsive to remote symbols, and not a few individuals of "paranoid condition" displaying the characteristic projection mechanism of moving against society as a whole. We realize also that once the ideological subculture had been firmly established in Russia and became fashionable, it attracted not a few individuals for other idiosyncratic reasons. These considerations notwithstanding, it may still be safely asserted that the psychological factors, taken separately or in tandem, cannot explain the rise and nature of the ideological movement in Russia. When Mikhailovsky availed himself of the psychological interpretation of repentance, he somehow brushed aside the fact that those "repentant nobles" appeared on the social scene after many of their privileges had been undermined. There is thus much more of the truth in Dostoevsky's pungent suggestion that the *intelligent*'s "love of the people was but *an outlet of his personal* sorrow about himself."[77] When others trace the rise of "new men" to the authoritarian family structure, they again ignore the fact that it was precisely the generation of young men and women let loose and forced to face the world on its own that so violently rebelled against the family. May it not have been that the very attenuation of the kindred group and the attendant dearth of familial security plunged these young men into the search for a substitute—a substitute that ultimately devoured their personalities and annihilated individual independence?

Although our analysis fails to account for individual variations, it accounts for the diverse social background, the age-homogeneous composition, the internal social structure of the groups, and the nature of social relations prevalent among their members. It also places the problem of ideologization within a broad social context and to that extent goes beyond plebeian social origin, Tsarist autocracy, parental harshness, and repentance. *In fine*, it discloses that the ideological movement in Russia was inextricably entwined with the whole fabric of her society and that, consequently, there was neither one single cause nor one single remedy.

Notes

1. B. Nazarevsky, *Biurokratiia i Intelligentsiia* (Moscow 1906), p. 5; *see also* A. Pazukhina, *Sovremennoe Sostoianie Rossii i Soslovnyi Vopros* (Moscow, 1886), p. 41.
2. James M. Edie, James P. Scanlan, and Mary-Barbara Zeldin, eds., *Russian Philosophy: The Beginnings of Russian Philosophy* (Chicago: Quadrangle Books, 1969), I, p. 315.
3. V. G. Belinsky, *Izbrannye Pisma* (Moscow, 1955), II, p. 158.
4. N. G. Chernyshevsky, *Polnoe Sobranie Sochinenii* (Moscow, 1939), I, p. 230.
5. Ibid.
6. Ibid., p. 231.
7. D. Pisarev, *Selected Philosophical, Social and Political Essays* (Moscow: Foreign Languages Publishing House, 1958), p. 567.
8. Ibid., p. 568.
9. V. Debogorii-Mokrievich, *Vospominaniia* (St. Petersburg, 1906), p. 77.
10. Eugenia S. Ginzburg, *Journey into the Whirlwind*, trans. Paul Stevenson and Max Hayward (New York: Harcourt, Brace & World Co., 1967), p. 113.
11. Merle Fainsod, *How Russia is Ruled* (Cambridge: Harvard University Press, 1953), p. 5.
12. Ibid.
13. A. I. Herzen, *O Razvitii Revoliutsionnykh Idei v Rossii* (St. Petersburg, 1907) p. 151.
14. Stepniak (S. Kravchinsky), *Underground Russia*, 2d ed. (New York: Charles Scribner's Sons, 1888), p. 27.
15. Isaiah Berlin, "A Marvellous Decade," *Encounter* 5 (October 1955): 28; *see also* N. Engelhardt, *Ocherk Istorii Russkoi Tsenzury v Sviazi z Razvitiem Pechati: 1703–1903* (St. Petersburg, 1904), p. 173; Sidney Monas, *The Third Section: Police and Society in Russia under Nicholas I* (Cambridge: Harvard University Press, 1961), pp. 133–96.
16. A. Yarmolinsky, "Censorhip in Russia: A Historical Study," *Russian Review* 3 (July 1917): 94–96.
17. A. M. Skabichevsky, *Ocherki Istorii Russkoi Tsenzury: 1700–1863 g.* (St. Petersburg, 1892), p. 179.
18. Ibid.
19. R. Gul, "Tsenzura i Pisatel v SSSR," *Sovremennye Zapiski* 66 (1938): 438; *see also* R. Gul, "Pisatel i Tsenzura v SSSR," *Novyi Zhurnal* 109 (December 1972): 240–257.
20. Waldemar Gurian, ed., *The Soviet Union: Background, Ideology, Reality* (South Bend, Indiana: University of Notre Dame Press, 1951), p. 19.
21. N. K. Karataev, ed., *Narodnicheskaia Ekonomicheskaia Literatura* (Moscow, 1958), p. 101.
22. Quoted in Christopher Becker, "Raznochintsy: The Development of the Word

and of the Concept," *American Slavic and East European Review* 18 (February 1959): 71; *see also* V. Evgeniev, "N. A. Nekrasov i Liudi 40-kh Godov," *Golos Minuvshago* 4 (April 1916): 114.

23. V. I. Lenin, *Sochineniia*, 4th ed. (Leningrad, 1952), XI, p. 204; Ibid., XX, p. 223; V. G. Baskakov, *Mirovozzrenie Chernyshevskogo* (Moscow, 1956), p. 5; Sh. M. Levin, *Obshchestvennoe Dvizhenie v Rossii v 60–70-e Gody XIX Veka* (Moscow, 1958), pp. 87–91; In attempting to bestow on Lenin's scheme somewhat greater precision, the present-day Soviet authors make it even less convincing. They distinguish, for example, three distinct camps in the first period; the reactionary-land-owning camp, to which they relegate most of the Slavophiles and such individuals as Pogodin, Shevyrev, Bulgarin, and Grech; the bourgeois-landowning camp, in which they include most of the Westerners and even some Slavophiles—Korsh, Botkin, Kavelin, Annenkov, Granovsky; and the revolutionary-democratic camp, headed by Belinsky and Herzen. Without going into details, it may be safely stated that these distinctions rest on the supposition that all ideologies are class-bound and hence are explainable in terms of class origin (position) of their exponents. By establishing the short iron chain that ties every individual to a corresponding class-position, it should be possible, so they believe, to "unmask" his class interests. The extent to which this classification—based as it is on such an assumption—is arbitrary and devoid of meaning can be seen from its inconsistency. The Soviet authors indiscriminately classify former peasants (Pogodin) in the camp of those who expound the interests of the reactionary landowners, proclaim the landowners (Annenkov, Korsh) and former serfs (Nikitenko) as apologists of bourgeois interests, and view Herzen and Belinsky as two closest revolutionary collaborators.

24. "Iz Razmyshlenii v Shlisselburge," *Minuvshie Gody* 1 (March 1908): 294; *see also* K. Breshkovskaia, *Hidden Springs of the Russian Revolution* (Stanford: Stanford University Press, 1931), p. 330.

25. B. H. Sumner, *Survey of Russian History*, 2d ed. (London: Duckworth, 1947), p. 330.

26. G. I. Shreider, "Gorod i Gorodovoe Polozhenie 1870 Goda," *Istoriia Rossii v XIX Veke* (St. Petersburg, 1907), IV, p. 5.

27. Ibid., p. 6.

28. Ibid., p. 4–5.

29. D. Mackenzie Wallace, *Russia* (New York: Henry Holt and Co., 1904), p. 165; Convinced, as Catherine II was, that "from the remotest antiquity we everywhere find the memory of town builders elevated to the same level as the memory of legislators, and we see that heroes, famous for their victories, hoped by town building to give immortality to their names," she acted in accordance with this precedence and embarked upon "town building" by administratively transforming some 216 villages into *Ackerburgerstaedte*.

30. Ibid., pp. 165–66.

31. Serge Elisseeff, "The Orthodox Church and the Russian Merchant Class," *Harvard Theological Review* 49 no. 4 (1956): 185; *see also* D. S. Mirsky, *Russia: A Social History* (London: The Cresset Press, 1931), pp. 215–16.

32. A. Ushakov, "Paralleli," *Vestnik Promyshlennosti* no. 9 (1861), pp. 92–96; quoted in B. Genkin, "Obshchestvenno-Politicheskaia Programma Russkoi Burzhuazii v Gody Pervoi Revoliutsionnoi Situatsii (1859–1861 gg)," *Problemy Sotsialno-Ekonomicheskoi Istorii Rossii*, eds. A. M. Anfimov et al., (Moscow, 1971), p. 104.

33. Valentine T. Bill, *The Forgotten Class* (New York: Frederick A. Praeger, 1959), pp. 141–42.

34. Shreider, *Istoriia Rossii*, IV, p. 5.

35. A. G. Rashin, *Naselenie Rossii za 100 Let: 1811–1913 gg.* (Moscow, 1956), pp. 124–27.
36. Solomon F. Bloom, "Business and Intellect in the Eighteenth Century," *Freedom and Reason: Studies in Philosophy and Jewish Culture*, ed. Salo W. Baron, Ernest Nagel, and Koppel S. Pinson (Glencoe: Free Press, 1951), p. 102.
37. Reinhard Bendix, *Work and Authority in Industry* (New York: John Wiley and Sons, 1956), p. 348.
38. B. N. Chicherin, *Vospominaniia: Moskva Sorokovykh Godov* (Moscow, 1929), II, p. 92.
39. V. I. Kovalevsky, ed., *Rossiia v Kontse XIX Veka* (St. Petersburg, 1900), p. 60.
40. Vladimir Il'ich (Lenin), *Razvitie Kapitalizma v Rossii*, 2d ed. (St. Petersburg, 1908), p. 442.
41. Lev A. Tikhomirov, *Russia, Political and Social*, trans. Edward Aveling (London: Lowry Co., 1888), I, p. 242.
42. Wallace, *Russia*, p. 238.
43. P. Kropotkin, *Memoirs of a Revolutionist* (Boston and New York: Houghton, Mifflin and Co., 1899), p. 264.
44. A. S. Glinka-Volzhsky, ed., *Gleb Uspenskii v Zhizni* (Moscow-Leningrad, 1935), pp. 62–63.
45. Stepniak (S. Kravchinsky), *Undergrond*, p. 68.
46. V. Figner, *Polnoe Sobranie Sochinenii v Semi Tomakh*, 2d ed. (Moscow, 1928), V, p. 215.
47. Ibid.
48. Stepniak (S. Kravchinsky), *Underground*, p. 81.
49. Figner, *Polnoe*, I, p. 191.
50. Ibid.
51. Ibid.
52. Ibid.
53. N. A. Charushin, "Kruzhok Chaikovtsev: Z Vospominanii o Revoliutsion-nom Dvizhenii," *O Dalekom Proshlom*, Part II (Moscow, 1926), p. 83.
54. L. A. Tikhomirov, *Vospominaniia* (Moscow, 1927), p. 54; for a recent analysis of the Chaikovsky circle, *see* A. V. Knowles, "The 'Book Affair' of the Chaikovsky Circle," *Slavonic and East European Review* 51 (October 1973): 554–566.
55. Stepniak (S. Kravchinsky), *Underground*, p. 96.
56. Ibid., p. 109.
57. P. Lavrov, *Narodniki-Propagandisty 1873–1878 Godov* (St. Petersburg, 1907), p. 65.
58. Vera Figner, *Memoirs of a Revolutionist* (New York: International Publishers, 1927), p. 180.
59. Stepniak (S. Kravchinsky), *Underground*, p. 231.
60. These and similar demands contained in the *Revolutionary Catechism* should in no way be attributed, as has been traditionally done, to the personal aberrations of Nechaev. In fact, the by-laws of the Executive Committee of the Will of the People organization consist of well-nigh identical requirements. *See* Robert Payne, *The Terrorists: The Story of the Forerunners of Stalin* (New York: Funk and Wagnalls Co., 1957), p. 22.
61. Ibid., p. 21.
62. Stepniak (S. Kravchinsky), *Underground*, p. 119.
63. A. D. Mikhailov, "Avtobiograficheskie Zametki," *Byloe* (February 1906), p. 169.
64. G. Plekhanov, "Ot Redaktsii," *Chernyi Peredel*, no. 1 (January 1880), p. 108.
65. "Zloba Dnia," *Narodnaia Volia*, no. 5 (February 1881), p. 1.
66. L. A. Tikhomirov, *Pochemu Ia Perestal Byt' Revoliutsionerom* (Moscow, 1896), pp. 108–9.

67. "An Unpublished Letter: Bakunin and Nechaev," *Encounter* 39 (July 1972): 81.

68. L. Deich, *Za Polveka* (Berlin, 1923), II, p. 67.

69. Stepniak (S. Kravchinsky), *Underground*, p. 74.

70. N. A. Morozov, *V Nachale Zhizni* (Moscow, 1907), p. 176.

71. Figner, *Polnoe*, I, p. 107.

72. Wallace, *Russia*, p. 233.

73. Ibid., p. 231.

74. Belinsky, *Izbrannye*, I, p. 161; *see also* S. A. Vengerov, *Peredovoi Borets Slavianofilstva: Konstantin Aksakov* in *Sobranie Sochinenii* (St. Petersburg, 1912), III, pp. 9–10.

75. Avrahm Yarmolinsky, *Road to Revolution: A Century of Russian Radicalism* (New York: The Macmillan Co., 1959), p. 103.

76. A. Nikolaev, *Khleba i Sveta: Materialnyi i Dukhovnyi Biudzhet Intelligentsii u Nas i za Granitsei* (St. Petersburg, 1910), p. 78; *see also* Lewis S. Feuer, *The Conflict of Generations: The Character and Significance of Student Movements* (New York: Basic Books, 1969), pp. 88–172.

77. F. M. Dostoevsky, *The Diary of a Writer*, trans. Boris Brasol (New York: Charles Scribner's Sons, 1949), II, p. 946.

Index

Engelhardt, N., 164
England, 90, 96
Erasmus, 20
Evgeniev, N., 165

Fainsod, M., 164
Fedotov, G. P., 3, 16
Feuerbach, L., 142
Feuer, L. S., 167
Fichte, J., 56, 59, 69, 111
Figner, V., 139, 166
Fischer, G., 17
Fonvizin, D. I., 5, 22, 36, 37, 38,
    42, 46
Fourier, Charles, 56, 59, 104, 142
France, 56, 96–97; Slavophile view of,
    90–91
Furst, L. R., 114

Genkin, B., 165
Gershenzon, M., 16, 116
Ginzburg, E. S., 144, 164
Gleason, A., 64
Glinka-Volzhsky, A. S., 166
Goethe, J. W. von, 52, 95, 98, 99, 103,
    106, 114, 142
Gogol, N., 49, 49, 63
Golovenchenko, F. M., 81
Goncharov, I., 49
Gooch, G. P., 47
Gorky, Maxim, 3, 16
Granovsky, T. N., 53, 56–57, 58, 59, 61,
    62, 68, 71, 95, 106
Griboedov, A., 5, 49
Gul, R., 164
Gurian, W., 164

Hegel, G. W. F., 60, 111, 142, 143
Heine, H., 15, 93, 18
Herzen, A. I., 27, 29, 32, 48, 52, 54–55,
    61, 62, 67, 69–70, 102, 106, 108, 109,
    114, 142, 144, 164; on freedom, 62, 95;
    on friendship and personal ties, 58; on
    village commune, 94; on individual in
    society, 96 passim
Homer, 35

Iakovlev (Bogucharsky), V. I.,
    109, 116
Ideology, 8–9, 15, 86, 130; ideological
    groups, 80, 154, 160; ideological
    orientation, 157–59; ideological
    relations, 68–70, 156–57

Intelligentsia: attitude to service, 37–38,
    definition, 4–5, 84; estrangement
    from social and political order, 52,
    55, 128; politicization of, 86; populist,
    Marxist, 8–14; relationship to *narod,*
    121–22, 127–28; to proletariat,
    130–33; social and ethnic composition
    of, 25–27, 147–49
Ivanov-Razumnik, R., 10, 17

Kablits (Iuzov), Ia.I., 128, 138
Kallash, V., 148, 138
Karamzin, H. M., 29, 40, 46
Karataev, N. K., 164
Karazin, V., 45
Karpovich, M., 146
Kautsky, K., 134, 140
Kavelin, K., 57, 75
Keep, J. L. H., 140
Kheraskov, M. M., 34
Khodasevich, V., 46
Khomiakov, A. S., 57, 64, 69, 90, 109,
    113, 142,
Kierkegaard, S., 72, 81
Kireevsky, I. V., 51–55, 57, 59, 63,
    94, 95, 114; on friendship, 106; on
    serfdom, 89; on Russia, 88 passim
Kireevsky, P. V., 109
Kluckhohn, P., 81, 113
Koltsov, A., 50
Kornilov, A. A., 112
Korsh, E., 57, 67
Koshelev, A. I., 93, 94, 138
Kostomarov, N., 33
Kovalevsky, V. I., 166
Krekshin, P., 30
Krieger, L., 63
Kropotkin, P., 152, 166
Krylov, I. A., 46
Kucharzewski, J., 16
Kucherov, S., 45

Lagardelle, H., 12, 18
Lampert, E., 64
Land and Freedom, 125, 131, 137,
    154–55, 159
Lavrov, P., 7, 117, 126, 128, 157, 115;
    on "critically thinking individuals,"
    7–9; on *narod,* 118 passim; on village
    commune, 119, 128
Leontiev, K., 138
Lermontov, M., 49, 71, 72, 74,
    142, 151

For Product Safety Concerns and Information please contact our EU
representative GPSR@taylorandfrancis.com
Taylor & Francis Verlag GmbH, Kaufingerstraße 24, 80331 München, Germany

www.ingramcontent.com/pod-product-compliance
Ingram Content Group UK Ltd.
Pitfield, Milton Keynes, MK11 3LW, UK
UKHW021447080625
459435UK00012B/405